Money for Millennials

Sarah Young Fisher & Susan Shelly McGovern

DK | Penguin Random House

Publisher Mike Sanders
Art & Design Director William Thomas
Editorial Director Ann Barton
Cover Designer William Thomas
Book Designer Ayanna Lacey
Proofreader Jennifer Weltich
Indexer Johnna VanHoose Dinse

First American Edition, 2024
Published in the United States by DK Publishing
1745 Broadway, 20th Floor, New York, NY 10019

Published in the United States by Dorling Kindersley Limited.

Library of Congress Catalog Number: 2023946039
ISBN: 978-0-7440-9248-6

DK books are available at special discounts when purchased
in bulk for sales promotions, premiums, fund-raising, or educational use.
For details, contact SpecialSales@dk.com

Printed and bound in China

www.dk.com

Reprinted from *Idiot's Guides®: Personal Finance in Your 20s and 30s,
Fifth Edition*

MIX
Paper | Supporting
responsible forestry
FSC™ C018179

This book was made with Forest
Stewardship Council™ certified
paper—one small step in DK's
commitment to a sustainable future.
For more information go to
www.dk.com/our-green-pledge

Contents

Introduction

Learning to handle your finances wisely and responsibly is an ongoing process that requires your time and attention at every stage of your life, whether you're just entering the workforce with your very first job; a millennial with an established career, home, and maybe a family; or a retiree enjoying the fruits of their labor. Personal finance is a big-picture event, not just a day-to-day or month-to-month process. And because the millennial generation ranges in age from their late 20s to their early 40s, where they are financially and their financial concerns vary significantly.

When you're just starting out, learning to budget and make your money last can be a daunting process, especially if you're not earning as much as you'd like to be. Whether you're dealing with financial issues on your own or with a partner, there are bills to pay, student loans to repay, a car payment to make, and that long weekend at the beach you and your friends are planning.

You'll need to think about getting some credit established because you likely will need to borrow money at some point for a house or other big-ticket purchase. And you'll want to start saving money in an employer-provided retirement account, such a 401(k).

As you get older, your financial responsibilities are likely to increase. You may have children, which, as you'll read in this book, are expensive. You might buy a house and incur the costs of being a homeowner. And before too long, you'll need to consider various investment vehicles and get your money working for you.

By learning the basics of personal finance now, especially if you're on the younger end of the millennial age range, you position yourself for greater financial success later in life. You'll have money to put aside for retirement, to help your kids with their college costs, and to live comfortably into your golden years.

This book provides a base to help you get started with saving money, paying back what you owe, and establishing a favorable credit history. It helps you understand how to stretch the dollars you have and put something aside for your future. When you finish, you'll have a sound understanding of how your personal finances work in various stages of your life, and you'll have a lot more confidence when it comes to handling your money and building a financially secure future.

How you manage your personal finances now affects nearly every aspect of your life in the future, so it's essential that you get started on the right foot.

How This Book Is Organized

We wrote this book in three parts:

Part 1, Financial Basics Everyone Should Know, discusses how a good foundation can be your start to a successful financial future. Understanding what kind of bank accounts you need and tracking your income and expenses in a budget helps you get an overview of your finances and learn to manage them with confidence. It's important to understand how much you earn, how much you spend, and how credit works.

In **Part 2, Life Events That Affect Your Finances,** we cover job strategies and job satisfaction, review the pros and cons of homeownership, and discuss how owning a home can impact your finances. We explore the potential financial implications of relationship changes, talk about some costs associated with children, and explain the importance of getting the insurances you need to protect your property and ensure you can care for yourself and those who depend on you.

And in **Part 3, Looking Ahead,** you learn about different types of investment vehicles, which might make sense for you, and some strategies that can help you make smarter investment decisions. We take a look at taxes that affect your bottom line, the importance of estate planning, and why it's never too early to start thinking about retirement.

At the back of the book, we've included a glossary of terms, a list of further resources you can use to continue your financial education, and some other helpful forms and worksheets.

Acknowledgments

We would like to thank the many people who provided time, information, and resources for this book. Especially, we thank our editors at DK and Gene Brissie of James Peter Associates.

About the Authors

Sarah Young Fisher is the former owner of Fisher Advisers, a financial consulting firm in Lancaster, Pennsylvania. She served as president of Lancaster-based RKL Wealth Management from 2005 until 2020. A Certified Financial Planner and Chartered Financial Consultant, Ms. Fisher is the coauthor of *Idiot's Guides®: Personal Finance in Your 20s and 30s*.

Susan Shelly McGovern is a freelance writer, researcher, and editorial consultant based in Shillington, Pennsylvania. She has written for online news services and various magazines, newspapers, businesses, and agencies.

Financial Basics Everyone Should Know

Most of us think about money pretty regularly. We think about when we'll be getting paid, how much we'll have left after all the bills are taken care of, if we can afford to take the vacation we've been thinking about, and how much we spent at the restaurant last night.

Not as many of us, however, regularly think about our overall financial picture and how, in the long term, it will determine the way we live and our ability to secure a healthy financial future.

Part 1 lays out the financial basics everyone should understand and practice. These include establishing financial goals, saving, analyzing expenses, budgeting, understanding debt, establishing and managing credit, and other important topics that are essential to financial health. Understanding these basic aspects of personal finance will give you a base upon which you can build for your future.

Chapter 1

Your Financial Base

Personal finance is important to all age groups, and perhaps especially so to millennials—a generation that faces unique challenges and opportunities regarding money and financial health.

A comprehensive study conducted by the Global Financial Literacy Excellence Center (GFLEC) at George Washington University examined the personal finances of more than 5,500 millennials and revealed some sobering facts. Millennials face a higher level of economic uncertainty than previous generations, the study concluded, and many lack the knowledge needed to successfully manage their financial affairs. Millennials also are faced with unprecedented student loan debt, and many struggle to save for their futures.

Those glum findings, however, do not need to define your financial situation nor your prospects for a healthy financial future.

By picking up this book, you've already demonstrated that you want to learn more about personal finance and how to be financially successful. That's a great first step toward taking control of and successfully managing your money.

Let's take a look at exactly what personal finance is and why it's so important to your life, both now and in the future.

Why Personal Finance Is So Important

Basically, personal finance is every aspect of your life that deals with money. Personal finance covers everything from buying a Netflix subscription, to finding an affordable apartment, to buying or leasing a car, to putting money into a retirement plan. Your personal finances affect your lifestyle, your relationships, and especially your financial future.

How well you accomplish your personal financial goals determines not only where and how you'll live, but also whether you'll have a family now or in the future and where those family members will live. Your personal finances impact what kind of vacations you can take, the level of charitable giving you're able to accomplish, and eventually the quality of your retirement.

To understand personal finance as it relates to you, you first need to understand your financial base. Your financial base includes the assets you have, such as a salary, bank accounts, investments within a 401(k), a vehicle, a house, personal property, and so forth.

Your financial base also includes what you owe, such as student loan debt, credit card debt, rent or mortgage payments, utility bill payments, or a monthly car payment.

Getting a handle on your financial base is necessary so you can figure out how to live within your means and start—or continue—saving money for your future. Retirement seems very far off when you're in your 20s, 30s, or early 40s, but the years go by quickly. The sooner you can get a handle on your financial future, with the accounts in place that you need, your debt under control, and an adequate source of income, the sooner you'll be able to take control of your money instead of letting your money control you.

How Your Finances Affect Your Life

By this point of your life, it's a pretty sure bet you've experienced how finances influence what you do, how you feel, and the way you live. Worrying about money—which, according to a survey by Capital One, is something 77 percent of Americans reported doing in 2023—is stressful and affects all aspects of your life.

Where You Live

You probably don't need anyone to tell you that affordable housing is an issue in America. The median home price shot up by more than 15 percent between 2021 and 2022, and rents rose by about the same amount—and even more in cities like Austin, Texas; Nashville, Tennessee; and Seattle, Washington.

The average cost to rent an apartment in the United States is $1,702 a month, and the median price of a home (the point at which half of all homes sold for more and half sold for less) in the second quarter of 2022 was $440,300. By any account, that's a lot of money.

We discuss housing and housing costs in greater detail in Part 2 of the book, but there's no doubt that your finances directly affect where you live. Roommates can be fun, but many single people prefer to live on their own, making paying the rent even more of a challenge. It's generally recommended that you spend no more than 30 percent of your monthly gross income—that's your income before taxes are taken out—on housing.

If you live in a state like Arkansas or Oklahoma, where average rents for apartments are less than $1,000 a month, the 30 percent rule might be easy to adhere to, especially if you're sharing the cost of the rent with another person. If you live in Washington, DC, New York, or Massachusetts, however, where average rents top $2,000 a month, the 30 percent rule becomes much harder to follow, especially for those who must come up with the rent on their own.

Being happy where you live is a huge factor in experiencing good quality of life, especially as many people have continued to work from home following the COVID-19 pandemic. Even if you don't work from home, it's likely that you spend a good chunk of your time there. Where you live is important, and it's directly affected by your financial situation.

What You Can Afford to Do

We all know people who post their lives on social media, offering frequent accounts of trips to fabulous places, dinners at the trendiest restaurants, and nights out on the town. Regardless of whether those folks are able to afford those luxuries or are running up serious debt splurging on them, it's hard not to feel envious of those types of experiences, especially if you're not able to participate in them.

The old saying that "the best things in life are free" may be true, but most people enjoy being able to try different things—and most of those things seem to cost money.

Getting and maintaining control of your finances means not having to sit out the bachelorette weekend in New Orleans because you can't afford to participate. It means you don't have to worry about the occasional $5 latte at Starbucks or nice dinner with friends or your family. It means you're able to rent that cabin on the lake for a week in the summer or fly to Seattle to visit your cousin.

Millennials are known to place high value on experiences. Having your financial house in order enables you to fully participate.

Your Health

Long-term stress—including financial stress—is detrimental to health. Stressing over your finances shows up through physical symptoms like sleep disorders, headaches, inflammation, high blood pressure, digestive issues, muscle tension, heart arrhythmia, and other worrisome signs.

Even worse, presentation of such symptoms can lead to medical appointments, tests, and procedures—all of which cost money, which brings about even more stress. This cycle can lead to chronic stress, which simply is bad for you.

Financial stress also affects mental health, leading to conditions like anxiety and depression. People who experience mental health concerns often have trouble managing their finances, which increases anxiety and can lead to feeling overwhelmed to the point that they're unable to even address financial concerns.

People who are financially well—who feel that they're able to fully meet money-related needs now and will continue to be able to do so in the future—feel secure and calm about their money. They're not overly stressed about being able to pay their bills or afford medications because their finances are well managed and maintained.

If you're among the more than three-quarters of Americans who worry about finances, be assured that there are ways to improve your financial wellness. You've come to the right place to learn how.

Your Financial Future

Ideally, planning for your financial future begins the day you land your very first job. Unfortunately, that often is not what happens.

Your financial future certainly includes your retirement, but there's a lot to plan for between now and then. A house? College for your kids or future kids? Financial security when you're in your seventies and eighties and beyond?

Financial planning is crucial for everything that's important to you.

Managing your money to plan for your future includes setting up the right kinds of accounts, putting money into savings, looking at various investment options, paying down debt, and other smart strategies you'll read about later in this book.

Regardless of your age or financial timetable, the time to start planning your financial future is now. Trust us—you'll be glad you did.

Evaluating Where You Are Financially

Many of you probably remember the Great Recession—the worst economic downturn in the United States since the Great Depression. The recession wreaked havoc in 2008 and 2009, causing the unemployment rate to double to 10 percent, gross domestic product to fall, home values to plummet, and the stock market to, at one point, drop 57 percent from its 2007 peaks. The government had to step in to prop up struggling banks and other companies, and the economies of practically every country in the world were negatively affected.

The effects of the recession lasted long after it officially ended, with many millennials who were graduating from high school or college at that time caught in the middle. Due to the high unemployment rate and dismal job market, they were unable to find jobs—in some cases for years. Just as they would have been beginning their careers and starting to plan financially, there were no jobs to be had.

To make matters worse, about two-thirds of those graduating from college at that time left with student loan debt, which many struggled to pay.

The job market eventually rebounded following the recession, but salaries haven't kept up with rising prices for years—a problem that was made worse by the COVID-19 pandemic. The pandemic also resulted in job losses for millions of people, including many millennials who were forced to dip into their savings or go into debt to stay afloat. A 2022 study by the consumer financial services company Bankrate showed that only about half of all Americans reported having more money in emergency savings accounts than what they owe in credit card debt.

These financial disruptions have taken their toll on many people, including millennials. Those who struggled to find jobs while trying to pay off student loans have had less ability to save money and build wealth than previous generations. New America, a nonprofit, nonpartisan think tank, found that overall, millennials earn 20 percent less than baby boomers did at the same stage of life, despite having more education, and more education debt. That, of course, makes it harder to save money, buy a house, start a family, and take other steps that typically have defined adulthood.

We're not trying to paint a gloomy picture of the financial lives of many millennials, but these are facts. We hope you graduated from high school, trade school, or college and didn't have any trouble landing a good-paying job. But if that's not the case, and you are one of the many millennials who report being very unhappy with their current financial situation, try not to be too discouraged. There are ways you can improve that situation and get on track financially.

Regardless of where you are on the financial spectrum, it's important to be realistic about your circumstances and take an honest look at what you have and what you owe. Consider your income—or lack of, if that's the case. Think about the expenses you have and how you're managing them. Take a good look at how much you owe, and consider how long it might take to get out of debt.

When you combine all those factors, you can determine your net worth and begin an honest assessment of where you are financially.

Assessing Your Net Worth

Your net worth, financially speaking, is everything you own minus what you owe. What you own are called assets, and any money you owe is a liability. Your net worth is simply the total of all your assets, less the total of all your liabilities.

To figure out your net worth, you'll need to take an inventory of everything you own and then figure out your outstanding debt.

Let's think about assets first. These would include the following:

- Checking accounts
- Savings accounts
- Retirement accounts
- Real estate (Meaning the current market value of your home, if you own it, and any other property you might have.)
- Vehicles (Again, the current market value.)
- Other (Such as additional accounts and investments like stocks or bonds.)

Liabilities include these things:

- Mortgages on your home and any other property you own
- Consumer debt (This includes credit card debt, student loans, car loans, and payday loans.)
- Personal loans
- Auto loans
- Other debt

Consider your assets and liabilities carefully because it's easy to overlook sources of both. Overlooked liabilities might include medical bills or unpaid tax bills. On the assets side, were any savings accounts set up for you when you were a kid? What about savings bonds?

Some families are great at buying US savings bonds for birthdays, and according to the US Bureau of Public Debt, $14 billion worth of those savings bonds are sitting unclaimed in government accounts. If you think you may have been given savings bonds but aren't sure, you can check by entering your Social Security number at this US Treasury Department website: treasurydirect.gov /indiv/tools/tools_treasuryhunt.htm.

You can find online net worth calculators to help you determine where you stand. When you've figured out your net worth, you have a financial report card of how you're doing.

If you do the calculations and find out your net worth is negative, you're by no means alone. About 13 million American households owe more than they own, according to the Aspen Institute, an international nonprofit. A big reason for negative net worth is home mortgages. If you purchased a home for $350,000 and only have paid $75,000 on your mortgage, for instance, your house is a much greater liability than it is an asset.

Typically, your net worth increases as your savings grow and the money you owe, such as a mortgage, decreases.

Establishing Short-, Mid-, and Long-Term Goals

Setting goals and sticking to them is an important step toward achieving financial security. Working toward your goals helps keep you on track with your spending and encourages you to save as much as possible.

As a certified financial planner, Sarah regularly works with clients to help them establish short-term, mid-term, and long-term goals. Your goals may change depending on your circumstances, but the important things are to be as consistent as you can and to get back on track if you get sidelined.

You'll read more about these goals as you progress through this book, but let's take a quick look at each of those categories now.

Short-Term Goals

Your first goal should be to build a budget that works for you. It's very difficult to set goals without having a good understanding of where you are financially, and to gain that understanding, you'll need a budget to track your spending. When you know exactly where your money is going, you can use that information to make better decisions about how to use your money in the future.

Another short-term goal is creating an emergency fund. This is money intentionally set aside for unanticipated expenses like a car repair or dental work not covered by insurance. Even putting aside a little bit of money every month can build an emergency fund over time. You can start small with the goal of growing the fund so you have money for larger expenses, such as a period of unemployment.

Paying off credit card debt should be another short-term goal. The sooner you get that taken care of, the sooner you can start building your savings accounts and thinking about forms of investing.

Mid-Term Goals

After you have a thorough understanding of your spending, have established an emergency fund, and have paid off or at least made a good dent in paying off your credit card debt, you can think about mid-term financial goals.

One important mid-term goal is to buy life insurance and disability insurance, especially if others depend on your income. You learn more about the importance of insurance in Chapter 10, but for now, remember that getting what you need isn't something you should put off.

Paying off any student loans is another mid-term goal. If you can reduce or eliminate those payments, you will free up cash you can use to increase your retirement savings or achieve other financial goals. You'll read more about paying down student debt in Chapter 3.

Other mid-term goals might include buying a home and perhaps later a vacation home. They might include saving to renovate your home, or pay for educational expenses, or be able to afford the expenses of having a family.

Long-Term Goals

Not surprisingly, the most important long-term goal for most people is to have sufficient retirement accounts. Entire books have been dedicated to this topic, and we spend more time on the topic later in this book, in Chapters 11 and 16.

This long-term goal, however, requires your attention early on because the earlier you start saving for retirement, the more time your money has to accrue compound interest, or interest paid on interest from previous periods, in addition to the principal.

To know how much you should save for retirement, you first must determine how much you'll need after you've retired. There are methods of figuring that out, as you'll read more about in Chapter 16.

Chapter Summary

When you understand that your financial situation will impact nearly every aspect of your life, you can take a hard look at the current state of your finances. If you're on track for saving and have debt under control, you're moving in the right direction. If not, now's the time to look ahead; set some short-, mid-, and long-terms goals; and come up with a financial strategy that will put you on track for a comfortable future.

Chapter 2

Understanding Your Spending

If we asked you how much money you spent last week, would you be able to give us an accurate answer? Or at least accurate within $15 or $20?

If you could, we'd applaud you. If you couldn't, we wouldn't be surprised.

Technology such as contactless card payments and autopay make it super easy to spend money without much accountability. A recent study by Upwise Capital showed that nearly half of the people surveyed were unsure about how much money they had in their bank accounts, and less than 30 percent reported checking their account balances more than once a week.

Not keeping accurate accounts of what you have and what you spend is not a healthy financial habit. Spending money without accountability might feel good while you're doing it, but like a fun night out with friends, it can leave you feeling pretty bad when it's over.

In this chapter, we make the case for getting a budget in place and sticking to it. Think of it as the budget challenge—something you'll be able to tell people you've done.

We never fully understood why, but a lot of people are resistant to making a budget and keeping track of everything they spend. We'd argue that by doing so you're rewarding your future self—setting up yourself and your dependents for a better financial future.

Why You Need a Budget

To avoid the traps many people fall into—too much debt, too little savings, too much spending—you've got to have a budget. A budget helps you live within your means while also saving for your long-term goals.

The years pass by quickly. If you have a child or children, we'll bet in some ways it seems like they were just born, even if they're now seven or eight or twelve years old. Or maybe it seems like you just graduated from college, even if it's been 15 years since you walked across that stage to receive your diploma.

You set goals—short-, medium-, and long-term—for a reason. It's because you want to be prepared for the future, whether that's 5 years from now or 35.

It takes a little time to set up a budget that's comfortable for you to use, but it's well worth it to get a clear picture of your financial situation and know what you need to do to be able to meet your financial goals.

What Your Budget Should Include

You can start your budget by simply identifying your spending categories and listing all the money you spend in each category. Most people use a monthly budgeting system, although some financial advisers argue that a weekly budget keeps you more accountable and is easier to use. You can figure out what works best for you, but for now, let's think about a monthly budget.

List all the money you spend in each budget category each month, either estimated or exact. Take some time to really think about your spending, right down to toothpaste and your afternoon pick-me-up coffees.

Chances are, you'll use an app or budget software to track your income and expenses, but take a look at the sample budget worksheet that's included here. You can revise it as needed, but it can help you begin to think about your categories of spending and see just where your money goes. You might be very surprised at what you find out.

Sample Budget Worksheet

Housing	Estimated Cost	Amount/Worth
Mortgage/rent		
Phone		
Internet		
Electric		
Utilities		
Furniture		
Appliances		
Maintenance		
Housing subtotal:		
Transportation	Estimated Cost	Amount/Worth
Gas/maintenance		
Tolls		
License/taxes		
Public transportation, taxis, car services		
Transportation subtotal:		

Sample Budget Worksheet ...

... Sample Budget Worksheet

Taxes	Estimated Cost	Amount/Worth
Federal		
State		
Local		
Social Security		
Property		
Luxury		
Taxes subtotal:		

Debt	Estimated Cost	Amount/Worth
Credit cards		
Car loans		
Student loans		
Personal loans		
Lines of credit		
Debt subtotal:		

Entertainment	Estimated Cost	Amount/Worth
Movies, concerts, theater, etc.		
Vacations		
Hobbies		
Pets		
Magazines and books		
Streaming services/cable		
Restaurants		
Entertainment subtotal:		

Personal	Estimated Cost	Amount/Worth
Food		
Gifts		
Clothes		
Shoes		
Jewelry		
Dry cleaning/laundry		
Hair/makeup/toiletries		
Gym		
Other		
Personal subtotal:		
Health Care	Estimated Cost	Amount/Worth
Copayments		
Prescriptions		
Doctor visits		
Optometrist visits		
Dentist visits		
Health care subtotal:		
Insurance	Estimated Cost	Amount/Worth
Car		
Homeowner's/renter's		
Disability		
Life		
Health		
Insurance subtotal:		

Sample Budget Worksheet ...

... Sample Budget Worksheet

Children	Estimated Cost	Amount/Worth
Day care/preschool		
Babysitters		
Toys		
Clothes		
Other		
Children subtotal:		
Charity	**Estimated Cost**	**Amount/Worth**
Donations		
Charity subtotal:		
TOTAL:		

Calculating Your Net Income

Before you can understand how much you have to spend, save, and give away, you have to understand what your net income is.

There's a difference between *gross income* and *net income*. Gross income is the total amount of money you earn—the amount you wish you'd see in your paycheck. Net income, often referred to as "take-home pay," is the amount that actually does show up in your paycheck—it's what's left of your gross income after taxes, insurance, retirement contributions, and whatever else needs to be deducted is deducted.

Let's say you earn $4,800 a month. You pay $618 in federal taxes, $198 in state taxes, $59 in Medicare taxes, $230 in Social Security taxes, $155 for health and life insurance (depending on how much your employer picks up), and $540 to your 401(k) retirement account.

With all those deductions, your net income stands at $3,000—a big difference from your gross income.

Obviously, your budget has to be based on your net income, not your gross income, which includes money you don't actually get. Yes, we feel your pain. Nobody likes to think about all that money that disappears from their paycheck, but that's the way it is. So figure out your net income, and we'll move on to expenses.

Analyzing Your Expenses

All expenses involve spending money, but there are different kinds of expenses, some of which you have far more control over than others.

When you're listing your expenses in your budget, you'll want to be sure you cover them all—not just the obvious ones like your rent, student loans, and car payments. In this section, you learn about routine and nonroutine expenses, fixed and variable expenses, and discretionary and nondiscretionary expenses.

Just a note here: there's no judgment involved when listing your expenses. Filling out a budget worksheet is not meant to be an exercise in shame; it's just what you need to do to fully understand where your money is being spent. As you've already read, you can't work to improve your financial situation if you don't understand what it is.

Routine Expenses

Routine expenses are the obvious ones—the ones you always know are coming. That doesn't mean they can't vary in amount from month to month, but they're the predictable ones like rent, insurance, food, and entertainment.

Housing

Your rent or mortgage makes up the biggest chunk of your housing expenses, but don't forget the other things you pay for. There's your utility bills, the sofa and loveseat you bought last month, the washer you needed to replace, the bill for carpet cleaning, and so on. You get the idea.

Debt

This is probably another big expense category, unless you don't use credit cards and are lucky enough to not have any student loans or owe on anything else. In addition to those just named, debt expenses can include car payments, a line of credit such as a home equity loan, a personal loan, the money your parents loaned you when you were unemployed that you're now repaying, and so on.

When listing your debt expenses, be sure to include both principal and interest payments.

Insurance

Any insurances you pay for—auto insurance, health insurance or copays for health insurance you pay to your employer, renter's insurance, and so on—should be included in this category.

Taxes

If you own a home or condo, you'll need to include local property taxes, even if you put the money in escrow and your mortgage company makes the payment for you. Also include the taxes deducted from your paycheck, as mentioned earlier.

Transportation

If you own a vehicle, this category will include routine costs such as oil changes and what you spend on gas and car insurance. Don't forget the expenses for your license plates and car registrations, too. If you pay tolls regularly when driving, include those as well.

If you don't own a vehicle, get a handle on and list what you spend on ride shares, trains, subways, buses, or however else you get from one place to another.

Health Care

Be sure to include any medical expenses you have to pay for, such as eye exams, glasses or contacts, dentist appointments, and wellness checkups.

If you pay for your own health insurance, that will be the amount you list, in addition to anticipated copays and other related expenses.

Entertainment and Vacations

Be honest when filling out this category because it's one of the first places we'll return to when we start talking about controlling expenses. You'll need to list the cost or anticipated cost of vacations. Think about what you have planned for the coming year, and divide it by 12 to get a monthly allocation, or base it on what you spent last year.

Also include what you spend monthly in restaurants, coffee shops, concerts (looking at you, Swifties!), greens fees, those last-minute weekend getaways, streaming services, books, and any other expenses.

This category takes a lot of people by surprise when they realize how much they've been spending.

Personal

This category includes food, clothing, shoes, jewelry, gym fees, costs of haircuts and pedicures, makeup, and toiletries.

Children

If you have kids, you know they're expensive. If you don't have kids but plan to someday, take note that expenses include day care, preschool, babysitters, clothing, toys, diapers, food, nursery expenses like furniture and lamps, and so on.

Pets

Fun fact: the US pet industry was worth almost $80 billion in 2023. If you have a pet, you'll need to list what you spend on food, treats, toys, vet bills, and those cute vests and kerchiefs you buy.

Giving

This is an often-overlooked category, but giving is an important habit to develop when you're young, even if you can only give a little. Supporting causes you care about provides a sense of ownership and community. You might contribute money to a place of worship, an organization that works for social change, a political candidate, your local animal shelter, or another organization you admire.

After you've listed all your expenses, add them up. Think about any categories of routine expenses you might have that aren't listed here, and be sure to add them.

Nonroutine Expenses

Nonroutine expenses are those that are less obvious, like birthday presents, unexpected car repairs, the out-of-town bachelorette weekend, a contribution you make to a GoFundMe event, and so on.

The best way to anticipate nonroutine expenses is to figure out all you had in the past year. Include car repair bills, unexpected medical bills, and anything else you can think of.

Add the cost of all those things, and divide the total by 12. That's how much you should set aside each month for nonroutine expenses.

Fixed Expenses Versus Variable Expenses

Some of your expenses are fixed, while others are variable. Fixed expenses include rent or mortgage payments; car payments; and any other payments that don't vary in amount, such as the monthly fee for your gym membership or streaming services. Variable expenses can include food, utilities, entertainment, and vacations.

Fixed expenses might be necessary, but that doesn't mean they can't be pared down. If your mortgage is putting a strain on your budget, perhaps you can refinance to lower it. You might love your gym, but if you're paying $45 a month that could go toward childcare costs or groceries, it might be time to lace up your running shoes and head for the nearest trail. You have to make car payments, but the payment for a used Toyota is sure to be significantly less than for a new Lexus SUV.

It may be easier to cut back on variable expenses than on fixed expenses. You can lower your utility bills by getting your toilet fixed so it doesn't constantly run anymore and turning down the heat when no one is home. You can control the cost of your food bills by shopping at a value store, or lower your entertainment costs by cutting back on the number of streaming services you subscribe to.

Discretionary Expenses Versus Nondiscretionary Expenses

After you've broken down your expenses into variable or fixed, you can add another category: discretionary or nondiscretionary.

Discretionary expenses are those that are not necessary—you don't absolutely have to have them. Discretionary expenses are the ones you'll have to look at if you need to reduce your spending. Unfortunately, these include those things most people most enjoy spending their money on, such as vacations, dinners out, club memberships, and leisure activities like golf or skiing.

Nondiscretionary expenses tend to be less fun, but they're necessary and include food, rent or mortgage payments, car payments, and utility bills. Nondiscretionary expenses are necessary, but you might be able to control or adjust them, as previously mentioned.

When you've considered all your discretionary and nondiscretionary expenses, there are basically two ways to use the information you've compiled: you can control your discretionary expenses by skipping a vacation this year or putting your gym membership on hold, or you can find ways to limit your nondiscretionary expenses, such as moving to a smaller apartment or getting a less-expensive vehicle.

Spending Ratios

When it comes to figuring out where you need to cut expenses, spending ratios are useful tools. If you're not familiar with what a spending ratio is, it's simply the percentage of money, as it relates to your gross income, that you use for a particular area of spending, such as housing or entertainment. If one area of expense becomes too great, you'll see that ratio is too high and be able to cut back.

To figure out your housing payment ratio, for example, you'll need to add up all costs related to housing, such as your rent or mortgage, homeowner's or renter's insurance, property taxes, and so on, and compare that number to your total income. As you read in Chapter 1, a popular standard for budgeting is to spend no more than 30 percent of your monthly gross income on housing costs. Thirty percent became the rule on thumb in 1981, when the US government determined people who spent more than 30 percent of their income on housing were "cost burdened."

This rule has come under fire recently because a national housing shortage, rising mortgage rates, and wages that haven't kept up with rent hikes have resulted in the average American renter now spending more than 30 percent of their income on housing. This is particularly true for people who live in cities like New York, San Francisco, or Washington, DC, where rents have traditionally been far above average, or for people with lower incomes, whose housing costs are taking increasingly bigger bites out their paychecks.

This trend is mirrored by homeowners, many of whom are spending larger percentages of their incomes on mortgage payments and other costs associated with owning a house. Data shows that nationally, homeowners spend an average of 28.4 percent of pretax income on mortgage payments, but homeowners in 21 states and Washington, DC, spend more than 30 percent.

For argument's sake, we'll use the 30 percent rule for housing costs. If you find you're closer to 35 or 40 percent, you'll definitely want to look for ways to decrease your housing costs.

To calculate your overall spending ratio, add up all your monthly payments and compare that number to your total income. According to an old rule of thumb, your total debt, including housing costs, student loans, car loans, and any others, should be no more than 36 percent of your total income. That number doesn't include your monthly expenses for food, clothing, and so on—just your debt. Because many people have debt ratios of much higher than 36 percent, that rule has been relaxed somewhat by lenders. The point is, if you have a lot of debt, work on getting the ration down.

Obviously, it's more difficult for some people to maintain healthy spending ratios than others. If you're earning minimum wage and your rent has increased three times during the past four years, your spending ratios likely have become difficult to control. If you have a steady and reasonable income, however, keeping track of spending ratios gives you an idea of what money you'll have available to save or invest.

Another ratio to consider is your savings ratio, which is the percentage of your monthly income you're able to save. Compare the amount of money you save each week or month to your income for that period. You should aim for at least 8 percent a year. If you're not saving that much, it's time to figure out where you can cut some expenses to increase the amount you put away.

How to Spend Less (or Make More) to Have Your Budget Work

Once you have a good grasp on exactly where your money is going, you have a better shot at controlling your spending and reducing it when necessary. If you're able to meet all your expenses, make regular payments on student loans, pay off your credit card bills every month, save a portion of your income each month, and have some money left for discretionary expenses, good for you! You're in good financial shape.

If, however, you're spending everything you earn and not saving anything—or worse still, you're spending more than you earn and running up credit card or other debt, or you're unable to pay your student loans or car loan—your financial condition isn't on solid ground, and you need to do something about it.

Basically, as we're sure you've heard, there are two ways to improve your financial condition: you can spend less or earn more. In most cases, we'd recommend looking for ways to cut your spending instead of looking for ways to make more money for the purpose of spending more. It's one thing to take an extra job or sell a personal possession for the purpose of paying off a debt or being able to save money to pay for a wedding, but it's another thing to work long hours at the expense of a relationship or your health just to have money to spend on things you don't really need.

We once met a young man who was married and had three young children. He and his wife both worked full-time. Mike decided to invest in a sandwich shop some friends were buying. His financial share in the business wasn't that large, but his involvement required him to work a lot of hours, for which he was paid a salary. It's true that he was earning extra money, but it came at a terrible expense for him and his family, and everyone suffered. When his mother called him out on his decision to take that much time away from his family, he told her he wanted to be able to buy his kids everything they wanted.

He wasn't putting the extra money he earned into a college fund or even saving it for a family vacation; he was buying his kids stuff they wanted but didn't really need. We thought at the time, and still do, that it was a terrible decision for Mike to take that time away from his family because he would never get it back. Having said that, we do understand that it's sometimes necessary for someone to take a second or third job just to earn enough to pay for the necessities.

Our preference and advice, however, is to go over your expenses, starting with those in the discretionary category, and figure out how you can spend less. Learn to separate *wants* from *needs*.

A good exercise is to delay buying something you want, such as a new dress for a friend's wedding or a new TV for your bedroom. Even if you've found exactly what you want, waiting for three days to decide whether or not you'll make the purchase often results in the item seeming less attractive or necessary.

You can find all sorts of tips for cutting expenses online and even get some help from an app like PocketGuard, which uses an algorithm to track your income, expenses, and savings goals to figure out how much you can spend every day, helping you avoid overspending.

When you fully understand your spending and you've identified areas in which you can cut back, you can create a budget you can live with. If your budget is too strict, chances are you won't be able to stick to it. If it's too lax, it probably won't adequately help you move toward your financial goals.

Staying Accountable to Your Budget Goals

A budget is of little use if you don't treat it as a financial road map. Staying accountable to your budget can be hard sometimes, especially when you run into unexpected expenses or something like an opportunity that seems just too good to pass up comes along.

But if you're careful to allow for little leeway when you're building your budget, and you follow some of these tips for sticking to it, you should be able to reduce some expenses and use that money to help secure your financial future.

Don't Spend What You Don't Have

Using credit cards to buy what you want at any given time is a dangerous game because getting into debt can trigger a cycle that's tricky to break out of. You'll learn a lot more about credit in Chapter 5, but suffice it to say now, that as of June 2023, the average credit card interest rate was 24.53 percent, according to Forbes Advisor's credit card interest rate report. That means if you owe $1,000 on your credit card, your interest for a year would be almost $250.

Have an Accountability Partner

An accountability partner can be a spouse, partner, relative, or friend you report your spending to. It even can be a journal in which you keep track of everything you spend.

Having someone other than yourself to answer to has been shown to make you think twice about what you do and just might keep you from buying that sweatshirt you really like but don't really need.

Use a Budgeting App

A good budgeting app can help you track your spending and categorize your expenses. NerdWallet has a recent list of recommended apps that includes Mint, YNAB, Goodbudget, EveryDollar, Empower Personal Wealth, PocketGuard, Honeydue, and Fudget. (You can find the list and descriptions of each app at nerdwallet.com/article/finance/best-budget-apps.)

The apps have different features and are recommended for different reasons, but NerdWallet reports that they all got great customer reviews. Most of these apps are either free or have a basic version that's free and then an upgradable version you have to pay for.

Keep Track of Your Accounts

Take the time to check your credit card and bank statements frequently. This can help you stay on track with what you're spending.

Some banks offer online tools that track every deposit, purchase, and payment you make with a debit or credit card, check, or online bill pay and send you reports of your transactions by email, either daily or weekly. This can be helpful because it's easy to use a credit or debit card at the store without really paying attention to how much you're paying.

Getting into the habit of checking your accounts—or letting an online tool do it for you—can let you know that you overspent at the grocery store or you were overcharged on an Amazon purchase. If you don't opt for automated reports, check your accounts at least once a week.

Plan for Seasonal Expenses Throughout the Year

Putting aside a little money in a separate account every month can give you the funds you need to buy holiday gifts, renew your gym membership when it comes due, or pay for the concert you go to every year over Labor Day weekend. Anticipate this type of spending so you don't end up having to take the money from someplace else—or, worse yet, put in on a credit card and then have to pay interest, too.

Don't Give Up

Sometimes it's difficult not to overspend. If you end up taking a friend to dinner because her partner just walked out on her and she needed someone to talk to, it's not the end of the budget world. Just figure out how you can cut back somewhere else and stay the course. One mistake doesn't negate all the effort you've put into your budget.

You can figure out the best methods for keeping yourself accountable for sticking to your budget. Find whatever works best for you, and stick with it. Budgeting becomes a habit, like running every day or stretching when you wake up in the morning.

Chapter Summary

Once you get a handle on your net income, you can budget your spending, understanding that some expenses are nonnegotiable while others can be adjusted. Keeping an eye on spending ratios can help you understand where you might be overspending and when you might need to employ strategies to help you spend less.

Chapter 3

Getting a Handle on Debt

Americans carry a lot of collective debt—about $16.38 trillion, according to Experian, a multinational data analytics and consumer credit reporting company. As a nation, we added $1 trillion, or 7 percent, to that debt in 2022, the largest annual increase in more than a decade. Consumer demand rose, despite inflation rates of about 6.5 percent, causing increasing prices for just about everything.

Experian also reported that millennials are the generation with the fastest-growing debt load, a fact attributed to a growing number who are still paying on student loans while also having children and buying homes, if they're able to consider homeownership. A sad statistic estimates that 34 percent of millennials making more than $75,000 a year believe they will never be able to pay off their student loans. To make matters worse, rising interest rates have resulted in higher rates for credit cards and car payments.

All told, according to Experian's State of Credit 2020 report, the average millennial nonmortgage consumer debt—which includes credit cards, student loans, car loans, personal loans, and any revolving debt such as a home equity loan (more about revolving debt later in this chapter)—stands at about $27,250. Millennials who are homeowners carry an average balance on their mortgages of about $232,370.

Debt isn't necessarily a bad thing because it allows consumers to buy homes and vehicles and continue their education and perhaps invest in a business. But carrying too much debt for too long can cause interest to accumulate, making it even more difficult to pay off your debt.

In this chapter, we look at different kinds of debt, the effects of debt, and how you might think about reducing or paying off your own debt.

How Debt Affects You and Your Finances

Increasingly, experts are looking at how debt affects not only your finances, but also your overall quality of life. You read in Chapter 1 about how personal finances affect your life, and the debt you carry clearly is a part of those finances. With three quarters of Americans stressed about money, you can bet that debt is a big contributor to that worry, which can lead to trouble sleeping, relationship problems, depression, and other ills.

In addition to your health, debt can negatively impact your financial future, too.

Retirement Savings

We're sure you know how important it is to save for retirement, but that becomes a challenging task when you're trying to pay down debt. The dilemma, of course, is that the longer you take to pay off debt, the more interest you'll end up paying over time. But using money you could be saving for retirement to pay off debt results in having less money saved when you're older.

A rule of thumb for retirement savings is that you should put away 12 to 15 percent of your annual salary each year, starting as soon as you're able. A lot of people, especially younger people with lower salaries, aren't able to do that, but it's a worthy goal. (You'll learn more about retirement plans in Chapter 6.)

If you have so much debt that you're not able to save any money, however, you need to rethink your financial situation and make some serious changes. You'll read some strategies for paying down debt later in this chapter.

Your Credit Score

A number of factors are considered when determining a credit score, and one of them is debt. The credit score folks refer to debt as "amounts owed," and it makes up about 30 percent of your score. That's because, according to FICO, the most widely used credit score, the amount of debt you owe usually affects your ability to pay all your bills on time. And if you can't pay your bills on time, it will be reflected in your credit score.

A low credit score can make your life difficult because it makes it harder for you to borrow money for a mortgage, car loan, or other purchase. It also can make it trickier to rent a house or apartment, set up accounts with utility or internet companies, and get the best deals on purchases for phones and other popular items. A poor credit score also means you'll have to pay higher interest rates on any loans you get. (You'll read more about credit scores in Chapter 5.)

Landing a Job or Leaving a Job

A lot of employers run background checks before making hiring decisions, and that background check is likely to include a credit check. Some states limit an employer's ability to check credit without your permission, but refusing to allow it also is likely to raise alarm bells. A poor credit score is especially problematic, of course, if you're looking for work in the financial field, but it's likely to cause concern for prospective employers in any area of work.

Alternately, owing a lot of money can force you to stay in a job you don't like in an effort to avoid going even further into debt. It limits your options, which can result in you feeling trapped and unable to achieve your goals.

Buying a Home

A high debt-to-income ratio, which is a comparison of how much you owe to how much money you earn, can limit your chances of being approved for a mortgage. If you are able to get one, you may be required to pay higher interest rates or have a higher down payment if you have a high debt-to-income ratio.

On the other hand, it's really important to have some well-managed debt on your credit report. A student loan that's been paid off or is being paid off is reassuring to most lenders, as are credit card bills that have been regularly paid on time. Well-managed debt can improve your credit score, which also is likely to encourage lenders.

Starting a Business

Too much debt can make it hard to borrow the capital you need to open a business because many banks are reluctant to approve small business loans for someone who already owes a lot of money. It also can prevent you from attracting investors or even partners who may feel threatened by your personal debt.

Affording Day-to-Day Expenses

Having so much debt that it impacts your ability to meet your day-to-day expenses is a problem many people face. If you're constantly struggling with paying bills or falling behind on monthly payments, it probably is time to take action to reduce your debt.

Different Types of Debt

As you read at the beginning of the chapter, debt occurs in various forms, including mortgages, personal loans, student loans, credit card debt, and so forth. Generally, though, most debt falls into a category of either secured or unsecured debt, and as either revolving debt or installment debt. Let's have a look at each type.

Secured Debt Versus Unsecured Debt

A secured debt is one that's backed by something of value, like a house or a vehicle. The item of value is known as collateral, and it's like insurance to the lender, who gets to claim it if the loan is not repaid.

A car loan is a secured loan because if you don't pay it back, the bank or whoever loaned you the money will lay claim to the car. The same thing happens if you're unable to pay your mortgage. After a period of time, your mortgage lender will take possession of the property, which will go into foreclosure.

An unsecured debt, such as a credit card or medical bill, is one that does not require collateral. A signature loan, which is a loan that requires only a promise to repay the loan and the signature of the borrower, is another example of an unsecured loan.

Unsecured loans generally carry higher interest rates than secured loans.

Revolving Debt Versus Installment Debt

A revolving debt is one that's open-ended, such as a credit card. After you pay down your balance, you can restart the loan. Revolving debt includes a maximum credit line up to which you can spend as many times as you need to. If your credit card has a $10,000 maximum credit line, you could charge $10,000 to it every month as long as you also paid it off each month.

The amount of available credit you have will vary, depending on how much credit you've already used. If you use $4,000 of your $10,000 limit, you'll have only $6,000 left to use. If you pay back $2,000 of the $4,000, your available credit would be $8,000.

Installment debts are closed-ended, or lump-sum loans. These include mortgages, car loans, and student loans. The lender gives the borrower a certain amount of money, which the borrower agrees to pay back at regularly scheduled intervals.

When you make a payment on an installment loan, you're paying back a portion of the principal amount borrowed, along with interest on the debt. Typically, the borrower repays the same amount every month, or whatever payment period has been agreed upon.

Now that you understand these debt categories, we'll have a quick look at some different forms of debt.

Common Types of Debt

Just as there are different types of spending, there are different types of debt. Within the categories of debt you've read about, there are different debt vehicles. In this section, you'll learn about some of the most common types of debt.

Credit Cards

As mentioned earlier, credit cards are a kind of revolving debt, enabling you to borrow up to the maximum allowed amount again and again. The amount you're able to borrow up to depends on various factors, including your credit score and your income.

Credit cards typically come with high interest rates, which is one of the reasons you can get into trouble with them if you're not careful.

Student Loans

Student loan debts are installment loans issued by a variety of lenders, including the federal government. Americans owe more in student debt than any other type of debt, except mortgages.

One reason so many people are having trouble repaying student loans is because interest starts to accrue on the loans as soon as they're distributed and continues, even if there's a period of deferment on the loan. The interest compounds—which is a good thing if you're *earning* it, but not if you're responsible for *paying* it.

Many people with student loans have repaid more than the amount of the principal of the loan but still have huge monthly balances because of the accumulated interest.

If you have federal student loans, there's not much you can do to get a lower interest rate because the rates are set by Congress. If your loans are through a private lender, you might be able to lower your interest rates by setting up automatic payments or looking for other discounts. Some lenders are willing to work with borrowers who don't miss payments and pay on time, and others, like some banks, may offer a loyalty discount if you also have a bank account at the bank.

The problem of student debt and the possibility of student debt forgiveness are front and center in current public debate, with even the Supreme Court weighing in. We'll see where it lands. Meanwhile, student debt income may be tax deductible if you meet certain income requirements.

Mortgages

A mortgage is typically the largest debt an individual will encounter, and it's the most common type of debt in America. More than 70 percent of Americans' total debt, in fact, is mortgage debt.

Interest rates on mortgages are usually one of the lowest of any consumer loan product, and you may be able to deduct the interest if you itemize your taxes. (You'll read a lot more about mortgage debt in Chapter 7.)

Autos

Car loans, as you read, are loans secured by the value of the vehicle. A car loan is given in a lump sum that you agree to pay back at regular intervals during a period of time, normally between three and six years.

Interest rates are normally lower than those on personal loans, due to the car serving as collateral. Auto loans account for about 9.2 percent of American consumer debt, with about 85 percent of car buyers using them.

Medical Debt

You may not hear as much about medical debt as other types of debt, but it's significant. The US Census Bureau reported that in 2021, nearly one in five households couldn't pay for medical care when it was needed. According to the Consumer Financial Protection Bureau, medical debt was the most common reason debt collectors contacted consumers in 2022, and it's a primary cause of bankruptcy.

Not surprisingly, lower-income people, who also are less likely to have adequate health insurance, are most negatively affected by medical debt.

What to Do About All That Debt

If you find that you're saddled with more debt than you'd like, there are steps you can take to reduce or eliminate it. First, however, you need to have a clear picture of exactly how much debt you have. Look up all your debt balances and add them up. Include student debt, car loans, housing costs, all credit cards, and any other types of debt.

When you've got a total, divide it by the amount of your gross (before taxes are taken out) monthly income. You can easily find an online debt calculator to help you do that. The resulting number is your debt-to-income ratio, which is an important metric in figuring out if you're in trouble with your overall debt.

If you're a two-income household and sharing the debt, combine your incomes and add up all the debt you're both responsible for.

A general rule of thumb is that a debt-to-income ratio of less than 36 percent is considered good. If it's between 36 and 42 percent, most experts recommend you take steps to lower it. If your debt-to-income ratio is 43 percent or higher, it's probably a good idea for you to consult a nonprofit credit counseling agency to help you get back on track. There are lists of approved agencies online; be sure you check first to find a reputable one.

The following table shows a few debt-to-income ratio examples. Some fall into the "good" category while others are in the "needs work to lower" category.

Sample Debt-to-Income Ratios

Annual Income	Total Monthly Debt Payment	Debt-to-Income Ratio
$40,000	$1,300	39 percent
$60,000	$1,800	36 percent
$80,000	$2,300	34 percent
$100,000	$2,800	34 percent

In addition to your debt-to-income ratio, other signs of having too much debt can include the following:

- You live paycheck to paycheck and are unable to save any money.
- Your debt balances stay the same despite making regular payments.
- You haven't been able to get an emergency fund established.
- You rely on credit cards for everyday purchases.
- You've been turned down for additional credit.
- You're opening new credit card accounts to pay for older ones.
- You're late paying your rent or other bills.

Methods for Paying Down Debt

There are many methods recommended for paying down debt. As long as you're making a real effort, probably any of them would work, although some may work more effectively and be faster than others.

The first thing you should do is to take a careful look at your budget and figure out where you can cut spending to get some extra money to throw at your debt. The more cash you can apply to paying down your bills, the better, and every little bit will help.

Consider a walk-in hair-salon chain with a $18 haircut instead of the $70 cut at the fancy place, for example. Realize that you really don't need another $50 sweatshirt. Put your two-dinners-out-a-week habit on hold until your debts are paid down—or better yet, eliminated.

If your debt-to-income ratio is between 36 and 42 percent, you can take steps to lower it on your own. Two popular DIY methods are the debt avalanche—the method we prefer—and the debt snowball. You also could consider consolidating your debt.

The Debt Avalanche

Start with the debt that has the highest interest rate. Stop using that card, and start making the highest payments on it you can, while continuing to pay minimum balances on all your other debts. This wipes out your costliest debt first, which will save you money in the long run. Just be consistent, and don't be tempted to skip any payments.

Also, don't close the account before the debt is paid off because that would negatively impact your credit score. Closing the account after the balance is paid off also may affect your score, but not as much. If you can leave the card open without using it, or keep it to use just in the event of a real emergency, that may be a better option than closing it. If you don't think you can refrain from using the card, however, you're probably better off closing the account.

The Debt Snowball

This method has you start by paying off your smallest balance first, regardless of the interest rate. When you've paid it off, stop using the card (or better yet, cut it up), and add the amount you had been putting toward it to the minimum payment on your next-smallest debt.

Repeat until you've paid off all your debt, remembering to pay minimum balances on all but the focus debt.

Debt Consolidation

Another method of reducing debt is debt consolidation, a process that combines multiple debts into a single payment. This can be a good idea if you can get a lower interest rate, but it may be difficult to do.

Basically, there are two ways to consolidate debt. If you're able to get approved for a debt-consolidation credit card, you could get a 0 percent interest balance-transfer credit card. That could enable you to transfer all your high-interest debt onto the 0 percent card and pay it off before the end of the 0 percent promotional period.

A couple drawbacks with this method: you need a really good credit score—usually between 580 and 680—to qualify for such a card, and you've got to be sure you can pay off the debt by the end of the promotional period. If not, the interest rate is likely to be as high or higher than it was on the debt you transferred onto the new card.

You also could get a fixed-rate debt consolidation loan and use that money to pay off your debt, after which you'd have to pay back the loan. You normally don't have to have great credit to get one of these loans, but the better your credit, the better interest rate you're likely to get. If you do get a debt consolidation loan, it's vital that you stop using credit cards while you pay back the loan.

There are other methods for paying down debt, such as getting a personal loan, home equity loan, or home equity line of credit or taking a 401(k) loan, but we would not recommend doing any of these things. The problem with these methods is that you're simply exchanging one type of debt for another, while putting your home or retirement savings at risk.

The best way to reduce or eliminate your debt is to cut your expenses, stop using credit cards, choose a method of paying off your debt, and stick to it until it's done.

Chapter Summary

Having too much debt can negatively affect your overall financial situation, so it's better to assess what debt you have and address it responsibly. Consider each category of debt you have, figure out your debt-to-income ratio, and determine if your debt level is too high. If so, create a plan, consulting a financial counselor if necessary, to get the debt paid down as quickly as possible.

Chapter 4

The Importance of Earning and Saving

Most of us understand that saving money is a good thing, for a lot of reasons.

Having some money saved provides peace of mind, perhaps minimizing the number of nights you'll toss and turn, wondering how you're going to pay for that unexpected car repair bill. Having money also gives you options that you wouldn't have without it, such as being able to upgrade from a one-bedroom to a two-bedroom apartment.

Starting to save money from as early an age as possible has the huge financial benefit of having that money work for you as you get older.

In this chapter, we explain why saving money is so important and why starting to do so while you're young is much better than waiting until you're older. We also consider various options for where to stash your savings, and we look at how much you should work toward putting away.

Why You Need to Be Saving Money Now

We have a two-word answer for anyone who asks about the importance of starting to save money at a young age: *compound interest*. Described by Albert Einstein as the "eighth wonder of the world," compound interest is the best argument for stashing some money in savings on a regular basis, even if it's just a small amount.

Compound interest is the interest that's paid not only on money you deposit, but also on the interest earned on that interest. That makes your money grow more quickly, which means you have even more money on which to earn interest.

Let's say that Anna, a 25-year-old who makes a little more than $50,000 a year, has $500 left from her tax return refund and decides to invest it. And let's say that her investment earns a compounding interest rate of 10 percent a year, which, although in no way guaranteed, has been about the average rate of return on the stock market for the past 100 years. If Anna lets her money sit for 5 years, it will have grown to $805. If she doesn't touch it for 15 years, she'll have about $2,089. And after 25 years, her $500 will have grown to about $5,417.

Notice how the rate at which the money is growing accelerates as more time passes. By the time Anna's money has been invested for 35 years, she'll have $14,051. And when Anna turns 70, and her money's been in that account for 45 years, her $500 investment will be worth $36,445. That is the beauty of compound interest!

Compounding interest is a compelling reason to start saving from as young an age as possible, but that's not the only reason. When you've got money saved in accounts and in an emergency fund, you can start thinking about investing money in stocks or bonds or exchange-traded funds (ETFs) or mutual funds, all of which you'll read about later in this book. Beginning to invest at a young age gives you the luxury of time, which means you can afford to take a bit more risk and tap into higher-risk, higher-reward investments. You'll be able to diversify your portfolio over time, which is beneficial, and weather any market ups and downs.

Plus, there are the practical-right-now reasons for saving, like giving you the ability to have a down payment for a house, or to start a college fund for your kids, or go back to school yourself. Having money gives you options.

Be Sure You Have an Emergency Fund

When you've gotten your budget set up and working for you, you'll see how much money is left after you've paid the rent or mortgage, been to the grocery store, paid the utility bills, made your loan payments, and met all your other monthly expenses.

If you don't already have one, the very first thing you should do with some of that extra money is establish an emergency fund. An emergency fund is just what it sounds like—money you save to see you through in case of an emergency, like if you get laid off from your job, or if you find out the foundation of your house has shifted and needs to be repaired, or if the mechanic tells you that the car you've had since college will cost more to repair than it's worth and it's advisable to get a new one.

Some people need an emergency fund to tap into because their income is uneven. If you're in an industry in which you earn a lot of money some of the time and next to nothing at other times, you should have an emergency fund you can pull from during the lean periods.

Research shows that 45 percent of Americans have less than $1,000 saved that they could get to quickly if needed. As a result, many people have gotten into serious debt problems because they encountered financial hardship and didn't have an emergency fund to turn to.

The fact is, you need money to live. If your income suddenly stops and you have no emergency fund to fall back on, what are you going to do, except use credit cards to pay for the things you need?

You can live just fine on your credit cards for a couple months, depending on your credit limits. But what happens when you've spent thousands of dollars on your credit cards and still haven't found a job so you can start paying them off?

It's best to set up a separate account for your emergency fund and resolve not to use the money for any other purpose. You'll want your cash someplace where it's available when you need it, like a savings or checking account, a money market fund, or a high-yield savings account. When deciding where to keep your emergency money, keep in mind that some banks offer cash bonuses when you open a new account. If you find one, be sure the bonus money goes right into your emergency fund.

Most financial advisers recommend having an emergency fund that can cover your expenses for between three and six months. Our feeling is that three months is generally okay for a household with two incomes, while someone living on a single income, or a household with a stay-at-home spouse, should try to save up for six months of living expenses. You can get an idea of how much you should have by figuring out your average monthly expenses and multiplying them by three or six months, as applicable. If your average monthly expenses are $3,000 and you're a single-income household, you should have an emergency fund of about $18,000.

We know that sounds like an awful lot of money, and it is. It will take time to grow your emergency fund to the level where it should be, but you can do it if you contribute to it regularly, regardless of what else is going on. Commit to saving something—as much as you're able to save—at regular intervals.

Your emergency fund serves the dual purpose of providing peace of mind that you'll be able to pay for unexpected expenses and assuring you that your finances won't be derailed by rent or other unplanned-for costs because you were not prepared.

Taking Advantage of a 401(k) Plan

Not meeting your employer's match in a 401(k) plan, if one is offered at your place of employment, is like leaving money on the table.

Contributing to a 401(k) plan, which is a plan that gives employees a chance to save part of their salaries in a tax-advantaged manner, or another type of employer-sponsored retirement plan, is an ideal way to start saving for the years after you stop working.

Many employers match employees' contributions to their 401(k)s up to a certain amount. Some employers offer a percentage of the employee's contributions. Either scenario is a win for employees, who should take full advantage of whatever is offered. By doing so, you're able to save more money more quickly, giving you more time to let it grow and work for you.

Where to Save Your Money

So where should you save the money that won't be put aside into an emergency fund or contributed to a 401(k) or other type of retirement account? You have some choices, and it's important to find the account or accounts that most fit your needs.

Some people are most comfortable with keeping all their funds in one bank, and for good reason. Having your finances in one place makes managing your money easier because you can have just one login to access multiple accounts and use one app to see everything in one place. Many Americans start with a bank and remain there, which can make it daunting to find another place to handle your money.

If you can get higher interest rates, or lower fees, at a different bank, however, it's worth considering moving at least some of your funds. The goal is to save money in an account where you'll earn some interest but still have access to it when you need it. Whenever possible, you want your money to be working for you—not just sitting there.

When deciding where to park your funds, consider the following:

- When will you need the money you're saving?
- How accessible does your money need to be?
- How much interest will you earn?
- Will the account provide the services you need?
- What kind of penalties might you incur if you need to get your money?

Let's look at some types of available accounts and consider some of their advantages and disadvantages.

Savings Accounts

Putting your money in a savings account at a bank or credit union is reliable and safe, and your money is available to you when you need it to pay bills or meet other expenses.

You'll have to do some looking around to find a decent interest rate, however. Some major banks offer next to nothing in interest on savings accounts—some are as low as 0.01 percent. Smaller banks, online banks, and certainly some credit unions, however, might offer significantly more.

Why? What banks pay customers to save with them depends on how much they need the deposits. Many big banks like JPMorgan Chase, Bank of America, Citigroup, or Wells Fargo are doing just fine and not overly concerned about getting people to open savings accounts with them. As a result, the interest rates they offer are minimal, and maybe almost nothing.

For example, in July 2023, Bank of America, the second-largest US bank after JPMorgan Chase, offered interest on just one type of savings account, the Bank of America Advantage Savings. There are conditions for having that account; if you don't maintain a minimum balance of $500, you'll have to pay an $8 monthly maintenance fee. And the interest you'll get? As of July 2023, it was 0.01 percent. That's lower than the July national average in 0.42 percent.

If you're willing to look beyond the big banks, you can do a lot better.

In its report for July 8, 2023, Forbes Advisor reported that SoFi, an online bank based in San Francisco, offered a savings account paying an annual percentage yield (APY), which is the real rate of return earned on an investment, of 4.30 percent. There's no minimum balance required, no fees, and you might qualify for a $250 bonus when you open the account. If you'd have $25,000 deposited in a SoFi savings account for 1 year, you'd earn about $1,075 in interest, compared to about $2.50 at the 0.01 percent.

Other banks mentioned in the Forbes Advisor report—all offering interest rates of more than 4 percent—are CIT Bank, LendingClub, Bask Bank, and Capital One.

We're not recommending any of these banks. We are telling you to do your research about wherever you choose to open any type of account. It's a good idea to explore your options, ensuring, of course, that the bank is a member of the Federal Deposit Insurance Corporation (FDIC), which insures your money in the event the bank fails. You'll also want to check on minimum required account limits and see if there are any fees associated with the account, such as a service fee for transactions over a certain limit.

High-Yield Checking Accounts

As with savings accounts, you can find high-yield checking accounts if you look around. Having a checking account in addition to a savings account is generally a good idea because it's designed for transactions. Checking accounts are also guaranteed by the FDIC.

As of early August 2023, some banks, particularly online banks, were offering interest rates on checking accounts of 4.26 percent. Most rates were not that high, but numerous banks had rates between 2 and 4 percent. Many had either low or no minimum balance requirements. Some banks capped the amount of money on which they'll pay interest, and other regulations may apply, but it's worth checking out what's available and thinking about whether one of these accounts makes sense for you.

Remember, the point is to make your money work for you.

Money Market Accounts

Money market accounts (MMAs) are a type of savings account that generally pay slightly higher interest rate than regular savings accounts. An MMA may have features of both a checking and savings account; many MMAs allow you to write checks and perform debit card transactions on the account. With some accounts, you can transfer money using the bank's app or access it through an ATM. As with checking accounts, some online banks offer relatively high interest rates on MMAs. Because these accounts are offered by banks, your money is insured by the FDIC.

The national average APY for money market accounts was only 0.59 percent in May 2023, but higher interest rates on MMAs can be found. Bankrate reported that as of July 2023, Western was offering an APY of 5.15 percent on MMAs with a minimum balance of $5,000, and VirtualBank had an offer for 5 percent APY with no minimum balance requirement. Schwab also has a money market fund with an APY of nearly 5 percent.

If you only need to make two or three payments from the account each month, a money market account might be worth considering. But there's usually a hefty fee if you make more withdrawals than permitted, and the bank may require a higher minimum balance than what's required with a savings account. To avoid fees, you'd need to remember to move money from your MMA to your checking account before you need it to pay a bill. Also, some money market accounts only allow you to access money over a certain amount. Remember that any additional interest you might earn is quickly eliminated if you have to pay for extra withdrawals or a low-balance fee.

Certificates of Deposit

Certificates of deposit, or CDs, are another option for saving, although you have to commit to leaving the money sit in the account, undisturbed, for a set amount of time. If you're willing to do that, you might get a higher yield than you would on a standard savings account.

The national average on a 1-year CD rate was 1.72 percent APY in July 2023, up significantly from the previous year, when it was just 0.3 percent. The increase is the result of the several rate hikes imposed by the Federal Reserve to combat inflation. Many financial analysts feel that if the Federal Reserve backs off on increasing interest rates, the rates CDs pay will not continue to increase. We'll see what happens.

Still, as with other types of accounts, there are good deals available for those who shop around. In July 2023, BMO Alto, part of the BMO Financial Group that offers online-only accounts, had a 1-year CD with no minimum deposit that paid 5.25 percent interest. CIT Bank had a 6-month CD with 5 percent interest. Be sure to do your homework.

Remember that money in a CD is not readily available, as it is in a savings or checking account. If you take your money out of the account before the specified amount of time has expired, you'll be charged a penalty. The amount of the penalty varies by each institution, but it can be pretty hefty.

If you pull out your money early, you could end up with even less money than you started with if the circumstances are right. You'd lose not only whatever interest you'd earned but also part of your principal.

Treasury Bills, Bonds, and Notes

Treasury bills, Treasury bonds, and Treasury notes—often just called treasuries—are safe savings vehicles because they're backed by the US government. They all are fixed-income securities the government offers to consumers and investors so it can fund its operations. You don't have to pay state or local income taxes on treasuries, and they come in different maturity lengths.

Treasury bills, bonds, and notes all are debt instruments, meaning the investor is lending the US government the amount it costs to purchase the bond. The investor receives interest or another form of payment, and when the bond reaches its maturity date, the face value of the bond is returned to the investor.

Treasury Bills

Treasury bills have the shortest terms of all government bonds, issued with maturity dates of 4, 8, 13, 26, and 52 weeks. You buy Treasury bills at a discount and, instead of receiving interest on your investment, get the full value of the bill when it reaches maturity. You might buy a $500 treasury for $450, for example, but when the bill matures, it will be worth the face value of $500. The extra $50 would be considered interest on your investment. Bills are available in varying increments starting at $100.

You can buy Treasury bills only in electronic form, either directly from the government at TreasuryDirect.gov or from a brokerage firm.

Treasury Bonds

Treasury bonds are long-term investments with maturities of 20 or 30 years. If you bought these bonds, you'd receive a fixed interest payment every six months and get the face value of the bond back when it hit its maturity. Because they're longer-term investments, Treasury bonds pay higher interest rates than Treasury bills or notes.

You can buy Treasury bonds at online auctions the US Department of the Treasury holds every month. Bonds are sold in multiples of $100, and the price of the bonds and their yield are determined during the auction.

After purchase, they can be traded in the secondary market and purchased from a bank or a broker, meaning you could get Treasury bonds either directly from the government or from a bank or broker. It also means you can elect to sell your bonds through a bank or broker before their maturity date after holding them for more than 45 days—although if you do, there's no guarantee you'll get the full face value.

Investors often buy Treasury bonds because they are safe vehicles for retirement savings that provide a steady stream of income. As with all Treasury investments, the interest on Treasury bonds varies due to different factors. In August 2023, interest rates were a little above 4 percent, significantly higher than normal.

Treasury Notes

Treasury notes are similar to Treasury bonds but with shorter terms. They come with maturity periods of 2, 3, 5, 7, and 10 years, and you earn a certain amount of interest every 6 months you hold them. Like a Treasury bill, if you buy the note at a discount, it will be worth the face value at maturity. Because they have shorter maturities, notes pay less interest than bonds.

Notes also are auctioned by the Department of the Treasury and sold on the secondary market, meaning you can buy them either at auction or from a bank or a broker. You can hold them to maturity to guarantee you redeem their full face value or sell them on the secondary market prior to maturity.

You only need a minimum of $100 to buy a Treasury note, so they're an easy way to begin saving in a safe vehicle.

Finding Ways to Save More

Because having some money saved is so important, it's a good idea to work out some strategies for saving as much as you can in as little time as possible. Building up an account can be a challenge, especially if you're a single-income household or your combined earnings are modest and are needed for living expenses. But if you look carefully at your budget, it's likely you'll find areas where you can cut back expenses and have some money to save.

The old adage is to put 20 percent of every paycheck into savings. That's part of the 50-30-20 strategy, which allocates 50 percent of what you earn to things you need, 30 percent to things you want, and 20 percent to savings. There's also a 80-20 strategy, where needs and wants are lumped into one category while retaining the 20 percent savings rule.

The all-items Consumer Price Index (CPI), which is a measure of inflation across the economy, reported that the cost of living rose 4 percent between May 2022 and May 2023. Between March 2021 and March 2022, the all-items index increased by 8.5 percent. Wages and salaries aren't keeping up with those increases, making saving money even more challenging.

Still, the old advice to "pay yourself first" bears repeating, even if you have to significantly reduce your discretionary spending. Fortune Recommends, an affiliate of Fortune Media Group, offers the following strategies for saving money quickly.

Increase Your Income

Try to increase your income by asking for a raise or getting a different job. Or you could add a second, part-time job if your schedule allows.

Before you consider asking for a raise, do some research to see how your salary compares to others who do the same job. If you find you're making less than others within your business sector or industry, it might be worth mentioning that to your boss and asking for more money.

Granted, hunting for a new job isn't always feasible, but it's easy to see what's available, and keeping your eyes open for opportunities can't hurt. Pew Research reports that 60 percent of workers who changed jobs between April 2021 and May 2022 got a pay raise.

If your job doesn't pay enough for you to save, you could temporarily add a second job, although as mentioned in Chapter 2, we would recommend that only after you've tried to accomplish saving more by spending less.

If you do consider a side hustle, be creative with what you choose. You might be able to earn some extra money by testing website usability or watching videos. If you have a property with extra storage space or parking space, it's possible to earn some additional cash by offering it on a site like SpotHero or Spacer. And of course there's Uber, Lyft, and other driving and task sites, which give you flexibility to work the hours and frequency you desire.

Switch Banks

To earn more interest, consider moving your bank accounts to another institution that offers higher interest rates. Or open an additional savings account with an online bank that offers higher interest rate yields.

Look for one that offers bonus cash or other incentives for new account holders.

Change the Way You Eat and Shop

If you've been out to eat or ordered in recently, you've likely noticed that it costs more than it used to. The CPI "food away from home" index (yes, there is an index for almost every expense category), rose 7.2 percent between April 2021 and April 2022. The increase for full-service menu prices for the same time period was almost 9 percent.

Shopping for groceries and cooking your own meals can save a significant amount of money that can be put toward savings. If you hate to shop, many stores offer pickup services for either a low or no additional fee.

A tip for saving money at the grocery store: buy generic or store-brand items. Name-brand goods can cost 25 to 35 percent more than generic—and sometimes they're the same product, just with different packaging. The next time you're in the grocery store, do some comparison shopping and see how the costs differ.

Review Your Insurance

Insurance can be expensive, but you can shop around and compare insurance prices to see if you can find a lower premium.

If you want to stay with your current insurance company, there may be ways to lower your premiums. The Insurance Information Institute says that increasing your car insurance deductible can reduce your premium by up to 30 percent. You also can ask if your insurer offers discounts for having a good driving record or having paid your premium on time. Or you may be able to bundle your policies to cut costs.

If your insurer doesn't offer such discounts, or doesn't want to help you find ways to save on your insurance, you can take your business to a company that will.

Save with Cash-Back Rewards

You could sign up for a credit card that offers cash back and put the rewards directly into your savings account. If you pay for everything—gas, groceries, trips to the dentist, and so on—with the cash-back card and pay it off in full every month, you could earn a fair amount of extra money.

Just be sure that you're able to pay off the card each month to avoid interest charges, which would defeat the purpose of the card.

Cancel Some Subscriptions

Make a list of all the subscriptions and memberships you have, everything from Amazon Prime to Netflix to your gym membership. Take a look at the cost of each one, and ask yourself how often you've used it in the past month. If it's no longer applicable, get rid of it.

You can always sign back up for some of these subscriptions for a brief time, such as when the next season of your favorite show is released. Some memberships even offer a free trial period you can take advantage of. Just be sure to cancel before you go into full subscription mode.

Saving even a little bit here and there can increase both your savings and your sense of accomplishment. Keep track of every time you're able to save money by resisting the urge to go out to eat or buying the generic laundry detergent instead of the brand name. You might be surprised at how quickly those savings add up!

Chapter Summary

Saving money isn't always easy, but saving now will make your future financial situation better and give you a chance to get your money working for you. We can't say enough about the importance of setting up an emergency fund because life can be so unpredictable. And taking full advantage of a 401(k) plan will help your savings significantly over time. Consider your savings options, and try to find something that will pay some interest while keeping your money safe. Look to cut some spending, too, where you can. These building blocks of saving will serve you well, both now and into the future.

Chapter 5

How's Your Credit?

The idea of credit is by no means new. In fact, the use of credit has been traced back to 4000 BC, when Sumerians were establishing the first cities and charging interest on loans they made to others who needed things they couldn't pay for. The methodology has changed since then, but the basic idea remains the same: people continue to desire things they can't pay for all at once, and they need credit to obtain them.

Not many people can pay cash for a home or a new car or all the furniture you need when you move into your first place. You need loans for those things and must accept that paying interest on those loans is the cost of doing business. America's economy is largely credit based, and there are a lot of things, ranging from getting a mortgage to using a credit card to buy a new bike helmet, that you can't do without it.

Having credit relies on a lender being willing to extend you a line of credit, which is basically a preset amount of money you can tap into as needed. To get that credit, however, you must demonstrate that you're creditworthy and not a risk to the lender. For that reason, you need to pay attention to your credit score, which is a number that informs lenders of your creditworthiness. Your credit score is largely based on a credit report that contains information about your credit history.

In this chapter, we look at how you build a credit history and why having a good credit score is important and can make your life a lot easier. We dive into credit cards, credit card interest, and how credit card debt adds up—topics that can be tricky to fully understand. We also discuss the importance of being vigilant about protecting your credit because identity theft becomes an increasingly concerning problem.

Let's start by looking at how you build a credit history and how that determines your credit score.

Building a Credit History

When you applied for your first credit card, your name and a lot of personal information were entered into a computer, and your credit history began. Since then, every time you applied for another credit card or a store card, took a vacation loan from your bank or credit union, or applied for a car loan, information was added to your credit history.

Your credit history is the record of everything pertaining to any credit you've ever had or applied for, all summarized in your credit report, which extensively documents your credit history and lists your credit score.

As noted earlier, if you want to borrow money for a car, a house, a vacation, debt consolidation, college, or a business, you'll need credit. If you go to a bank to borrow money and have no history of ever having any credit, you don't stand a good chance of getting the loan. The bank will be reluctant to take a chance on you because it has no indication of whether you'll pay back the money or default on the loan.

Lenders have become more selective when issuing credit cards, too. Credit cards used to be easier to get than they are today. Due to high rates of student debt, more stringent industry regulations, and other factors, a percentage of millennials who apply for credit cards are denied—something that actually can end up hurting their credit score.

Still, Bankrate, a consumer financial services company, reported at the end of 2021 that nearly three quarters of people between the ages of 30 and 50 have at least one credit card. How those cards are used are contributing factors in their owners' credit histories and credit scores.

Your credit report includes lots of information about you and your credit history, including the following:

- Your name
- Your Social Security number
- Your date of birth
- Your address from the time you first got a credit card until now
- Everywhere you've worked
- How you pay your bills

Whenever you apply for a loan or for credit, the place at which you applied will check out your report with a credit agency, which is a company that collects information about the debts of individuals and businesses and compiles credit scores. There are three major nationwide credit agencies:

- Equifax (equifax.com)
- TransUnion (transunion.com)
- Experian (experian.com)

All three agencies probably have the same basic information about you and your credit history. They get that data from banks, finance companies, credit card suppliers, department stores, mail-order companies, and various other places that have had the pleasure of doing business with you. Smaller, regional credit bureaus supplement the information.

Knowing and Understanding Your Credit Score

All the information about you and your credit history is evaluated and used to determine your credit score, which lenders rely on as a very powerful predictor of your future bill-paying ability.

The best-known and most widely used score is the FICO score, which is based on a system developed by the Fair Isaac Corporation. The mathematical equation used to calculate your score takes into account 22 pieces of data from your credit report, and the resulting number, which can range from 300 (the lowest) to 850 (the highest), identifies you either as a low-risk or high-risk candidate for a lender.

Why Your Credit Score Matters

FICO scores are regarded as providing the best guides to future risk based solely on credit report data, and lenders look most favorably on those whose scores are 740 or higher. The general rule of thumb is that the higher your score, the less risk you pose to a lender. Historically, people with high FICO scores have repaid loans and credit cards more consistently than people with low FICO scores. Although there's no single "cutoff score" used by all lenders, it's important to know and understand your score.

A potential lender looks at your credit report and your credit score when deciding whether or not to give you a loan. The lower your score, the less likely it is you'll be offered a loan. If you are offered one, it undoubtedly will come with a higher interest rate or more restrictive terms. Mortgages and other loans can be difficult to obtain with a less-than-optimal credit score, making it important to maintain good credit or improve your credit score if necessary.

As you read in Chapter 3, employers are increasingly checking out the credit reports of prospective employees before hiring. It's standard practice in some industries, such as the defense, banking, financial, and medical fields, but other employers also are engaging in the practice. If you're turned down for a job because of something in your report, you're required, under federal law, to be notified of your right to get a copy of your report at no charge.

You can work to improve your score by paying off credit cards, getting rid of excess cards and using only one or two, and paying all your bills by the due date. Over time, as you do these things, your credit score should increase.

A look at the average credit score by age, shown in the following table, indicates a rising trend in scores as people get older, as of the second quarter of 2021.

Average Credit Score by Age

Age	Average FICO Score
18 to 24	679
25 to 40	686
41 to 56	705
57 to 75	740
76+	760

How Your FICO Score Is Determined

Your credit score is calculated by compiling information in five categories:

- The debt you have counts for 30 percent of your rating. That's a compelling reason for controlling debt!

- Your payment history constitutes 35 percent of the rating. One or two late payments won't make a difference in your score, but a pattern of late payments will.

- The duration of your credit history counts for 15 percent of the rating and is a partial explanation for why credit scores tend to increase with age.

- The amount of new credit counts for 10 percent, so watch how many credit cards you apply for.

- The types of credit you've used counts for 10 percent. Although this isn't a huge factor, having a mix of revolving and installment credit can reflect favorably on your score.

Income is not a factor in determining FICO scores.

Usually, the FICO score is given with four reason codes, in order from the strongest negative reason to impact your score, the second strongest factor, and so on. It's important to understand how you scored, so be sure to review your credit report at least once a year (we explain how to access your report later in this chapter) and especially before making a large purchase, like a house or a car.

If your score isn't what you'd like it to be, you can work to improve it.

Factors That Can Affect Your Credit Score

It's important to be aware of a few major factors that can affect your credit score.

Your level of revolving debt is one of the most important factors considered for your FICO score. Even if you pay off your credit cards each month, your credit card may show the last billing statement in relation to your total available credit on revolving charges. If you think your FICO score should be higher, work to pay down your revolving account balances.

Shifting balances impacts your score, too. Don't transfer your credit card balances from one card to another to make it appear that you're being diligent about paying off debt. And don't open new revolving accounts. These tactics won't improve your credit score.

The length of time your accounts have been established also can influence your score. This can hurt you when you're first starting out, but consumers with longer credit histories tend to be lower risk than those with shorter credit histories.

Too many accounts with balances can ding you, too. Having too many open credit card accounts with running balances is a dangerous sign that you might not be able to make your payments should your employment status change.

Too many credit inquiries within the last 12 months also influences your score. Borrowers who seek several new credit accounts are riskier than people who aren't seeking credit, although these have only a small impact on your FICO score. Inquiries have much less impact than late payments, the amount you owe, and the length of time you've used credit.

Canceling one or more credit cards may negatively impact your credit score, but that isn't always the case. Credit advisers often urge clients to leave credit card accounts open, whether or not they're using them, because closing a card can impact your credit utilization ratio, which is a measure of how much of your total available credit you are using at any given time.

Closing a card will reduce your amount of total available credit, potentially increasing the amount of that total you're currently using. That can ding your score, but you can get around it by paying down *all* your credit card accounts— not just the one you want to cancel—to $0 before canceling the card.

That, of course, isn't possible for everyone, so it may be better to just leave the account open.

Who, Besides You, Can Access Your Credit Report?

The Fair Credit Reporting Act limits who can see your credit report. The list of who can access it is still pretty long, but the reporting act does set some guidelines. For instance, even though they are increasingly running credit checks on prospective employees, employers are required to get consent before pulling an applicant's credit history.

Your credit report can be released by a reporting agency under the following circumstances:

- In response to a court order or a federal grand jury subpoena

- To anyone to whom you've given written permission, such as a potential landlord

- To anyone considering you for credit or collection of an account

- To anyone who will use the report for insurance purposes

- To determine your eligibility for a government license or benefits

- To anyone with a legitimate business need for the report in connection with a business transaction with which you're involved (This includes your landlord when you apply to rent an apartment as well as your cell phone and utility companies.)

When you realize how often your credit report can be accessed, you can begin to see how important it is that you keep it clean. But even if your credit record is perfect, your report might not be, and that could affect your credit score.

With so much credit information floating around out there, it's easy for mistakes to be made with that information. Human error is a big factor, and somebody who misreads some information about you can mess up your credit report royally. A recent study showed that one out of four people who took the time to thoroughly review their credit reports discovered a mistake that eventually was corrected. That's why it's important to know how to access your report and to keep an eye on it.

Accessing Your Credit Score and Credit Report

You can find out what your credit score is for free using a credit score app like NerdWallet, Intuit Credit Karma, Experian, myFICO, or OneScore. In addition to letting you check your score, these apps may let you check your credit report (there are other methods for doing that as well), offer suggestions on how to improve your score, explain the main factors impacting your score, notify you if there's an unexplained change in your credit score or report, and more.

Most of these apps are considered safe to use, especially if they're through your bank or one of the three major credit bureaus, Equifax, TransUnion, and Experian. As with everything you do online, however, be wary of scammers, and never provide payment or personal information to a company you don't know.

You also may be able to get your credit score from your credit card company, bank, or loan company, as many have started including scores for their customers. It might be included with your statement, or you can access it by logging into your account.

Credit reports from Equifax, TransUnion, and Experian usually do not include credit scores, but you can get a free copy of your credit report each year from each of the companies. You can request your free report by going to AnnualCreditReport.com. The site enables you to request all three reports at once, or you can request to get them separately at various intervals, which lets you monitor your reports throughout the year.

You can order additional reports from some or all of the three companies more than once a year, but you may have to pay for them. You are allowed additional free reports under these circumstances:

- You receive notice that you were denied credit, insurance, or employment based on your credit report. You must request a copy of your report within 60 days of receiving the notice.

- You are unemployed and preparing to apply for a job within 60 days of your request.

- You believe your credit report is not accurate due to fraud.

- One of the nationwide credit bureaus has placed an initial fraud alert on your credit file.

- You receive public welfare assistance.

- Your state law allows for more than one free credit report per year.

Some websites offer free credit reports, but proceed with caution because there may be stipulations such as you have to buy a product or service in order to get your report.

When you receive your report, look it over carefully. If you discover a mistake, contact all three credit agencies by certified mail, inform them of the mistake you've discovered, and request that they investigate. If you don't get a reply within 60 days, send another letter. Remind the companies that they are required by law to investigate incorrect information or provide an updated credit report with the incorrect information removed. With financial breeches and identity theft at an all-time high, you need to be vigilant and scrutinize your report for anything that doesn't look right.

If you see information you don't like on your credit report that, unfortunately, isn't a mistake, don't despair. The Fair Credit Reporting Act mandates that negative information on your report be removed after a certain period of time. Even if you declare bankruptcy, that information is supposed to be removed from your report after 10 years.

The trick, of course, is keeping your credit report healthy and in good shape. In this case, preventive maintenance works best.

Managing Your Credit Cards

Credit cards are a wonderful thing … until they're not. At the end of the first quarter of 2023, Americans collectively held about $988 billion—close to $1 *trillion*—in credit card debt. The average debt per cardholder was about $5,733.

Spending slowed during the COVID-19 pandemic but is back to prepandemic levels, a trend reflected on many credit card balances. To make matters worse, interest rates have shot up, including on credit card debt.

You read about reducing or eliminating debt in Chapter 3, and we hope you'll do that, if necessary. The key, however, is knowing how to manage your credit cards so you don't find yourself with mounting debt that you have to struggle to pay off.

Everyone should have a credit card. But you don't have to pay for everything you buy with it. Many financial folks advise that you never use a credit card to buy anything that will be gone or finished by the time you pay for it—groceries, concert tickets, restaurant meals, coffees, pedicures, movies, and so on. That's not always feasible, we know, but there's a lot to be said for using debit instead of credit and not encountering those bills every month.

A word of caution: contactless devices have made buying and spending easier than ever. We strongly suggest you link a debit card to your phone or wearable device, or carry a debit card, and use that instead of having only credit available. It's fine to have credit linked to your device, too, but if you rely only on credit, you're likely to be surprised at how much you've spent when the bill comes.

Understanding Credit Card Fees

In addition to charging interest, credit card companies often tack on fees that can cost you hundreds of dollars a year. Fees vary per card, and all the ones your credit card company can charge you are outlined in the long cardholder agreement that comes with your new card. (You read that, right?)

In the following sections, we explain some of the most common fees. The good news is that some are avoidable.

Annual Fee

Some credit cards do not have annual fees. Others, like the highly prestigious Centurion Card from American Express (commonly called the Amex Black Card), charge a $5,000 annual fee, and perhaps even higher.

Credit cards that charge an annual fee typically are reward cards, offering perks like cash back or travel rewards. In other cases, someone who does not have a bank account or whose credit score is low may only be able to secure a credit card by agreeing to pay an annual fee.

If you have a card with an annual fee and you use it to pay for everything you buy so you rake in the cash back, or you put all your points toward airline tickets or hotel discounts that you actually use, the annual fee can be worth the price.

In some cases, however, the card owner pays the fee and doesn't claim the rewards, or the card sits largely unused, defeating the purpose of paying the annual fee.

Plenty of credit cards come with rewards and perks and no annual fees, so think carefully before you agree to one that has the fee. Read the fine print and figure out if the rewards offered by a card with an annual fee justify the cost.

Late Payment Fee

Every time you're late with a credit card payment, you're charged a late fee. These fees normally range from about $30 for the first late payment up to $40 for subsequent late payments within a specified time frame.

Fortunately, late fees are easy to avoid if you set up autopay to cover your minimum payment due every month. You can (and should, if you're able) pay more than the minimum, but if you forget to do it, you're covered.

Some credit cards don't charge late fees, so look around when choosing one.

If you're a long-time cardholder and you've forgotten to make an on-time payment, you always can call your credit card company and ask them to waive the late fee as a courtesy. It's not guaranteed they'll agree to your request, but it doesn't hurt to try.

Cash Advance Fee

Cash advances can be a huge help if you have an emergency, but they come at a cost. You're typically charged a 3 percent or a 5 percent cash advance fee, which, depending on how much you borrow, can be costly.

The interest charged on the advance is generally much higher than the regular interest rate you pay on purchases. And the monthly payments you make will be applied to your regular balance before the cash advance, meaning you can end up paying the higher interest rate for longer.

Returned Payment Fee

If you schedule a payment for your credit card without having enough money in your bank account to cover it, your payment is likely to be returned. If that happens, you may be charged a fee, normally up to $40.

This fee is easily avoidable by ensuring you have sufficient funds in your account before scheduling your payment.

Balance Transfer Fee

Transferring debt from one credit card to another can be advantageous if the card you're transferring to has a lower interest rate or an interest-free period. But you're likely to be charged a fee for the transfer, usually between 3 and 5 percent. Cards are available with no balance transfer fees, although you'll probably need a good to excellent credit score to get one.

Be aware, however, that transferring balances too often can negatively affect your credit score.

Foreign Transaction Fee

Some credit cards come with a foreign transaction fee, meaning you'll be charged an additional fee, usually about 3 percent, every time you use the card to make a purchase outside the United States.

You can find cards that don't charge for foreign transactions, however. If you're a frequent traveler or plan to travel, it's worth finding one.

Making Sense of Interest and How Credit Card Debt Accrues

Credit card debt can be a little difficult to understand, so let's take a closer look.

Credit card companies make money—a lot of money—collecting interest from cardholders who don't pay off their balance each month. This interest is usually expressed as an annual percentage rate (APR), which is the yearly rate charged for a loan.

The amount of interest a credit card company charges varies significantly depending on a number of factors, but as you read earlier, the average APR on credit cards in mid-2023 was 24.5 percent—a huge amount that can add up quickly.

Each month you get a credit card statement. Take a look at it, and you'll see it shows your new balance and a minimum payment due. You probably have between 21 and 25 days from the time you get your statement until the date by which you must make a payment.

If you don't pay off the entire balance each month, you'll accrue interest on your average daily balance, which is the card's balance at the end of each day divided by the number of days in the billing cycle. The number of days in the billing cycle depends on the number of days in the month, ranging, of course, from 28 to 31.

That interest is added to the amount you still owe on your balance. This increases daily because the balance of your account is multiplied by the daily periodic rate and the interest it added to your balance each day.

This daily accumulation of interest adds up fast and can significantly increase your balance. When your next statement arrives, it will contain your latest purchases added to the balance from your last statement, along with the interest you've accrued.

If you carry a $2,000 balance on your credit card throughout the year and your APR is 24.5 percent, the interest accrued will be about $490—about a quarter of your balance. Considering that the average debt of a credit cardholder is about $5,733, it's easy to see how credit card companies collectively generate $120 billion in interest and fees every year, according to the Consumer Financial Protection Bureau.

Knowing When You're in Trouble and Where to Find Help

You read about some DIY methods of paying down credit card debt in Chapter 3, and hopefully you would never need to take more drastic measures to alleviate your debt. People get into serious debt all the time, however, and sometimes other options become necessary.

Credit Counseling

Credit counseling has been available for more than a half century to advise, serve as an intermediary with creditors, lower interest rates, and consolidate monthly bills. Many reputable, nonprofit companies provide these services, but be aware that numerous scam companies have surfaced during the past decade or so. If you get involved with one of the latter, you could end up with even bigger problems than you started with.

If you're thinking of seeing a credit counselor or counseling firm, it's important that you keep a few things in mind. For example, ask what the total monthly fee will be. You should never have to pay more than $50 a month for the services of a credit counselor. Some predatory firms charge as much as 10 percent of their customer's payments, which ends up totaling a couple hundred dollars a month.

Check with your local Better Business Bureau or Consumer Protection Agency to see if any complaints have been filed or any current investigations are underway about the firms you're considering.

Never sign a contract at the first meeting. Be certain you have time to understand the agreement, the repayment schedule, and the fees. Never disclose your bank account number before you've signed a contract.

Be wary if a counseling service doesn't suggest other options besides its own debt management plan. Remember, it might be possible to sell some personal property or refinance your mortgage to lower your debt rather than embarking on a debt management plan.

Lack of affiliation with the National Foundation for Credit Counseling or the Association of Independent Consumer Credit Counseling Agencies may be a reason to avoid a firm. These affiliations don't guarantee you're getting the best firm, but it does mean the company obtains a majority of its income from grants and donations rather than from fees alone.

And remember, if it sounds too good to be true, it probably is.

Debt Settlement

Debt settlement companies charge clients a fee to settle their debt with a credit card company or other debt collectors. Typically, a debt settlement firm gets a credit card company to agree on a reduced balance that's considered payment in full and then charges the client for this service. Debt settlement also is known as debt arbitration or debt negotiation.

Credit counselors typically get creditors to agree they won't continue to try to collect from a client when the client is in the credit counseling debt management program, but debt settlement companies often don't provide that service. That can result in creditors charging late fees and penalty interest charges as well as continuing to pursue collection.

Before considering a debt settlement company, check to see if your credit card company has a standard policy for how much debt they'll forgive. If it does, you'll do as well negotiating with the company on your own as you would using a debt settlement company.

Bankruptcy

If you absolutely don't have enough money to pay what you owe, bankruptcy is a possible option. Achieving bankruptcy can give you a fresh financial start by erasing your debt. However, it definitely is not for everyone.

Basically, there are two types of bankruptcy, chapter 7 and chapter 13. To qualify for chapter 7 bankruptcy, your income has to be below a certain level. For chapter 13 bankruptcy, your debt must be below a specified amount.

Even if you qualify for bankruptcy, however, certain types of debt, called priority obligations, won't be eliminated. You'll still be responsible for priority obligations, which can include child or spousal support, federal student loans, and certain income taxes.

Also, filing for bankruptcy can have long-lasting financial consequences, including a decreased credit score, less ability to borrow money, and a potential loss of tax refunds and assets.

If you are ever at the point that you're thinking about filing bankruptcy, consult a bankruptcy attorney first. He or she can help you decide if it's the right move for you. Attorney fees vary, but they can be expensive, potentially running into thousands of dollars. If you need a lawyer, ask about spreading out the costs, or call the Legal Aid Society in your area to see if no- or low-cost legal aid is available.

Keeping Your Accounts Safe

Hopefully, you have not experienced identity theft yourself, but you've certainly heard about it because it's become increasingly common in the past decade. In fact, studies show that nearly one third of Americans have experienced identity theft, which is what happens when someone obtains and uses your personal or financial information in some way without your permission. Identity theft can damage your credit status, sometimes taking years to recover from.

The US Federal Trade Commission (FTC) received more than 5.88 million fraud reports in 2021, an increase of 19 percent from 2020. Financial losses associated with identity theft were more than $6.1 billion. Credit card–related identity theft is the most common form of this criminal act.

One problem with identity theft is that it's not always easy to recognize, especially if you're not diligent about checking your accounts and keeping an eye out for suspicious transactions or applications made in your name. Be aware of these possible signs that someone has stolen your identity:

- Information on your credit reports for accounts you didn't open
- Being denied for loan applications, including store credit accounts
- Debt-collection calls for accounts you didn't open
- Bills for items you didn't buy
- Unusual mail or mail missing

If you notice any of these or other signs of possible identity theft, you should contact the FTC online at IdentityTheft.gov or by calling the FTC Identity Theft Hotline at 877-438-4338.

Also notify the fraud department at all your credit card issuers, your bank, and any other places where you have accounts. Most credit card companies and banks have features that let you temporarily block access to your cards or accounts. If you feel your identity may have been compromised, do that as soon as possible to prevent someone from accessing and potentially draining your accounts.

You also should contact the three major credit reporting agencies, Equifax, Experian, and TransUnion. Ask the credit reporting agencies to place fraud alerts and a credit freeze on your accounts. A credit freeze blocks access to your credit reports, which will protect you because if someone attempts to access your credit reports and open fraudulent accounts, the lender or card issuer won't be able to access the information they need to approve opening the account.

It's difficult to stay completely immune from identity theft or other security breaches, but there are steps you can take to protect yourself and family members.

Beware of emails, texts, or phone calls from numbers or people you don't know. Don't ever open suspicious links within emails or texts, especially if they come from someone you don't know.

Learn to recognize phishing emails, which often appear to be from a company you know and trust, like a bank. If an email or text claims there's a problem with a payment you've made and the sender needs your personal or bank information to fix it, do not respond. That's just one example of phishing. Countless articles have been written about how to avoid phishing scams. You'd do well to read more about it to help you avoid becoming a victim.

Never share personal information—including your bank account numbers, Social Security number, date of birth, etc.—with anyone you don't completely trust.

Collect your mail every day, and place a hold on it while you're away. Be especially careful if you live in an apartment where mail tends to be left where other people may have access to it.

Review your credit card and bank account statements frequently, immediately reporting anything that appears unusual.

Finally, never carry personal information, like a Social Security card or passwords, with you.

Chapter Summary

Building a credit history and maintaining a good credit score will make it easier for you to borrow money, get additional credit cards, and sometimes even land a job you want. That makes it important to know how a credit score is determined and what you can do to build a good credit report, along with understanding how credit cards and credit card interest and debt work. Credit is an interesting and complex subject, but getting a handle on it now will make it easier for you to manage your credit as you move forward.

Life Events That Affect Your Finances

It's likely at your age that you're undergoing, or getting ready to undergo, some important life events that will significantly impact your financial situation. Maybe you've got a new job or are getting ready to change jobs. You might be thinking about buying a house or condo or moving in with your partner. Maybe you're considering marriage or starting to feel ready for a kid or two.

These and other major life decisions require planning, both personal and financial. You probably spend a lot of time at your job, so it's important that it's rewarding on a personal and a financial level. Homeownership is a big deal and not something to be done without a lot of consideration. Personal relationships can have a big effect on personal finances, and you need to understand the connections between those things. Having children is a huge financial commitment that requires a lot of planning, and understanding what insurances you need to protect the important people and things in your life is vital.

Part 2 walks you through the financial implications of these life scenarios to provide some perspective and help you prepare for them.

Chapter 6

How's Your Job Going?

Endless research has been conducted exploring the habits and attitudes of millennials, now the United States' largest living adult generation. You've no doubt heard some of the conclusions: millennials are technologically savvy, they're more racially and ethnically diverse than older adults, they're highly educated, they value experiences over things, they love avocado toast—the list goes on and on.

A lot of that research examines how millennials work. Recent Gallup polls tell us that millennials are known for frequently changing jobs, they remain open to new employment opportunities, and they're the least-engaged generation in the workplace.

We don't know if those claims are accurate or generalizations. We know plenty of millennials who have had lots of different jobs, but we also know some who are still working for the first company that hired them. As far as remaining open to new job opportunities, that seems like a good thing, wouldn't you say? And the reason that more than half of millennials reported not feeling engaged with their work was primarily because they didn't experience close relationships with their colleagues or employers. That might say as much about the companies they work for as their own attitudes.

Other polls reach different conclusions, including one that found workers of all ages leave jobs and start new ones for the same reasons: they want to make more money, they're looking for greater career development and advancement, and they want to work for a company with leaders who care about them.

Jobs are important, and hopefully they mean more to you than simply a means of generating a paycheck. In this chapter, we look at why jobs are key to your current and future financial situations, some factors that may affect the way you work, and some work benefits that might make your job more palatable.

The Changing Job Market

Anyone who's been in the job market for any amount of time is likely to be feeling a little shaken about all the changes we've seen since the beginning of the COVID-19 pandemic.

The pandemic changed the job market and how we work in some very profound ways. About 20.5 million jobs were lost between March and April in 2020, the largest one-month decrease ever recorded. Hiring rebounded in a huge way by the middle of the year, however, and employment was back to prepandemic levels by February 2021.

In addition to the unprecedented job market volatility, the pandemic fundamentally changed the way millions of Americans work, moving us out of workspaces and into our homes, where many struggled to deal with children who were out of school; working around spouses, partners, or roommates who were also working from home; balancing home and work responsibilities; and learning new technology to accommodate a new working environment.

Hopefully, you managed to avoid losing your job, or if you didn't you have found a new one that's comparable to or better than what you left. Maybe you've returned to the workplace, or perhaps you're still working from home, either because you must or because you choose to. Maybe you're one of the nearly one and a half million people who work for delivery services, spending hours on the road as required by your job. Whatever you're doing, we hope you're finding some satisfaction in the work, along with earning enough to keep you on track financially.

Looking forward, the overall job market has slowed from its peak performance in early 2021, and it appears that the Great Resignation—the trend during which millions of employees quit their jobs—appears to be over. Generally, however, the market remains favorable for workers.

Regardless of what work you do, it's important that you're getting paid what you're worth. To understand if that's the case, you need to know how your salary compares to others.

Getting Paid What You're Worth

Everyone who works wants to earn what they're worth, yet many workers feel that they are underpaid. This was especially true during the early 2020s, when inflation was very high, causing the costs of almost everything to go up. More than half of all workers who responded to a survey by Bankrate said their incomes haven't kept up with rising household expenses.

If you're in a job where you're underpaid, or you feel like you're underpaid but you aren't sure, you should take action. Being underpaid can set you up to continue to be underpaid in the future because employers often base salaries of new hires on what they earned in previous jobs. It also can be damaging to your self-worth and cause you to become unmotivated and disengaged at work.

Not earning what you're worth is detrimental to your financial future. If you are underpaid even by 5 percent and your annual salary is $50,000, you're losing out on $2,500 a year. Multiply that by 10, and you discover that over 10 years, you will have lost $25,000 in potential savings or investments that could have been working for you and maybe earning high returns.

Being underpaid affects both your short-term and long-term net worth.

If you're not sure how your pay stacks up to others who do the same work, job site Glassdoor has a "Know Your Worth" tool at glassdoor.com/salaries /know-your-worth.htm that lets you review salary data by job title and geographic location. Checking that should be your first step.

You also could ask others in the same job how much they earn, but that's often awkward and can have repercussions if it gets back to your boss that you were questioning coworkers about their salaries. If you are going to ask around, find someone at a different but comparable company who is doing the same job as you.

If you discover or confirm that you are underpaid, you can consider asking for a raise. This is not something many people are comfortable doing, but it's often the best thing you can do. Payscale, a compensation software and data company, found that 70 percent of employees who asked for a raise got one, although only 39 percent got the amount they asked for.

Before you ask, think about your job responsibilities and put together a list of your achievements you can show your employer. Also, be sure to mention characteristics that make you a valuable employee, like your willingness to take on new projects at short notice and how you always inform your supervisor about the progress you're making or raise flags about problems you encounter and your proposed solutions to those problems.

If you know your company is doing well and have found that you're underpaid, asking for a raise is a reasonable action. Be prepared and confident when you do so, and you may be pleasantly surprised at the outcome.

Should You Go Back to School?

If you're established in a career, you might find that you can improve your skills and knowledge through on-the-job workshops, training courses, and other programs that enable you to keep moving up within your field.

In some cases, however, you might consider going back to school to earn a degree, an advanced degree, or a certificate to help you progress in your career, either within your current field or into a different one.

Experts recommend you consider advancing your education if your skills are outdated, you want more responsibility within your company or with a different company, or you're looking to change to a new area of work. It also can make sense to return to school if you've started a degree but haven't finished it and having the degree would provide more opportunity for advancement.

Finding the Right School for You

Returning to school doesn't necessarily mean enrolling in a college or university. Many career and technology centers that teach high school–aged students during the day offer night programs for adult learners in fields such as electronics, computerized machining technology, and electromechanical technologies. You normally have to pay tuition, but it generally is reasonable, and for some programs, the cost of course materials is covered.

Community colleges, where tuition is usually much less than four-year institutions, also offer a range of course opportunities for adult learners. Many of them partner with four-year colleges and universities, meaning you could start classes at a community college and finish at a four-year school. If you're looking to move into a different field, see what's available in your area.

Regardless of how you choose to continue your education, you'll need to consider how you'll pay for it (more on this coming up) and how it will affect other areas of your life. Squeezing in classes and homework when you're working full-time can be challenging, and juggling a job and school with family responsibilities can be particularly demanding. That's not to say it can't be done, however.

Recognizing that students come from many different backgrounds and are at various stages of life, many colleges and other schools have revamped adult programs to accommodate busy lives and tight budgets. Most colleges and universities offer all-online or hybrid learning, meaning you can complete your classwork when and where it's most convenient for you.

You could look for a school that offers accelerated programming or certificate or credential programs that count toward a degree. This enables you to take only one or two courses at a time, or, if you're able, load up on courses to finish a program sooner. Schools that cater to adult learners have programs that might enable you to earn a bachelor's and a master's degree in the time it would ordinarily take to achieve a bachelor's. With some research, you may be able to find a program that tailors the courses you take to meet your education and career goals.

Paying for Continuing Education

The cost of earning a certificate, degree, or advanced degree can be daunting, but you may be able to get some help. Many companies, large and small, offer tuition reimbursement or tuition assistance programs as an employee benefit. There are some tax advantages for companies that offer these programs, so be sure to check if your employer is one of them.

You'll read more about this in Chapter 14, but some tax credits are available for students, such as the Lifetime Learning Credit. Be sure to look into whether you might be eligible for one because they could provide helpful assistance.

Before applying to any type of learning institution, inquire what scholarships or grants may be available. Many colleges offer very specific scholarships, some of which may be designated for adult learners. Others have work-study programs in which you may be able to get free or reduced tuition if you agree to take a job at the school. Ask to speak to someone in the financial aid office to help you find out what may be available.

You also can look into scholarships or grants offered by nonprofits, private companies, and other organizations, such as the College JumpStart Scholarship (jumpstart-scholarship.net) or the Return2College (return2college.com) award.

Also check out federal grants like the Pell Grant and the Federal Supplemental Educational Opportunity Grant, both of which are based on financial need and offered to students regardless of age. If you plan to apply for federal student loans, remember that you'll need to complete the Free Application for Federal Student Aid form (studentaid.gov/h/apply-for-aid/fafsa) and renew it each year. If you're going to apply for student loans, please do your homework carefully and weigh the pros and cons of taking on that debt.

Don't be tempted to withdraw money from your 401(k) or other retirement account to pay for school costs, and don't raid your emergency fund. If it's absolutely necessary, you could borrow funds from your 401(k), which is different from taking an early withdrawal and not subject to the same taxes and penalties. You'll read more about 401(k) loans in Chapter 11, but understand that although it's possible to set up a loan, it's by no means an ideal solution. Any money you put into the 401(k) until the loan is paid off is applied to the loan, not your retirement savings. That puts you at a disadvantage for saving for your future.

It really pays to do your research here. You can get information about more than 8,000 colleges at Universities.com, a site that offers rankings, tuition costs, and in-depth information about colleges across the United States.

Taking Advantage of Employer-Sponsored Benefits

You read about the advantages of a 401(k) plan in Chapter 4, but that's just one employer-sponsored benefit to consider. If you've got a job that offers health insurance, a 401(k) or another type of retirement savings plan, and other perks, consider yourself lucky. These benefits greatly increase the value of your earnings and give you an opportunity to save money for your future.

The key, of course, is to take full advantage of any opportunities offered through your job. Let's look at what employer-sponsored benefits are and why they're so important.

What Are Employer-Sponsored Benefits?

An employer-sponsored benefit plan, which is a package of benefits an employer offers employees, provides one or more types of benefits at no cost or minimal cost to employees. Typically, these benefits include health insurance and a retirement savings plan, although some employers may offer life, disability, dental, and vision insurance; education reimbursement; and other perks. Paid time off for vacations, sick days, and personal days is another nice benefit offered by most employers.

An often-overlooked benefit that employers pay is half of your required contribution to Social Security and Medicare, or 7.65 percent of your pay. If you're self-employed, you have to pay both halves of those taxes yourself, which takes away money from what you could be saving.

Benefits account for about 32 percent of an employer's cost of compensation for an employee, with salary making up the other 68 percent. When you think about it, that's a big add-on to what you earn.

Employee benefit programs are by no means a new concept in the American workplace. As early as 1875, the American Express Company offered a pension plan to employees. Montgomery Ward established a group health, life, and accident insurance plan for employees in 1910, and Baylor University Hospital offered a group hospitalization plan to its workers in 1929.

Employees benefit from these plans by getting discounted services, and employers get some tax advantages when they provide benefits. Benefits also play a role in attracting and retaining good employees.

Health Insurance

Studies have shown that employer-covered health insurance is the benefit employees want most when they're looking for or working in a job. About 60 percent of Americans access health insurance through an employer, with the rest having to buy a plan on their own or get coverage through a government-sponsored program like Medicare or Medicaid. Employers with 50 or more full-time employees are required to sponsor plans.

Many employers used to cover the full cost of their employees' health-care policies, but as the price of coverage has risen, workers are increasingly being asked to contribute to the costs. In 2023, workers paid an average of about $5,600 toward the cost of employer-sponsored health care for themselves and their families. Employees with single coverage paid about $1,240. Employers picked up the remaining costs, paying about $6,230 for single coverage and about $15,750 for family coverage.

If you're covered by health insurance provided by your employer, be sure you carefully read and understand the policy. Know what you're responsible for as far as copays, deductibles, prescriptions, and other costs. Attend your company's annual benefit meeting to ascertain any new deductibles, changes in the plan, and so on.

You'll need to consider all those costs, plus any amount taken out of your check to help pay for the plan, when you're making a budget and figuring out your monthly expenses.

Consider yourself fortunate, however, because having to pay for health insurance on your own can take a huge bite out available funds and, ultimately, savings.

Retirement Plans

You've read about 401(k) plans, which are a popular type of retirement savings vehicle many employers offer, but they are not the only type of employer-sponsored retirement plan. The US Bureau of Labor Statistics reported that in 2020, 67 percent of nonunion workers and 94 percent of union workers had access to some type of retirement savings plan. Generally, these plans fall into one of two categories: defined benefit plans or defined contribution plans.

A defined benefit plan is a retirement plan that guarantees a specific amount of retirement income, while a defined contribution plan doesn't guarantee income but does enable employees to invest money for retirement, often with some employer assistance.

Defined benefit plans, also known as pension plans, used to be much more common than they are today. Although with most pension plans both the employer and employees contribute, companies that offer the plans have to invest significant amounts of money in order to have enough available for employees when they retire, and that involves risk and responsibility. Pension plans have become increasingly rare among private companies, but public employees who work for a federal, state, county, or municipal government are likely to still qualify for pensions.

If your company offers a pension, you'll need to be employed for a specified amount of time before you're vested, or eligible to benefit from it. When you leave the company, you may have to decide whether to take your pension money as a lump sum or in installments.

Defined contribution plans, which are much more common than defined benefit plans, include 401(k) plans, 403(b) plans, employee stock ownership plans, and profit sharing plans. All of these plans have different features, but they all stand to benefit employees who take advantage of them.

When you contribute to a 401(k), the most common type of defined contribution plan, your contributions go into a mix of investments that you determine. These are most commonly mutual funds containing domestic and international stocks, money market funds, and bonds. Your employer serves as the plan sponsor and works with a third-party administrator (TPA) and a record keeper to ensure the plan remains in compliance and your money continues to be invested according to your wishes. The TPA should be able to answer any questions you have regarding your 401(k) or other type of defined contribution plan.

The money you contribute to a defined contribution plan and some defined benefit plans is deducted from your paycheck before it's taxed, which is advantageous for you. If you leave your job for a different one, you can either take your 401(k) plan with you, leave it where it is, or roll it over into an individual retirement account (IRA), which is a tax-advantaged personal retirement savings plan. Like a traditional 401(k) plan, contributions to a traditional IRA are tax deductible. If you contribute to a Roth IRA, your contributions are after-tax dollars, meaning you've already paid tax on them before they go into the account. So although those contributions don't reduce your taxable income, you realize the benefit of a Roth when you start to withdraw the funds because the money you'll take out is completely tax-free under current tax laws. Withdrawals from a regular IRA are considered taxable income.

Student Loan Repayment

A recent benefit offered by some employers, notably government agencies and some private employers, is a student loan repayment assistance program. Under this program, employers can provide up to $5,250 in student loan assistance each year as a tax-free benefit for employees.

As part of the Coronavirus Aid, Relief, and Economic Security (CARES) Act passed by Congress in March 2020, employers are able to make up to $5,250 in tax-free annual payments directly to their employee's federal student loans. Employees don't have to pay tax on this money because it's not considered income. The CARES Act was supposed to remain in place only through 2020, but it 2021, Congress passed a combined spending bill and continuation of coronavirus relief funds called the Consolidated Appropriations Act. Although it's possible that the tax-free aspect of the employer-provided student loan assistance program could be rolled back in the future, the Consolidate Appropriations Act assures it will remain in place through 2025.

A company might provide a lump sum payment or repeating payments, either to the employee or directly to the student loan lender. Employees may be required to provide proof of completion and that they've satisfied any minimum grade requirements before employers will make payments to a lender or reimburse an employee. Some employers offer assistance as a signing bonus, while others let employees trade in unused vacation time for money to be applied toward their loans. Others tie the contributions to the employee's retirement savings. Members of the military and those in some government jobs receive service-based assistance.

Time Off

Paid time off (PTO) is a valuable commodity—just ask anyone who's self-employed or works for an employer that doesn't offer it. A paid time off policy combines vacation, sick, and personal time into a bank of hours that employees can use as needed. Time can be taken for any reason at the employee's discretion, providing flexibility that many employees find extremely useful.

Employers who don't offer a PTO policy often give employees time off that's designated for specific purposes, like vacation time and sick leave. Some employers offer paid personal days or mental health days, too.

About 6 percent of employers offer unlimited PTO, a policy that has been shown to increase trust between employees and their employers, increase retention, and help with recruitment of employees.

Regardless of what types of benefits come with your job, it is to your advantage to use them. They increase the value of your compensation and contribute to increased job satisfaction and engagement.

What Happens If You Lose Your Job?

The thought of losing their job is scary for most people. In addition to placing you in a vulnerable financial position, it can affect your self-esteem and your sense of purpose and belonging. Many people strongly identify with the work they do, and losing a job forces them to reevaluate their values and role in life.

We witnessed a lot of job loss in the early days of the pandemic, when more than 50 million Americans filed new claims for unemployment benefits between March and the end of June 2020. Service industries were hit the hardest, but the damage was widespread, affecting clerical or office workers, health-care workers who were laid off as hospitals suspended elective medical procedures, maintenance and repair workers, those in manufacturing, sales workers, employees in the construction industry, and more.

Job loss comes in different forms. You can be fired, laid off, or furloughed, all with the same result. A company normally fires an employee as the result of an action by the employee that the company deems unacceptable. Being laid off means losing a job due to changes within the company, perhaps shutting down a division or restructuring the workforce. A furlough is a mandatory, temporary leave of absence, during which an employee is either not paid or receives reduced pay, with the understanding that they'll return to work when notified to do so. Companies typically furlough workers to reduce their business costs while assuring employees will be available to return when they're needed. A lot of furloughing occurred during the pandemic when businesses were forced to temporarily shut down.

Regardless of the circumstances, if you lose a job, there are steps you can take to minimize the damage. The employment website Indeed advises avoiding burning any bridges with your former employer and asking for written notification of your termination. Help make the transition as easy as possible for your coworkers by informing them of ongoing projects or actions, and meet with HR to find out the circumstances of your severance with the company.

Find out if you'll receive severance pay, how long you can keep your health insurance, how to best manage your retirement plan, and so on.

From a financial perspective, it's important to assess your financial needs and make a plan for the time during which you're unemployed.

File for Unemployment Benefits

You can apply for unemployment benefits regardless of the circumstances under which you lost your job. You may qualify if you quit a job for a reason such as health issues or transportation problems, but probably not if you quit because your start time was too early, or if you were fired. You're most likely to qualify if you were let go through no fault of your own, such as if your company needed to lay off employees to conserve funds or do some employee shuffling to better meet its staffing needs

Unemployment benefits vary from state to state, so you'll need to check with your state's unemployment department on the regulations that apply to your specific state if you attempt to collect.

You should file for unemployment compensation during the first week you're out of work. In some states, eligibility for payments may start on the day you apply—not the day your job ended.

The amount of money you'll get in benefits is tied to how much you made when you were working. Most states have minimum and maximum amounts you can receive. You'll need to have worked consistently for a period of time before losing your job and earned a minimum amount to qualify for benefits. If you do qualify, you should start receiving payments within a few weeks of applying.

If your claim is rejected or you feel you've been approved for less money than you should have been, most states allow you to appeal.

It's important to understand what your state requires and provides, so be sure you do some research before applying.

Analyze and Adjust Your Spending

Because you don't know how long you'll be without employment income, it's important to identify where you can curtail spending. It may be necessary to give up some activities you enjoy, but remember, it's a temporary situation.

This might be a good time to download a (free, of course!) spending tracker app so you can see exactly where your money is going. Mint, Goodbudget, EveryDollar, and PocketGuard come highly recommended from personal finance company NerdWallet.

Contact Your Lenders and Creditors

Notify your mortgage lender or landlord if you're unable to make your payments. Explain your situation, and ask if there are options regarding payments. The bank may offer a repayment plan, or your landlord may be willing to give you a break and let you pay later.

Call your creditors, too. If you're paying back student loans, you might be able to adjust or delay your payments, so be sure to inquire. Try to continue paying at least the minimum fees on credit cards, and stop using them completely, if possible.

If you owe money to anyone else, ask if you can arrange to pay later.

Review Your Health Insurance Options

If you're going on your spouse or partner's health insurance, you'll probably have to sign up within 30 days of your last day of work.

If that's not an option, consider COBRA (the Consolidated Omnibus Budget Reconciliation Act; www.dol.gov/general/topic/health-plans/cobra), which allows you to continue on your employer's insurance plan for 18 months. The problem is, you'll have to pay for it—105 percent of the combined cost you and your former employer paid while you were working, so the cost may be prohibitive.

You also can check out the federal Health Insurance Marketplace plans, commonly referred to as Obamacare, at healthcare.gov. (You'll read more about health insurance and different types of plans in Chapter 10.)

What About Your Retirement Account?

Do not—we repeat—do not raid your retirement account.

Tapping into your 401(k) or other retirement account to cover expenses during unemployment might seem like your only option, but avoid doing so if in any way possible. You're almost sure to encounter penalties—10 percent on an early withdrawal from a 401(k), and depending on the type of account, you may have to pay income tax on the money as well. Even more importantly, you're robbing yourself of money you're going to need in the future.

Instead, think about how you might generate some extra cash. Sell the sports gear, electronics, baby equipment, or other items you no longer use or need. Offer to give piano lessons or tutor neighbors' kids. People who can do odd jobs are often in demand, as are painters and yard-care providers. You can consider a gig job like DoorDash or Uber, but be mindful about state laws regarding income when you're receiving unemployment benefits.

Losing a job and being without work and an income can seem traumatic and discouraging, but try to remain optimistic. Hiring company ZipRecruiter reported that the median length of unemployment for laid-off workers in March 2023 was just nine weeks.

Let us leave you with this: if you're out of work for nine weeks and not overly stressed because you have an emergency fund to pay your bills and keep you going, give yourself a big pat on the back. Well done!

Chapter Summary

A job you enjoy is great; a job that you enjoy and that pays enough to allow you to be saving, paying off debt, and living comfortably is even better. If you've reached that level of employment, be happy and enjoy. If you're still working toward that level, that's okay. You may have to advance your skills by getting some additional training or going back to school. That can be advantageous but also pricey, so you'll need to do some careful budgeting and planning before deciding whether it's smart for you to do so. Be sure you're taking advantage of all employer-sponsored benefits available to you, and be prepared in the event you would lose your job and have to rely on unemployment benefits for a period of time. Remember that it never hurts to be aware of other job opportunities in your area—just in case.

Chapter 7

Thinking About Buying a House?

Owning a home has long been considered a piece of the American dream, but doing so has gotten more difficult for many people due to lack of savings needed for a down payment, increasing mortgage rates, soaring housing prices, credit problems, and other issues.

Despite the difficulties of finding an affordable home, nearly three quarters of Americans still view owning a home as a high measure of achievement and security—more so than graduating from college, having a successful career, or raising a family, according to a recent study by the financial services company Bankrate.

You read in Chapter 1 how the Great Recession affected the millennials who were graduating from high school or college around that time and looking to break into the job market. With few jobs to be had, many were forced to live at home and work jobs for which they were overqualified and underpaid. That situation, coupled with the need to start paying off student debt, delayed their ability to save and put millennials behind previous generations for the age at which they could purchase their first home. As a result of that and other factors, many delayed getting married as well.

It wasn't until 2022 that more millennials owned homes than not, according to a report from RentCafe, an internet listing service that lets renters search for apartments and houses to rent across the United States. By the end of the year, 51.5 percent of millennials were homeowners, the study showed. The average millennial was 34 years old when they reached the homeowner milestone—2 years older than the generation before them, Gen X.

Homeownership remains a lofty goal for many, but it is not for everyone. Market research firm YouGov conducted a survey to find out the reasons why people don't own homes. In addition to those already mentioned, 14 percent of respondents said they simply have no interest in becoming a homeowner, regardless of circumstances. Many people are perfectly happy with renting a place and leaving the responsibilities of homeownership up to someone else.

Let's begin this chapter by examining the pros and cons of owning a home.

The Pros and Cons of Homeownership

If the thought of owning a home seems appealing to you, think about why that is. Maybe you like the thought of owning instead of paying rent every month, or it seems like owning provides better security than renting because a landlord can't decide to sell and tell you you've got three months to find another place to live.

You might think you'll be able to assure your financial future by investing in a home and selling it for a profit down the road. Or maybe you just like the thought of owning a house, having friends and family over, being able to paint the walls any color you want, and grow tomatoes in the backyard.

All of those can be good reasons for buying a house, but there are some downsides to owning a home as well. Not only is it expensive to buy a house, but it's also expensive to maintain a house. Roofs leak. Appliances break. Termites decide they like the wood framing in your basement.

Depending on the type of house you have and how much property comes with it, keeping up with chores can feel like a full-time job. There can be grass to cut, leaves to rake, weeds to pull, rooms to paint—all things you wouldn't have to do as a renter.

Only you, or you and your partner, can decide if buying a house is the right decision. Consider some of the advantages and disadvantages of homeownership.

On the Plus Side

Historically, owning a home has been a way to achieve long-term financial security. The housing market has traditionally increased in value decade after decade (largely due to inflation), rewarding homeowners with equity and the ability to borrow money against the value of their homes. Although records show that overall home prices fluctuate, flattening out and then rising again, the value of homes tends to increase.

Owning a home also provides some federal tax benefits, which you'll read more about a little later in this chapter.

If you have a fixed-rate mortgage, or a mortgage on which the interest rate remains constant during the life of the loan, you'll pay the same monthly amount for principal and interest until the mortgage is paid off. Your monthly costs can change due to fluctuations in the cost of insurance or property taxes, but you won't have to worry about your mortgage costs going up every year like rents can.

Other than dollars and cents, an advantage to owning a home is the freedom you have to adapt it to meet your needs or the needs of your family. If your kids start driving and you get another car, you can enlarge your driveway if space permits. If you want to add a home office to accommodate an ongoing work-from-home situation, that's your call. You can tear out a wall to create open space or build a patio in your backyard. It's your home to adapt as you'd like.

On the Minus Side

It costs a lot of money up front to buy a house. You'll read more about these costs in a bit, but you'll need a down payment and closing costs to cover things like property taxes, home insurance, interest, title-related costs, inspections, appraisal fees, mortgage insurance, loan-origination charges, escrow account funds, government recording fees, and more. Generally, closing costs for the buyer run between 2 and 6 percent of the loan amount, which can add up to a hefty amount.

Maintenance costs on a house also can be expensive, and although you get some tax benefits from owning a home, there are taxes you'll have to pay, namely property tax, which in some areas is very high.

Home equity is a good thing, but it doesn't happen overnight. Most of the payments you make in the early years of a mortgage go toward interest, meaning you don't gain equity quickly unless the property values in your area increase significantly in a short time. If you're able, however, you can apply extra money to your principal each month, which will help you build equity faster.

Owning a home can tie you down if you decide you want to look for a job in a different location or move for another reason. In a tight housing market, such as we're currently experiencing, you'd probably be able to sell a home fairly quickly. In a down market, however, it could take a long time to sell a home you no longer want.

How Much Home Can You Afford?

If you're thinking about buying a home or have decided you're going to, you're probably wondering how much house you'll be able to afford. As you know, property values vary tremendously, depending on the size and condition of the home, how much land is included, the location, and other factors.

You can compare the typical cost of a house in every state in Zillow's March 2023 home value list, shown in the following table.

State	Typical Home Value	State	Typical Home Value
Alabama	$206,044	Montana	$427,886
Alaska	$345,363	Nebraska	$243,012
Arizona	$409,038	Nevada	$412,244
Arkansas	$178,744	New Hampshire	$429,421
California	$728,134	New Jersey	$451,559
Colorado	$539,640	New Mexico	$279,763
Connecticut	$358,906	New York	$411,304
Delaware	$358,686	North Carolina	$309,861
District of Columbia	$627,158	North Dakota	$242,261
Florida	$383,063	Ohio	$205,800
Georgia	$306,278	Oklahoma	$188,453
Hawaii	$834,583	Oregon	$485,475
Idaho	$435,374	Pennsylvania	$243,859
Illinois	$236,049	Rhode Island	$413,948
Indiana	$222,592	South Carolina	$273,977
Iowa	$200,038	South Dakota	$284,308
Kansas	$210,742	Tennessee	$291,354
Kentucky	$190,037	Texas	$294,336
Louisiana	$182,959	Utah	$506,072
Maine	$351,375	Vermont	$332,149
Maryland	$387,872	Virginia	$360,873
Massachusetts	$558,313	Washington	$562,936
Michigan	$218,684	West Virginia	$146,578
Minnesota	$315,122	Wisconsin	$262,652
Mississippi	$162,292	Wyoming	$325,091
Missouri	$227,347		

To determine how much of a mortgage you're likely to be able to get, consider your gross income, or the amount you make before taxes are taken out. The recommended guideline is that you should spend no more than 28 percent of your gross monthly income on your mortgage payment. Some financial advisers, and many mortgage lenders, will tell you that it's okay to spend more than 28 percent of your monthly income on your mortgage. Many recommend not going higher than 33 percent, and some may even go 1 or 2 percentage points higher. Remember, however, that many people have made themselves "house poor" by buying a more expensive home than they reasonably could afford.

When you're thinking about applying for a mortgage, you must pay close attention to all your expenses as they relate to your income. Although the recommended maximum for your mortgage payment is 28 percent of your gross monthly income, the historical maximum for your total monthly debt is 36 percent of your income. That means all your debt other than a mortgage—such as your car payment, credit cards, student loans, child support payments, and other bills—should total no more than 8 percent of your gross income.

If you have very high monthly expenses because of high credit card or other debt, reduce the debt as much as you can before you apply for a mortgage. Those expenses will work against you on your mortgage application.

You need to take a realistic look at your gross income and all the expenses you'll be faced with once you've bought a house. Then consider how much you can afford for a down payment, or the money you pay upfront when purchasing a home, and you'll be able to determine how much you can afford to borrow.

Many good mortgage calculators are available online, such as Quicken Loans' Mortgage Calculator (quickenloans.com/calculator-mortgage).

What Kind of Home Makes Sense for You?

Many people associate buying a home with a single-family residence, but that's not the only option available. You also might consider a townhome, a condominium, a double house, a duplex, or an apartment.

A single-family residence is designed as a separate structure and is the most common type of residential housing. This standalone home has the advantage of outdoor space where you can have a large fenced-in yard, patio, or pool, if you wish.

Some neighborhoods have homeowners associations (HOAs), and those monthly, quarterly, or annual fees will need to be considered as part of your budget. The fees go toward a variety of items depending on the neighborhood, such as common-area maintenance, trash pickup, snow removal, and so on.

A townhome—a concept that originated in Europe in the 1600s—is a home that shares one or two walls with properties on either side. A condominium, or condo, is similar to a townhome but usually is part of a larger, multistory building. Townhomes and condos generally are smaller and cost less than single-family dwellings, perhaps enabling you to become a homeowner more easily. The lower sales price also means you'd need less for a down payment, which is typically a percentage of the cost of the home.

A townhome or condo also involves less work than a single-family home because they're usually part of a larger community association that takes care of tasks like mowing the lawn and removing snow. These services vary from community to community, so you'd need to look at a copy of the bylaws to find out what is provided.

On the downside, a community association can impose restrictions on what you can do with your home, such as what color you can paint your front door and whether you're allowed to add another room. Plus, you normally have to pay an HOA fee to cover the cost of the association handling the mowing and snow removal and so on, so you'd need to factor that into your budget.

A townhome or condo community may have shared outdoor space and amenities such as a pool or tennis court, but you'd be subject to rules regarding when and how you could use them.

Some people enjoy having close neighbors, while others prefer homes that are farther apart. If you're looking for space, a townhome or condo would not be your best option because you're often subjected to noise, additional traffic, and frequent interactions with your neighbors.

In a double house, two homes are side by side and share a common wall. Each dwelling in a double home can be quite large, and each half often includes some property. Double homes generally are less expensive than single homes and can be a good value.

Another example of non-single-family housing, a duplex holds one complete living unit above another complete living unit. Duplexes are popular investment properties, and the owner often lives in one unit rents the other.

We normally think about renting apartments, but they also can be purchased, particularly if you live in a large city. An apartment is a living unit contained within a larger building with other living units.

Overall, the choice of home comes down to your budget and your personal preferences on where and how you want to live.

Financing Your Home

Because not many people have a few hundred thousand dollars available to hand over for a home, we rely heavily on mortgages. A mortgage is a loan you get from a bank or other lender to buy a home. You borrow the difference between the cost of the house and the money you have for a down payment and agree to pay back the loan during a specified period of time and at an agreed-to rate of interest.

On one hand, mortgages are great because they provide a means for buying a house. On the other hand, they can be financially crippling if they're not managed properly. In a worst-case scenario, people get loans they're unable to pay back and their homes go into foreclosure, or the legal process in which ownership of a house transfers from the homeowner to the mortgage lender.

To avoid the danger of that occurring, be conservative when calculating how much house you can afford.

You'll also need to consider what you have for a down payment. Generally, a 20 percent down payment is considered ideal, and there are benefits of paying that much up front if you're able. It's a difficult task for many younger people, however, considering that wage growth has been slow, the cost of renting is high, and the average student loan debt is more than $37,000 per borrower. That doesn't leave a lot left over each month to save for a down payment.

If you can come up with a 20 percent down payment, you won't have to buy private mortgage insurance (PMI), which is insurance that protects the lender if you default on your mortgage. A higher down payment also can give you access to better interest rates than you'd get if you don't put as much down, and it lowers the amount of money you need to borrow, which means your monthly payments will be less. Also, in a hot housing market, a larger down payment can make it easier to find a mortgage lender.

If you qualify for a government-backed mortgage such as through the Federal Housing Administration (FHA) or from the Federal National Mortgage Association (Fannie Mae) or the Federal Home Loan Mortgage Corporation (Freddie Mac), you'll qualify for a lower down payment than if you were borrowing from a private lender. If you're a veteran, you may qualify for a loan backed by the Veterans Benefits Administration (VBA), and if you're a buyer in a rural or certain suburban areas, you may qualify for a loan backed by the US Department of Agriculture (USDA), both of which come with much lower down payment requirements than a conventional mortgage, which is not federally guaranteed.

These government-backed mortgages were created to make homeownership more affordable and, along with reduced down payments, often come with lower rates than a mortgage that is not backed by a government agency. They're often available to people who may not qualify for private mortgages because of income or poor credit.

There are different types of mortgages that vary tremendously in time needed to pay them back, the frequency of payments, and other factors. The two most common types are a fixed-rate mortgage (FRM), which, as you read earlier, is a mortgage with an interest rate that stays the same over the life of the loan, and an adjustable-rate mortgage (ARM), which has an interest rate that can fluctuate.

Fixed-Rate Mortgages

With more than three quarters of people who get mortgages choosing FRMs, they're by far the most common type. They're also the easiest to understand: you agree to pay a certain amount of interest on your mortgage for as long as you have it. If you pay 4 percent interest the first month, you'll pay 4 percent interest the last month as well. The rate doesn't change, and neither does your monthly payment. You receive a schedule of payments, and you know exactly how much you must pay each month. So if you like to know precisely how to plan your long-term budget, you'll probably like FRMs. It removes the guesswork.

The interest rate a lender charges on a mortgage or another type of loan depends on inflation and the state of the general economy. Interest rates are controlled by the Federal Reserve System, which is the central bank of the United States. The Federal Reserve, as it is widely known, determines the interest rates it charges to banks. If the Fed charges banks high interest, your mortgage rate will be high; if rates are low, a mortgage you take out should have a low rate.

The Federal Reserve raised interest rates 11 consecutive times between March 2022 and May 2023, leaving speculation as to whether it would continue to raise the rates or leave them alone. The average rate on a 30-year mortgage at the beginning of July 2023 was about 6.5 percent, according to Bankrate, more than double the rate of about 3.2 percent at the beginning of 2022.

A problem with FRMs is that if you obtain a mortgage when interest rates are relatively high and the rates fall, you're stuck paying the higher rate. You can refinance your mortgage, or trade it in for a new one to take advantage of low rates, but this process requires time and involves significant expense.

Still, there are reasons why more people have FRMs than any other kind. They're easy to keep track of, for example, and although you'll have to factor in increasing costs of taxes and insurance, you can count on making a specific payment each month.

Adjustable-Rate Mortgages

ARMs differ from FRMs in one big way: the interest rate does not stay the same for the entire term of the loan. Because of that, your monthly mortgage payment varies as well. Homebuyers generally are attracted to ARMs because they offer some initial savings, like a lower beginning interest rate and no points. (Points are prepaid interest paid as a fee to a mortgage lender to cover the cost of applying for the loan. You learn more about these later in the chapter.)

With ARMs, you generally agree to pay a fixed interest rate for a certain amount of time, after which your rate and monthly payment may fluctuate. The interest rates for ARMs are tied into various indexes that determine how they'll rise or fall. The indexes used for the interest adjustment are based on the current interest rate scenario available at the time the ARM rate is adjusted. Your lender will specify what index is used to determine your rate.

Most ARMs also include annual caps, so your interest rate can't keep increasing forever. However, if the interest rates rise dramatically, you could end up paying hundreds of dollars more on your monthly payment down the road than you do initially. On the other hand, if interest rates stay low, an ARM can be a good deal.

The initial savings of an ARM over a FRM can be tempting, and it can be a good idea to take advantage of those lower early rates if you don't plan on living in the home for a long time.

But don't get sucked into an adjustable-rate deal, especially when interest rates are low, unless you fully understand how it works and are willing to take the risks. Get all the information you can about different types of mortgages before you decide what type is best for you.

Comparing 30- and 15-Year Mortgages

Most people take out a 30-year mortgage, which is one you'll pay back over 30 years. You also can get a 15-year mortgage, which you'll pay back over 15 years. Paying off your house more quickly can save you a lot of money during the length of the loan.

Consider this comparison: Let's say you buy a house for $300,000, putting 20 percent, or $60,000 down, giving you a mortgage of $240,000. To keep it simple, we'll assume that the interest rate on both a 15-year and a 30-year mortgage is 6 percent fixed, although interest rates on 15-year mortgages generally are less than those paid over 30 years.

With a 15-year mortgage, your monthly payment, including principal and interest, would be $2,025 a month. After 15 years, the total cost of your house, including the down payment, principal, and interest, would be $424,547.

With a 30-year mortgage, your monthly payment would be $1,439, and after 30 years, the total cost of your house would be $578,011—a big difference from the total cost with a 15-year mortgage.

But although a 15-year mortgage makes perfect sense on paper, it's not the best choice for everyone. Let's look at some pros and cons of each type of mortgage.

Pros and Cons of 30-Year Mortgages

Pro: Your monthly payments are lower, which is desirable for many people. Lower monthly payments allow you to put away more money for present and future expenses, such as home repairs, a college fund, or retirement.

Con: Higher interest payments over a longer period of time. You'll end up paying more during the life of the loan.

Pro: More time to pay back a mortgage may mean you could buy a more expensive home because your monthly payments would be lower than with a 15-year mortgage.

Con: It will take longer to build up home equity.

Pros and Cons of 15-Year Mortgages

Pro: You own your home sooner. You'll be finished making mortgage payments earlier and be debt free, enabling you to invest your money or use it in another way.

Con: Your monthly payment is significantly higher, leaving you less money to save, invest, or use in other ways.

Pro: You'll end up saving thousands of dollars in interest. As noted, interest rates on 15-year mortgages normally are lower than on 30-year mortgages, and you're only borrowing the money for half the time, which drastically reduces the cost of borrowing.

Con: A 15-year mortgage can be harder to qualify for because it requires larger monthly payments.

Pro: You'll build equity in your home sooner because you're reducing the amount of your loan more quickly.

When deciding between a 15- and 30-year mortgage, consider your lifestyle, your job security, and other factors before choosing.

And remember that unless it comes with a prepayment penalty, you can make extra payments on the principal of a 30-year mortgage, which would enable you to pay it off early. Some people apply a bonus or their tax refunds to additional payments, while others make systematic payments each month.

Another tactic is to pay half a mortgage payment bi-weekly, or every time you get paid. This results in an extra full mortgage payment every year, which dramatically reduces the amount of interest you'll pay over the length of the mortgage.

Finding the Best Lender

According to Bankrate, borrowers who carefully compare offers from at least three different mortgage lenders save a considerable amount of money over borrowers who accept the first mortgage offer they get.

After you've gotten your credit score and debt-to-income ratio in shape and figured out how much you can spend on a house, gather rates and terms from a number of lenders, including banks, credit unions, and online lenders. In addition to interest rates, pay attention to the following details:

- Annual percentage rate
- Down payment requirements
- Terms of the loan
- Mortgage points
- Mortgage insurance
- Closing costs
- All other fees

When you have an idea of what you're working with, you'll want to get a mortgage preapproval, which is a written verification from a lender that you qualify for the amount of money you've applied for. Lenders will review your credit history, salary, credit scores, assets, and other factors before granting preapproval. You'll need to provide information and materials such as your Social Security number, photo ID, pay stubs, tax returns, statements for all your financial accounts, a list of your debt, information about a down payment, and more. A preapproval is desirable because a seller will normally look more favorably on a potential buyer who is preapproved than one who is not.

Try to get preapproved by every potential lender you researched. Different lenders have different preapproval requirements, so it's possible you'll be preapproved by one lender but not by another.

You should get loan estimates back within three days of submitting your application. Be sure to read them all carefully to ensure there are no errors or information you did not expect as you compare what offer is best for you.

Understanding Closing Costs

You read a little bit earlier about closing costs that cover things like property taxes, home insurance, interest, title-related costs, inspections, appraisal fees, mortgage insurance, loan-origination charges, escrow account funds, government recording fees, and more.

How Much You'll Pay for Closing Costs

Closing costs for the buyer run between 2 and 6 percent of the loan amount, meaning that on a $300,000 home loan, you'd pay between $6,000 and $18,000 in addition to your down payment.

Paying closing costs as a one-time, out-of-pocket expense is the most cost effective, but coming up with that amount of money can be prohibitive. You may be able to pay the costs over time by rolling them into your mortgage loan, but then you end up paying interest on those costs for as long as you have the mortgage.

You might be able to negotiate to lower some of the fees associated with the closing costs. Also, some states, counties, and cities offer low-interest loans for first-time home buyers who need help with closing costs, the down payment, and other fees. You can find information online regarding first-time home buyer programs in your state.

After you've applied for a mortgage, your lender will give you a loan estimate document that outlines projected closing costs and other information. Closer to your closing date, your lender will give you a final summary of closing costs in a closing disclosure document. Be sure to read these documents carefully and ask the lender to clarify any information you don't understand. Meanwhile, you can find calculators online that can help you estimate what your closing costs will be. NerdWallet (nerdwallet.com/article/mortgages/closing-costs-calculator), Credit Karma (creditkarma.com/calculators/mortgage/closing-costs), or Freddie Mac (myhome.freddiemac.com/resources/calculators/closing-costs) all offer free calculators.

The house buyer pays most of the closing costs, but the seller is responsible for some fees, such as the real estate agent's commission and sometimes a real estate transfer tax, which is a tax imposed on both the buyer and the seller when a property is sold. Buyers can ask the seller to assume some of the buyer's closing costs, but sellers generally only agree to do so when there are more homes for sale than buyers, something we haven't seen in a number of years. Lenders can place limits on how much sellers are allowed to contribute toward closing costs, based on the type of loan.

What Closing Costs Cover

As a buyer, you'll pay the bulk of the closing costs. Some common costs you'll pay include the following:

- Appraisal fee. A lender will order a home appraisal to be sure the amount of the loan isn't greater than the value of the property.

- Discount points. These are optional fees you pay upfront to lower your interest rate. One discount point is equal to 1 percent of your mortgage amount and generally lowers your interest rate by about a quarter of a percentage point.

- Escrow account funds. Your lender will set up an escrow account, which is an account specifically designated to collect and pay property taxes, home insurance, and, if required, mortgage insurance premiums. You'll need to put up money equivalent to about two months of taxes and insurance premiums to fund the account.

- Loan-origination charges. This is a fee the lender charges for underwriting and processing your loan.

- Flood determination fees. This money pays a company to determine if the property is in a flood zone.

- Government recording fees. These fees pay to update records on who has owned the property.

- Government-backed loan mortgage insurance. Loans backed by government agencies such as the VBA, USDA, or FHA have fees that must be paid at closing or folded into the loan.

- Pest inspection. In some areas, lenders require an inspection to check for termites.

- Prepaid expenses. These are the costs you'll need to prepay for home insurance, property tax, and interest on your loan.

- Tax monitoring fees. These determine how much property tax you'll need to pay and confirm that they've been paid up to the date of settlement.

- Title search fee. A title search is done to ensure the person claiming to own the property is the proper owner.

- Lender's title insurance. This is to compensate the lender if there's an error in the title search and someone makes a claim on the home.

- Owner's title insurance. This compensates the homeowner if there's an ownership claim on the property.

You can see how all these fees can add up to the hefty costs you'll need to pay at closing. If you feel that you won't be able to handle the costs, ask your lender about rolling them into your mortgage.

One word of warning when it comes to the closing process: in an average or down housing market, buyers normally have a home inspector conduct an inspection before agreeing to purchase the property. If any problems are discovered, like a leak in the roof or mold in the basement, the seller usually agrees to pay for necessary repairs. In a very busy housing market, like we've seen recently, many buyers have waived inspections to increase their chances of getting the house. This is done at the peril of the buyer and is not recommended.

How Owning a Home Affects Your Taxes

Owning a home provides some good tax advantages. When you buy a house, Uncle Sam gives you a little housewarming gift and lets you deduct three of the biggest homeowner expenses from your federal income taxes:

- Your mortgage interest
- Your property taxes
- Your private mortgage insurance

Other one-time deductions also are available to you, such as the points you pay at closing, but interest, property taxes, and PMI are the long-term biggies.

These deductions are great news for homeowners. When paying the mortgage bill every month starts to seem like more than you can bear, remember that, come April, you'll be happily filling out Schedule A (Form 1040), Itemized Deductions, which is a part of your federal income tax return. If you itemize deductions, the interest you pay on your loan, the property taxes you pay on your home, and your PMI all lower your tax liability. That's a good thing!

Tax deductions can be itemized and subtracted from your adjusted gross income if they're greater than the standard deduction the tax laws allow. The deductions and personal exemptions are subtracted from your income before you figure out how much tax you have to pay. If your total income is $45,200 but you have $8,500 in deductions and personal exemptions totaling $4,050, you'll pay tax on only $32,650 ($45,200 − $8,500 − $4,050 = $32,650).

When you become a homeowner, you get the privilege of taking some pretty hefty deductions. If you haven't itemized your deductions before buying the house, be sure you find out all the deductions you're entitled to before you pay this year's taxes. Deducting your mortgage interest, up to $10,000 in property taxes, and PMI can take quite a large chunk out of your taxable income.

Points usually are the responsibility of the buyer, but a seller who really wants to sell sometimes can be convinced to assume responsibility for paying some or all of the cost of the points. If you can convince the seller to pay the points, which is next to impossible to do in a tight housing market, you win in two ways: you don't have to pay the points, and you still can deduct them from your income tax. If you and the seller split the points, you still get to deduct the total amount. One point is 1 percent of the value of your mortgage loan.

In addition to deducting mortgage interest and points, you can deduct some of the property taxes and other expenses that are finalized at settlement. Some of the expenses you pay at closing can be deducted from your income tax, and some are considered capital expenses when you sell your home. You can find tax calculators online to help you figure out how much you'll save on taxes as a homeowner. If an accountant or tax adviser assists you with your tax return, take your settlement sheet with you when you meet.

The Downside to Taxes

There are tax advantages to homeownership, but there also are taxes you'll need to pay, and they can be quite expensive. Property taxes, which are taxes levied by the municipality and/or school district in which you live, can be especially hard on the wallet.

Property tax rates vary significantly but usually run somewhere about 1.5 percent of the value of your property. Because paying property taxes can be prohibitive, many lenders require that homeowners pay money into an escrow account to cover the cost of the taxes when they come due. An escrow account is a special account used to hold money designated for a particular purpose, such as property taxes. Your taxes are paid monthly out of the account, which is a much easier way to pay them than making one large, annual payment.

In most areas, you pay local property taxes (also known as your school tax), county taxes, and sometimes some oddball taxes from your municipality. Taxes can vary, depending on the quirks, wishes, and wealth of the municipal boards that impose them.

The majority of property taxes you pay go toward funding your local school district. A portion also goes to the borough or township where you live, and some goes to your county. You normally pay your taxes to a local tax collector, who distributes them to the proper places.

The average American household pays $2,690 a year in property taxes, according to US Census Bureau data. In some states, though, the taxes are much higher. Residents of New Jersey, the state with the highest property taxes, pay an average of $5,420 a year. Illinois, New Hampshire, Wisconsin, Connecticut, Vermont, and Texas also have much higher-than-average property taxes.

You can be assessed for your taxes once a year, twice a year, or more often. Property taxes have gotten so high in some areas that officials are allowing residents to pay their taxes quarterly to relieve the burden of huge lump sums. Making a quarterly payment, however, may mean you also have to pay an additional fee for the convenience.

Many property owners and legislators agree that property taxes are not an equitable means of raising money to support public education and other services. Elderly people whose children graduated from high school 40 or 50 years ago still pay property taxes if they own homes. And people who don't own property enjoy the same services without having to pay the high taxes, although their landlord does pay the property taxes. Property tax is an issue in almost every state, and movements are underway in some states to reform it.

A concerning aspect of property taxes is that the municipality imposing them can raise them by reassessing your home. Every now and then, municipal governments declare a major property reassessment. When that happens, look out. At that point, the municipality probably has reached its upper allowable tax limit and is looking for a way to make more revenue. If it can't increase your tax rate, it can reassess the value of your home. You can challenge your assessment by filing an appeal, which can be approved or denied.

You can expect to pay various other taxes in addition to your property tax. You might be charged additional taxes for streetlights, fire hydrants, trash collection, sewage, water, and the like. Unfortunately, these taxes are not tax-deductible.

All this means you have to be careful when breaking down your expenses for your tax return. The bank might pay $2,000 to your municipality for your taxes, but only $1,550 of the $2,000 is deductible on your taxes. It's a good idea to keep copies of all bills and the payments you make so you have them handy when tax time comes around.

Getting Help When You Need It

Buying your first house—or any house—is a big decision, and you're going to need some help. Some people insist on doing it themselves, but that's not advisable, especially for first-time buyers.

First, you should secure the services of a good, reputable real estate agent who can walk you through the process of finding and purchasing a home. A good agent can be your best friend when you're searching for the home of your dreams.

You also might want to identify a mortgage broker to help you locate and obtain the mortgage that makes the most sense for you. You'll have to pay for a broker's services, but if you don't have time to shop around for the best mortgage, or if you feel intimidated by it all, it might be worth your while to hire one. If you apply for a mortgage and are turned down, you should call a broker.

Be sure to check the qualifications of anyone you hire to help you in the process of buying a home.

The Continuing Costs of Homeownership

You don't stop spending money after you've closed on your house and moved in. You've read about the high cost of property taxes, but there are other costs related to owning a home to consider as well.

Zillow, the real estate listings site, and Thumbtack, a home renovation platform, teamed up on a study that found that the cost of essential home maintenance projects averages about $6,400 a year, which breaks down to about $530 a month.

Experts recommend making a monthly schedule of tasks, which can help you avoid serious issues that can cost a lot of money to remedy. Be especially aware of water issues because even a small amount of water from a leak around a sink or bathtub can cause significant damage.

Appliances don't last forever, including furnaces and air conditioners. You can prolong the life of your heating and cooling system by changing filters at regular intervals and having them inspected at least once a year.

A leaky roof can result in serious damage to your home, so keep a close eye out for problems like loose shingles or soffits. Also, keep your rain gutters cleaned to prevent water from building up and possibly entering the house.

Homeowner's insurance is required to get a mortgage, so this expense is no surprise. It's likely that these fees will be paid out of your escrow account. (You'll read more about homeowner's and other insurances you need in Chapter 10.)

As mentioned earlier, if your residence is part of a homeowners association or condominium association, you'll need to pay a monthly or quarterly fee to cover services provided by the association.

These are just a sampling of expenses you'll encounter as a homeowner. Some financial analysts claim that buying a home is not an investment because it does not meet the criteria of being liquid and producing income. But homeownership remains a dream and a financial goal to aspire to for many people.

Chapter Summary

Purchasing a home is a complicated process, so it's best to take your time and do your homework before proceeding. Be sure to conduct a careful assessment to help you understand how much you'll be able to spend on a home and how much you'll likely be able to borrow, remembering that you'll encounter a lot of up-front costs and closing costs when buying a home. You'll need to know about different types of mortgages and consider which is best for your situation and also think about what type of lender you'll want to approach. Understand that owning a home offers both tax advantages and tax liabilities because you'll need to pay property taxes, which in some areas are daunting. And don't forget to calculate the ongoing costs associated with homeownership. We're not trying to discourage you from buying a home, but going into the process with eyes wide open can save you some unwelcome surprises.

Chapter 8

Finding That Special Someone

Life keeps changing, and those changes can affect your finances in a big way. Events and milestones like finding that special someone, moving in together, getting married, and maybe getting divorced are part of life and can affect you physically, emotionally, and financially.

The millennial generation is spread out over an age range—about 27 to 42—that can bring about a number of those important events. Maybe you're still single, either by choice or because you haven't yet met the right person. You might be living with a partner, engaged and planning a wedding, or married. Maybe you're raising a young child or are trying to keep up with a couple of teenagers and thinking about sending them to college. (More on kids in the next chapter.) Or maybe your marriage ended in divorce and you're on your own again.

In this chapter, we discuss some of these events that change your life— along with your finances. What happens to your budget when you move in with a partner? How are your taxes affected when you get married? How would a divorce affect your finances? Let's get started.

Living Together

So you've met somebody you really, really like. Okay, you're in love. You're spending a lot of time together. Actually, you're together almost all the time. You talk about a future together, but neither of you feels like you're quite ready to start shopping for an engagement ring. And then one day you're just hanging out when it happens: your significant other asks you to move in.

This scenario has become commonplace, as the number of unmarried partners living together nearly tripled between 1999 and 2019, according to US Census figures. As of 2019, 17 million unmarried partners were living together in the United States.

Couples live together for a variety of reasons. Some do it because it's convenient; it eliminates running back and forth between two apartments or houses and shuffling belongings all over the place. Some couples use living together as a sort of "trial run" for marriage; they reason it makes more sense to see whether it will work out before they get married than risk a divorce later.

Financial considerations also can factor into a couple's decision to live together rather than get married. Many couples set a goal of saving a specific amount of money, paying off student loans, or putting back enough for a down payment on a house before taking the plunge. Some want to establish their careers before getting married and live together while they do.

Whatever the reasons, plenty of couples choose to live together. Although cohabitation is common and widely accepted, it still can be a sticky arrangement. There are financial and legal ramifications as well as the less-tangible emotional aspects to consider.

You're on your own to figure out the emotional particulars of living together, but we can tell you some things you should know about the legal and financial aspects.

Financial Pros of Living Together

Living together definitely comes with some financial advantages:

- If you each had an apartment before you moved in together, you'll cut your housing costs by about 50 percent by sharing your space. That makes more sense than paying rent on an apartment that was empty most of the time, anyway.

- You'll also be sharing costs for utilities, so you'll see some savings there.

- If you were living a considerable distance apart, you'll save money on transportation.

- You'll also realize some tax advantages by living together instead of opting for marriage. Although you're living together, you'll continue filing your tax returns as singles. That can save you some money, especially if you and your significant other earn above-average salaries. Even with changes to tax laws that lessen tax-rate disparities, many married couples still pay more combined income tax than two singles filing separately.

Financial Cons of Living Together

Although living together does have some financial benefits, it's not all a bed of roses. In some instances, you'd be better off financially if you were married. Consider the following:

- Some employers offer health and dental benefits to spouses of employees but not to unmarried partners.

- If an employer offers life insurance and the employee dies, benefits automatically go to the spouse of the deceased. An unmarried partner must be named as a beneficiary to receive the benefits.

- If you live together in a house or condo that's in only one of your names, the significant other may have no claim on the property, despite having invested $30,000 in the new kitchen.

- If a person dies while employed, the spouse might be eligible for some Social Security benefits upon reaching age 60. An unmarried partner isn't eligible for these benefits.

- Unmarried couples may not be eligible for money-saving "family" memberships in clubs and organizations.

We're not trying to turn marriage into a business transaction, but as you can see, there are financial advantages and disadvantages to living together instead of getting married that you might want to consider.

One thing to remember, though, is that marriage implies love and commitment that extend far past the savings account. If you're putting off marriage because you might be taxed at a higher rate, you might have to ask yourself whether you're looking for an excuse to stay single.

Getting Married

You're tying the knot! Congratulations and best wishes to you both! Before you blissfully embark on your honeymoon, though, you need to think about some financial matters.

Paying for the Wedding

If you're engaged and planning a wedding, chances are you've been thinking a lot about money as you ponder how much to spend and how to pay for it. We leave that up to you, with only a warning to think long and hard before taking on a lot of debt to pay for your special day.

With some planning, you can put on a lovely wedding without a $30,000 price tag, the amount the average wedding cost in 2022, according to wedding website The Knot. Many websites, blogs, apps, and articles can help you plan a wedding that won't break your budget. Here are few favorites:

- Airtable (airtable.com/templates/wedding-planning/expxNBai7rjuqdJ06) offers a wedding planning template that includes a spreadsheet, calendar, and to-do list, all in one place.

- The Knot's (theknot.com) Wedding Budgeter is a personalized tool that helps you log costs and stay on track with your spending. It also gives estimates on vendor costs to help you figure out what to look for and who to hire.

- WeddingWire (weddingwire.com) has a budget tool that helps you track and compare your spending goals with actual spending. It also has a detailed schedule to help you avoid late fees or missed payment deadlines.

- Jessica Bishop's *The Budget-Savvy Wedding Planner and Organizer: Checklists, Worksheets, and Essential Tools to Plan the Perfect Wedding on a Small Budget* can help keep you organized and on track with your spending.

Your Combined Finances

A large number of divorces are caused by financial problems. Sometimes these problems are a result of gambling or another type of addiction. Often, though, financial problems occur because the couple doesn't work together on their financial health.

If you're planning to marry, it's absolutely essential that you and your intended sit down and carefully and thoroughly discuss how you'll handle your finances after the wedding. You should establish some goals to work toward together and be sure you know about each other's debts, spending patterns, and investments. Talk about your college debt, credit card debt, or other liabilities. Get familiar with one another's credit scores, and understand what each of you earns and saves. As a married couple, you'll need to work together to handle your finances.

You also need to decide how you'll set up your bank accounts as a married couple. It's not necessary to have joint accounts, although most married couples do have at least some of their money pooled. Some couples, especially when both people are earning, both keep separate accounts and joint accounts. Separate accounts give individuals freedom and independence, while joint accounts offer the convenience of allowing either spouse to sign a check or make online payments. This is a decision you and your partner need to discuss and figure out based on what works best for the two of you.

While contemplating marriage, be sure to consider your spouse-to-be's financial personality. Learn your partner's attitudes concerning savings and the best means for saving money for your future together. Do you have 401(k) plans? Any stocks? What about savings bonds you got as gifts when you were a kid? Talk about saving to buy a house. What about saving for kids, if you want to have them?

Talk, too, about how you'll operate within a budget, and together plan the budget you'll use. You don't want the stresses of adjusting to married life to be aggravated by a misunderstanding of how you'll be handling your finances. Iron out as many financial considerations as possible before the wedding to avoid conflicts afterward.

You also should discuss how your marriage will affect your employer benefits. If one of you has a much better package than the other, set it up so you're both covered by the better deal if possible. Consider health benefits, retirement savings plans, and anything else that might affect your financial situation. Check to see whether either employer offers compensation to an employee who gives up benefits to be covered by the partner's plan.

What About Prenups?

Prenuptial agreements—legal documents that spell out how assets will be divided in the event the marriage fails—used to be primarily for very wealthy people. But even if you don't have lots of money, some matrimonial lawyers and financial advisers strongly recommend a prenup, especially if one person has a child or children from a previous marriage or relationship. A prenuptial agreement also might make sense if one partner owns a business or makes a lot more money than the other. Some families with significant means favor prenuptial agreements to protect the family money in the event of a divorce. Such an agreement could be important if one partner has major assets independently and doesn't want to risk losing them. Prenups primarily deal with finances, but they also can include provisions for issues such as pets and social media imagery.

The average cost of hiring an attorney to draw up a traditional prenuptial agreement can vary dramatically, depending on the complexity and the amount of assets to be considered. Sarah recently oversaw the proceedings for a prenuptial agreement for a family member that garnered legal fees of $5,500. Online sites like HelloPrenup (helloprenup.com) offer agreements for a flat fee—$599 as of this writing—or you can get agreements online from sources like LegalZoom (legalzoom.com), an online legal document provider.

Whether or not to have a prenuptial agreement is something you and your betrothed have to decide together. If you can't agree on the need for one, or if you feel your partner is pressuring you to have one and you don't want it, it might be a good idea to get some financial or relationship counseling before the wedding. It might just be a matter of not fully understanding the other's concerns or wishes.

Filing Jointly or Separately?

The American tax system is far from simple, and it's long been a thorny issue for some couples as they marry. As mentioned earlier, the taxes a couple has to pay after marriage might be higher or lower than the combined amount they would have paid if they had remained single. If the amount is more, it's referred to as the *marriage penalty*. If it's less, it's called a *marriage bonus*.

Typically, a marriage penalty happens when two people who make about the same amount of money marry. This is true for both low- and high-income couples because combining salaries and doubling your taxable income can push a couple into a higher tax bracket. The US tax system is set up as a graduated tax, starting at zero and increasing in implements of 22 percent, 24 percent, and 37 percent. If your combined income bumps you into a higher tax bracket and you end up paying more taxes, it can negatively affect your net income.

It used to be that the deduction a married couple took didn't even come close to adding up to the total of the deductions of two people filing separately, but tax revisions have come a long way in closing the gap.

A marriage bonus typically occurs when a couple with very unequal salaries files jointly. The amount earned by the person with the lower income generally isn't enough to put the couple into a higher tax bracket. Because income tax brackets for married individuals are much wider than those for single filers, the couple might actually fall into a lower bracket and pay less in taxes.

To see which way is more advantageous to you, run your returns both ways—jointly and separately—through a tax program such as TurboTax before filing for the first time.

Divorce

Statistics show that between 40 and 50 percent of marriages in the United States end in divorce, an act that can wreak havoc with your finances. If you're looking at a divorce, it's extremely important to pay close attention to financial issues and be sure you get what you're entitled to. Many people have been forced to dramatically alter their lifestyles after divorce due to financial considerations.

Divorce and Your Finances

Let's review the legal steps of divorce and the money-related actions you should take at each point.

Deciding to Divorce

When you and your spouse have decided to divorce, you should consult a lawyer or begin some legal research of your own. The more you know, the better prepared you can be.

You'll need to learn your state's laws regarding issues such as child custody and support (if you have children), alimony payment or custodial support, debts incurred after separation, valuation of marital property, and so forth.

Any joint bank accounts should be frozen or closed at this time, and you should organize all financial papers and documents.

Separation

Although physical separation doesn't always happen, normally one spouse leaves the household to live elsewhere. Obviously, this can cause financial problems. If you're paying a mortgage and keeping up with expenses of a home, finding cash to rent an apartment or other accommodation can be difficult.

Each person should document all debts incurred, including moving expenses. Money spent on improvement or repairs to the marital home should be noted. Keep track of any joint bills you pay, and be sure you have adequate insurance policies for the current living situation. Start thinking about tax issues at this point, too, and decide whether you'll file jointly or separately.

Legal Matters

Next comes the actual filing for divorce. One spouse files the complaint or petition for divorce, officially beginning the divorce process. The other spouse will need to file an official response to the complaint or petition.

A request for temporary court orders follows. One spouse files a request for temporary court instructions regarding issues such as alimony, child custody and support, and visitation. The request also may ask for one spouse to pay the other's legal fees. All child support and alimony payments should be documented to assure that court orders are being followed and for tax purposes.

Legal discovery is next. This is a series of procedures used to obtain information about your divorce case. It involves financial fact-finding and identification and consideration of the value of all marital property. Child support and alimony payments to be made after the divorce is final will be set during this period.

You should make a list of all assets such as stocks, bank accounts, real estate, cars, and so on. You may need to hire a financial planner who specializes in divorce issues at this stage.

Then comes the settlement. Following the discovery process, legal and financial settlement negotiations will begin. If both parties are in reasonable agreement concerning division of property and other matters, these negotiations can be fairly simple. Lawyers representing each party can conduct these negotiations, as can a mediator both parties agree to use or an arbitrator with the power to make binding decisions that will be transferred back to the court. An arbitrator normally is used when a couple is not cooperative as to the division of property and other matters.

The legal settlement can be long and drawn out or fairly simple, depending on circumstances and people involved. Be sure all legal and financial issues, such as alimony and child support, child custody, and tax implications are addressed at this time.

The settlement agreement is a formal document that sets forth the terms of the divorce settlement.

The judgment of divorce finalizes the divorce and ends proceedings.

Aftereffects

After the divorce is final, you'll need to be sure all your legal documents, such as deeds and wills, reflect your change in marital status and any changes in ownership. Also check and update all bank records, stock certificates, insurance policies, and other documents, making sure to change any beneficiary designations that no longer apply.

Final Financial Thoughts on Divorce

If you and your spouse are willing, you can work together during the divorce process to ensure it has as little negative impact on your finances as possible. Remember that a long, drawn-out divorce almost always costs more than an amicable one that proceeds smoothly.

An important fact to keep in mind is that alimony, sometimes called separation maintenance or spousal support, is no longer tax deductible for the person paying it and is considered income for the person receiving it. Child support payments also are not tax deductible but are not considered taxable income.

One spouse may be directed by the court to help with expenses incurred by the other spouse other than child support. These could include paying premiums on insurance policies or paying some or all the mortgage.

Divorce is not a simple matter, financially. If it happens, be sure to get the professional advice you need. Keep in mind that you likely will need a new postdivorce budget to help you adjust to financial changes in your life. Plan carefully to avoid unnecessary problems.

Chapter Summary

Life changes can be challenging in many ways. As you move into your 30s and 40s, you'll encounter events and changes that can affect you financially as well as mentally, physically, and emotionally. There will be happy occasions and difficult times, and you'll need to be prepared as best as you can to deal with them. What you can do, however, is keep an eye on your financial situation, think about how you can minimize the impact of life changes, and keep yourself moving forward financially.

Chapter 9

Growing Your Family

Having children changes your life in so many ways. There's the excitement of deciding you're going to adopt a child or finding out you're pregnant, then experiencing a range of emotions as the proceedings or pregnancy progresses. The process of preparation builds, culminating in the moment you bring home a baby or child to welcome into your family.

And then come the nights of getting up to feed and comfort the baby, the days of keeping up with a toddler who seems intent on discovering every potential hazard available, and the times of pondering the effects that having a child or children can have on your finances.

Nobody can really explain the life-changing effects of kids, but if you're lucky enough to be a parent, you'll discover them firsthand. You can, however, anticipate the financial implications of raising children.

The Cost of Raising a Child

Money might not be the main thing you're thinking about when you're expecting a child, but you should be prepared for the costs you'll incur and how your budget may have to be adjusted.

In 2015, the US Department of Agriculture estimated the average cost of raising a child from birth until age 18. When adjusted for average inflation of about 2.5 percent since then (even though, as you know, inflation rose to much higher than 2.5 percent starting in late 2020 and extending into 2022), the cost of raising a child in 2022 came out to $277,108, or $15,395 per year. And that's only up to age 18, which doesn't factor in the cost of college.

Remember that cost is the *average* cost of raising a child. Families with fewer financial resources spent less, while those with greater resources spent more. Households with before-tax incomes of less than $59,200 spent about $9,500 a year on children, while families with incomes of more than $107,400 spent about $21,000.

That's a big gap, but when you think about it, a lot of spending is controllable when children are very small. They don't need dozens of fancy outfits, a changing table in every room, a designer changing bag (Dior offers a Blue Dior Oblique Canvas changing bag for $3,300), or a stroller that costs upward of $2,000. Those choices are on the parents—the baby doesn't care.

The bigger issue to think about is whether your household income will be impacted due to costs associated with the pregnancy and birth or because one or both parents will take time off work to care for the baby. You'll also need to consider childcare costs if both parents are working or plan to return to work.

Costs of Prenatal Care, Childbirth, and Baby's Medical Care

When expecting a child, it's important to be realistic about expenses you might incur. According to the Health Care Cost Institute, the national average for out-of-pocket childbirth costs for someone with health insurance was $2,854 in 2020.

Check the provisions of your health insurance policy to find out exactly what pregnancy and childbirth expenses are covered by your employer's plans—both of you, if you have separate plans—and what you might have to pay for yourself. Don't forget to consider any deductibles or copays you might be responsible for.

There also is the cost of prenatal care to consider, and any costs associated with the baby's medical care after delivery. Remember that these costs can vary dramatically from state to state, city to city, and even hospital to hospital.

Estimating the expenses you'll be responsible for can be cumbersome, but the more you learn up front, the fewer surprises you'll have later. The best thing to do is call your insurance company and ask a lot of questions, such as those in following the list. Be sure to make a note of who you spoke to and the date of the conversation.

- Does my policy provide benefits for prenatal care, labor, and delivery?
- Do I need a referral from my primary care provider to see an OB-GYN or other specialist?
- Does my policy cover tests such as ultrasounds, amniocentesis, and genetic testing?
- Will I need preauthorization for any prenatal care?
- Which doctors and hospitals in my area are in my network of care?
- What medical costs incurred by my baby following delivery are covered?
- Which costs may not be covered?
- What length of hospital stay is covered for the mother?
- What length of hospital stay is covered for my baby?
- Does my policy cover a private room or a shared room?
- Does my policy cover alternative delivery options, such as a home birth with a midwife (if applicable)?

If you have to pick up some or even all of the cost, many hospitals and birthing centers will work with you on setting up a payment plan. Those costs should be incorporated into your budget and planned for accordingly.

Costs of Adopting a Child

The cost of adoption varies tremendously depending on the type of adoption you pursue. Generally, you can adopt a child through the public welfare system, through a private adoption agency in the United States, or through a private or public agency outside the United States.

Adopting a child through a public agency is by far the most economical option and normally starts with becoming a foster parent. Adopting from foster care generally costs less than $1,000, according to the Child Welfare Information Gateway, a service overseen by the federal Office of the Administration for Children and Families. Costs are intentionally kept low to encourage people to foster and adopt children who need homes.

If you choose to adopt through a private agency within the United States, the Child Welfare Information Gateway sets costs at between $30,000 and $60,000. Those fees cover expenses for a home study, placement, counseling, training, and legal documentation, and they can vary from state to state and among agencies. You also can work with an attorney to pursue a private adoption on your own, resulting in slightly lower costs—between $25,000 and $40,000, according to Gateway.

Intercountry adoption is a popular option, but it can take a long time and costs between $20,000 and $50,000, depending on the type of agency you work with. Intercountry adoptions can be complicated because you need to deal with passports and travel visas and also navigate the legal system in the country from where you're adopting. You could face language barriers and normally have to pay for extra expenses such as airplane tickets and hotels.

There are pros and cons to each of these adoption methods, so you'll need to consider your goals, motivations, and budget before deciding how you want to proceed.

What About Time Off After Your Little One Arrives?

If your employer offers paid family and medical leave, which would enable you to continue getting a salary while you stayed home to care for the baby, consider yourself fortunate. According to the Kaiser Family Foundation, a nonprofit that focuses on major health-care issues in the United States, fewer than one in four workers had access to paid leave in 2021.

Most federal employees have access to 12 weeks of paid parental leave following the birth or adoption of a child, and 13 states and Washington, DC, have passed laws that require companies to provide some form of paid leave. With no federal law legislating paid time off, most private employers are not required to provide it, and many do not.

In 2023, Annuity.org, a financial consulting organization, compared state laws and other factors and came up with the 10 best states for paid family leave:

1. Oregon (12 weeks; $1,446 maximum weekly benefit)
2. Washington (12 weeks; $1,327 maximum weekly benefit)
3. New York (12 weeks; $1,068 maximum weekly benefit)
4. New Hampshire (6 or 12 weeks, determined by insurance; $1,696 maximum weekly benefit)
5. California (8 weeks; $1,357 maximum weekly benefit)
6. Colorado (12 weeks; $1,100 maximum weekly benefit)
7. District of Columbia (12 weeks; $1,099 maximum weekly benefit)
8. Delaware (12 weeks; $900 maximum weekly benefit)
9. Massachusetts (12 weeks; $1,084 maximum weekly benefit)
10. Rhode Island (6 weeks; $978 maximum weekly benefit)

If your employer doesn't offer paid maternity or paternity leave, check at work to see if you're covered by short-term disability insurance, which might cover you for time off due to pregnancy and childbirth. If short-term disability won't kick in, you could take time off under the Family and Medical Leave Act, which stipulates your employer must offer you the same job or a similar job when you return but does not have to pay you during the leave.

Considering Childcare Costs

The cost of childcare is cumbersome for many families, often the most expensive cost associated with raising a child. But although it's expensive, childcare is essential for families who need it so parents can work, go to school, or tend to other obligations. We saw during the COVID-19 pandemic what happened when childcare facilities had to shut down. Many parents, especially mothers, left their jobs to care for children—a move that negatively impacted their finances.

Despite a well-recognized need for affordable, dependable childcare in the United States, costs continue to go up, outpacing inflation by more than 3 percent. The problem is intensified by an exodus of childcare workers. According to the Center for American Progress, 8.4 of the prepandemic childcare workforce did not return to work when the pandemic ended.

In 2023, Care.com, an online marketplace for those looking for care for their children, aging parents, or others, released its tenth-annual Cost of Care Report. The report concluded that childcare is unaffordable for the majority of US families, particularly those who are low or middle income. It found that families, on average, spend 27 percent of their household income on childcare expenses, and that 59 percent of parents surveyed said they'd spend more than $18,000 per child for childcare in 2023—a cost that is clearly prohibitive.

When considering the costs of childcare, think about how much you earn compared to what you pay. If you're paying for two children in daycare, you need a pretty decent salary to simply cover those costs. Would it be smarter for you or a spouse to stay home and care for the kids for a few years to cut the daycare costs? Do you have a trusted relative or neighbor who could care for them on a part-time basis while you work part-time?

If childcare costs are affecting your ability to pay bills and keep up with other expenses, try to come up with some alternatives. There's no formula for balancing childcare and work; only you and your partner can decide what's best for your family.

Childcare Tax Breaks and Credits

But there is some good news: the federal government offers a couple of tax breaks that can help with some of the costs.

The child and dependent care credit is a tax credit that can save you thousands of dollars when you file your taxes. The childcare credit is based on childcare expenses. Generally, the maximum credit is 35 percent of childcare expenses up to $3,000 for one child or $6,000 for two or more children.

To claim the credit, you'll just need to save childcare expense receipts for the year and record the appropriate information on your tax return. You'll need to file IRS Form 2441, Child and Dependent Care Expenses with your return, and you'll need either the Social Security or employer identification number for the provider.

You also should take advantage of any assistance available from the federal child tax credit, which is a partially refundable tax credit available to taxpayers with dependent children under the age of 17. The credit is based on various factors, including income. If you qualify, it could be worth $2,000 for each qualifying dependent child.

You can claim the child tax credit on your federal tax return Form 1040 or 1040-SR. You'll need to fill out Schedule 8812, Credits for Qualifying Children and Other Dependents, which you submit with your 1040.

Ongoing Costs of Raising Children

Kids don't get less expensive as they grow, that's for sure. In addition to childcare costs, you'll have ongoing expenses like diapers, formula and food, creams and wipes, clothes, toys, and other items when they're babies and toddlers.

As they grow, you'll pay for their housing, food, transportation, health care, clothing, schooling, and a whole lot of miscellaneous items like bikes, skateboards, video games, summer camp, sports lessons, allowances, and more. Participation in sports can be an expensive endeavor, especially if your kids are on travel teams and lodging and food costs are involved.

Your budget will have to change to meet the needs of your family. Hopefully, your income will increase to keep up with your changing financial needs. And you can encourage your kids to pick up part-time jobs as teenagers to help offset some of their expenses.

Starting a College Fund

If everyone started saving for college costs on the day their first child was born, they'd be in pretty good shape by the time that baby reached 18 or 19 years old. Unfortunately, that's not the route most people take, and it's understandable. Life and daily bills get in the way, meaning that often, the college fund is the last account on your deposit list each month.

If you're not convinced that starting to save for college early is important, consider these numbers from T. Rowe Price Investment Firm. They are the amounts parents need to save per month and per year at 10 percent interest in order to have $100,000 saved when it's time for college:

- Parents who start saving when their child is born need to save $161 a month, or $1,938 a year.

- Parents who start saving when their child is 8 need to save $447 a month, or $5,364 a year.

- Parents who start saving when their child is 13 need to save $1,140 a month, or $13,681 a year.

Why the different amounts? Remember our discussion about compound interest in Chapter 4? It can go a long way in making savings in a college fund work for you. Let's look at some different types of plans so you get an idea of what you'll be dealing with.

529 Plan

A 529 college savings plan is the most common means of saving for a child's college education. There are tax advantages to these accounts, along with the potential to earn some interest on the money you invest.

With a 529 plan, you make after-tax contributions to the account. That means income taxes have already been deducted from the money you're contributing. Because taxes are deducted when you contribute, you won't have to pay them when you start taking money out of the account.

Your money is invested in accounts in which the risk is dependent on the age of the child. An account for a baby might be highly invested in stock initially and then transitioned to lower-risk investments as the child gets closer to college age.

A 529 college savings plan generally doesn't yield super-high returns, but over time, you could earn some interest. An advantage of 529 plans is that any return on your money you earn is exempt from federal taxes, and the withdrawals you take from the account are tax free when used for education expenses like tuition, books, housing, or fees.

If for some reason your withdrawals are used for something other than education-related expenses, your contributions won't be taxed, but the earnings on your contributions will be, plus you'll have a 10 percent federal income tax penalty.

Every state offers at least one 529 plan, and you're free to invest in a plan from any state you want. So feel free to look around at what different states have to offer and see which plans have historically gotten the best returns. Some states even have a state income tax credit for a 529 contribution. Also, a recent tax law change enables 529 funds now to be used to provide up to $10,000 a year per beneficiary at a secondary public, private, or religious school.

Coverdell Education Savings Account

Coverdell education savings accounts (Coverdell ESAs) were the main college savings vehicle before the 529. Coverdells are still in use, but only families under a certain income are able to use them. Unlike 529s, the funds may be used to cover elementary, secondary, or higher education expenses.

These days, most people prefer the flexibility and tax advantages of a 529 account over a Coverdell. Also, contributions to a Coverdell are limited to $2,000 a year per student—much less than what you can contribute to a 529 plan. Coverdell plans are not tax-deductible, but, like a Roth IRA, money you put into an account can grow tax-free until you need it, and withdrawals are usually tax-free.

Custodial Account

You also can save money for college in a custodial account, which is a type of account you control for your child until he or she is of legal age, which is 18, 19, or 21, according to your state's laws. When the child reaches legal age, control of the account automatically transfers from you to them. Prior to that, the child's name is on the account and the money in it belongs to them, not you, even though you control it.

An account manager will invest the money you contribute to the account. A custodial account doesn't have the tax advantages of a 529 plan, however. Any return your money earns in the custodial account is taxed in the year of the realized gain.

Withdrawals from a custodial account don't have any penalties as long as the money is used to benefit the child, whether or not that benefit is an educational expense.

One problem with custodial accounts is that because the money is in the child's name and technically belongs to them, it can reduce eligibility for financial aid or other financial perks.

If you're considering this type of account as a college fund, it's a good idea to speak with a financial adviser before making a decision.

High-Yield Savings Account

You read about these types of accounts in Chapter 4, but not in the context of using one as a vehicle for saving college funds. Although you might not earn as much interest as with some other types of accounts, there can be advantages to using a high-yield savings account, perhaps as a complementary source of savings for your child's education.

If your child decides to pursue interests other than college, there are no restrictions on the money in the account—either you or your child can use it for anything. Also, you can withdraw the money at any time without penalty.

Whichever way you decide to save for a child's college costs, getting an early start will give you a tremendous advantage. You can't plan for every contingency, but having money set aside can give you and your child options for the future, which is always a good thing.

Chapter Summary

Starting and growing a family can be one of life's most rewarding experiences, yet it comes at a cost—often a high cost. When planning a family, remember that there are costs associated with having or adopting a child and with raising a child. Take time to consider those costs and determine how you can best adjust your finances to accommodate a growing family.

Chapter 10

Protecting Your Stuff with Insurance

Many of us have a kind of love-hate relationship with insurance. You know you should have it, but you don't like that it takes a bite out of your budget, especially when you might not even need it.

Still, it's better to have insurance than not to—and better yet to have it and never need it.

How Insurance Works

Insurance is a method of sharing risk among a large group of people. Everybody pays for it, whether you use it or not. Hopefully, you make your payments on time, never need to make a claim, and recognize how lucky you are. If you do need it, however, your contributions to that pot of money will have been well worth it.

If you learn one thing about insurance from this chapter, let it be this: insurance is meant to protect the important things in your life—your life itself, your health, the health of your family, your home, and your lifestyle—against big losses. If you get sick and can't work, you'd better have insurance to cover your lost income, even if you're supporting only yourself. If you have a house and it burns down, you'd better have insurance to rebuild and replace the stuff you lost. Whenever you walk outside and get into your car, there's the potential for an accident, and you need to be insured just in case.

Although some insurance companies, including GEICO and the United Services Automobile Association (USAA) sell directly to the public, most insurance is sold through agents or brokers who work for insurance companies like Allstate, State Farm, Nationwide, Liberty Mutual, and thousands of others. The agents earn commissions from the insurance companies based on how much and what type of insurance they sell. Insurance agents aren't the only people out there who work on commission, and there's nothing wrong with a commission system, but be aware that that's how the insurance industry works.

If an agent is going to get a big commission for selling a certain type of policy or a policy for a specific company, you can be sure they'll make every effort to do so. Some agents are really good at making you believe you need something that's completely unnecessary. In fact, some analysts say that nearly 50 percent of insurance agents and brokers try to sell you policies that generate the highest commissions for them.

You can ask an agent how much commission they make on the policies they recommend to you. You might be surprised to find out some commissions are as much as 50 percent of what you'll pay for the policy. If you don't know what you want or need, you could be suckered into buying unnecessary coverage while helping the agent get big commissions.

After you read this chapter, you'll have a better understanding of what you need and don't need. Don't let an agent talk you into buying something you don't need, for which you'll end up paying a large premium, which is the amount of money you pay every month. Be sure he or she understands your situation so you get the kind of coverage you really should have.

If you don't know anyone who sells insurance, you'll have to take your chances with a referral or someone you find on your own. Choose someone with a Chartered Life Underwriter (CLU), Chartered Financial Consultant (ChFC), or Certified Financial Planner (CFP) designation, which demonstrates that the agent has taken courses to further educate him- or herself about the industry. It also implies that the agent has pledged to practice ethically.

You also could use a service such as Angi (angi.com) when searching for an insurance agent, or look for an established insurance company within your community and ask to see a list of agents and their qualifications.

You can buy insurance online, but if you're purchasing for the first time, it's a good idea to work with a reputable agent who can help you figure out exactly what you need and explain the ins and outs of various policies. Getting the right insurances is important. Buying online can be quick and efficient, but there's a lack of personalization, and you won't have the opportunity to develop a relationship with an agent who you can call if you run into trouble.

Figuring Out What You Need— and Don't Need

Make no mistake about it: you can buy as much insurance as you want. You can insure all your electronics, your road bike, your drum set, your toaster oven, and your snowboard if you want to. You can pay $44 a month to buy health insurance on your 5-year-old golden retriever and still be out the $500 deductible and 20 percent of costs for care in the event she needs it. You can insure your lawn mower, your microwave, and the locket you wore when you were a baby. Before you start buying insurance on everything you own, however, consider what you really need.

If you buy a lot of little insurance policies hoping to cover every possibility for loss, you'll end up spending a lot more on the policies than you would fixing the things that go wrong. If your computer or smartphone breaks, by the time you pay the deductible, spend an hour or two filling out the claim, and try to cut through the inevitable red tape, you're probably better off having it fixed on your own.

When it comes to insurance, think big. Forget the little stuff, even if it's tempting because it doesn't seem to cost very much. In many cases, the same coverage offered with "specialty" policies, such as mortgage life insurance or flight insurance, is already provided for in your regular life insurance policy.

Remembering that the goal of buying insurance is to protect the people you love and the things you value, here is a breakdown of insurances you should have depending on where you are in your life. Your insurance needs will change as you age.

- If you're single with no dependents, you need health insurance; auto insurance; homeowner's insurance if you own a place; and enough life insurance to cover your burial, final expenses, and any outstanding loans. If you rent, you should have renter's insurance in place of homeowner's insurance. Disability insurance also is important for you now.

- If you're married with no kids, you need some life insurance, especially if your spouse doesn't work or if you own a home. Auto and homeowner's or renter's insurance are necessary, as are health and disability insurance.

- If you're married with kids, you'll need to bump up the amount and types of insurance you have. If you don't have life insurance yet, you definitely need it now. Term life insurance, for which you pay a certain amount per year and your survivors receive a certain amount if you die, is probably your best bet. You still need health and disability insurance, too, along with auto (pay special attention to this one after the babies get to be teenagers and start driving!) and homeowner's insurance. It's a good idea at this point to reexamine all your policies to be sure you're adequately covered. Having kids makes you responsible for them, and you want to be sure they'd have plenty to get by on if you suddenly became disabled.

What about insurance you don't need? The list could include the following:

- You probably don't need dental insurance. If your employer provides it, that's great, but unless you have some sort of condition that makes extensive dental work necessary, you probably can cover standard cleanings, exams, and X-rays out of pocket. The average cost of an exam and cleaning is about $125, according to health insurance company Humana, and the average cost of an individual dental insurance policy is about $50 a month.

- The same thinking applies to vision insurance. If you don't need glasses or contacts and only get an eye exam once a year or once every couple years, you probably are better off paying out-of-pocket. The average cost of an eye exam is about $150 without insurance, according to vision insurance provider Vision Service Plan. You can get inexpensive vision insurance plans, some as low as $5 a month, but you'll encounter deductibles and copays.

- Credit life and disability insurance probably isn't necessary either. This type of insurance is sold by credit card companies and pays a small amount to your beneficiaries if you die with a credit card balance.

- You can skip life insurance on your children. Life insurance is used to protect income, something children generally don't have. If you feel that you wouldn't be able to afford a funeral and final expenses if your child were to die, you could consider purchasing a child rider on your own life insurance policy for the amount you would need for the child's funeral and burial expenses.

Now let's look at the essential insurance you do need: life, health, disability, property (homeowner's or renter's), and vehicle.

Life Insurance

If you are young and healthy with no dependents and no debt, maybe you don't need life insurance. For everyone else, life insurance is a good idea.

The point of life insurance is to provide for those who depend on you. Your life insurance also would be used to pay off any debt you owe, should you die. So if you have college debt, credit card debt, a car loan, mortgage, or any other type of debt, think about who would be responsible for paying it if you died and whether having to pay off your debt would negatively impact their finances. If your parents cosigned a loan for you, they would be responsible for it if you died. If you die with a big chunk of your mortgage unpaid and the house is in both your name and your spouse or partner's name, he or she would be responsible for the rest of it, without the benefit of your income.

If you have a job that includes benefits, you might be covered for life insurance through an employee-provided group policy. If so, be sure you understand the terms of the insurance and how much would be paid out in the event of your death. A standard plan usually offers a payout of twice the amount of your annual salary.

Also, find out if it's possible for you to increase your coverage if you pay for additional insurance, which could allow you to bump up the payout to four or five times of the amount of your annual salary at an affordable rate as part of a group policy.

If it's just you, you should have enough life insurance to cover your funeral and other final expenses and any outstanding loans. If you're married but have no kids, you should have life insurance if your spouse would have to dramatically change his or her lifestyle if you died. If you have kids and support a family, you definitely need life insurance.

Term Life Insurance Versus Cash Value Insurance

In general, there are two basic types of life insurance: term life insurance and cash value insurance.

Term life insurance is a policy in which you pay an annual premium in exchange for a predetermined amount of money that will be paid to your beneficiaries if you die during the term you're insured. Cash value insurance combines a life insurance policy with a type of savings or investment account, and you actually earn interest, or appreciation, on part of the money you pay into the plan.

Most people benefit more from term life insurance than cash value insurance when they're young. Cash value insurance is actually a type of investment vehicle. It might make sense for older people who use it as part of their estate planning or for families who want to pass along life insurance to their heirs.

Term life insurance is the least expensive kind of life insurance. In exchange for your annual premium, term life gives a predetermined amount of money to your beneficiaries if you die during the term you're insured. All you need to do is continue to pay the premium.

Unless you have a type of term life insurance called level term life insurance, which enables you to pay the same premium for the life of the policy, your premium will keep increasing as you get older. This can make it harder to pay, especially if your income decreases. It's a good idea to review your policies periodically to be sure they continue to make sense for you.

Cash value insurance might sound like a better deal because you think you'll be getting something back from it. Your premiums not only ensure your survivors receive money if you die, but in addition, some of the money from the premiums is credited to an account that should increase in value as long as you keep paying premiums.

An agent who sells cash value life insurance will tell you that after you pay on the policy for so many years (usually 15 or 20), your policy will be all paid up and you won't have to make more payments. The problem is that, compared to term life insurance, cash value insurance is much more expensive to buy when you're young—it can cost up to eight times as much—and the only reason you might be able to stop paying premiums at a certain time is because you've already paid in a great amount of premiums.

There's an argument for buying a cash value policy at a young age. When you buy term life insurance, you need to provide proof of insurability to get a new policy when the current term expires. If it turns out you're uninsurable due to an emerging disease or other medical problem, you could end up without life insurance. A cash value policy can't be cancelled as long as you continue to make the premium payments.

Agents often receive a higher commission on cash value policies than they do on term policies. For that reason, some agents might try to steer you in that direction. Think carefully about what type of plan is better for you. At this point in your life, unless there are special circumstances, it's likely you'll do fine with a term policy.

How Much Life Insurance Do You Need?

Knowing how much life insurance you need isn't always easy to determine. As stated, if you're single or married with no children, you can get away with less than if you have a family to support.

To ensure that your family can continue the lifestyle to which they are accustomed, you'll need to look at several things when considering how much life insurance you need.

Other than your mortgage, what kind of debt do you have? If you have debt, you need to have enough life insurance to pay it off, in addition to being able to continue to support your family.

The next thing to consider is how much money you spend every month. If you haven't already prepared a budget, take a good look at your bank statements or use a personal budget software package to determine how much you need each month. This is important because you can't ensure your family will have enough money to live comfortably if you don't really know how much money that requires. The point of having life insurance is to protect your family and help them achieve the goals you would have been working toward if you had continued to earn.

In addition to long-term financial goals, your spouse would need to have money to fill in the gap left by the loss of your salary. Your household bills and expenses would remain relatively the same, after all.

To get an idea of the amount of life insurance you should buy, use this formula:

1. Calculate how many years your family would need replacement income for your salary. Using the year your youngest graduates from high school or college as an end date probably is reasonable.

2. Multiply your salary by the number of years your family would need replacement income for your salary.

3. Add to that number the balance of your mortgage; the total of all other debt such as college loans, car loans, and credit card debt; and funeral costs.

4. Add to that an estimated amount for the cost of college for your children.

5. Subtract from that number the amount of savings you have in place, including retirement savings, college funds already saved, and proceeds from group life insurance.

After you do the math, you'll know about how much insurance you need.

Shopping for Life Insurance

You'll want to shop around before choosing a life insurance policy to ensure you get a good price from a reliable company.

You can get instant quotes from different insurance companies by using an online insurance broker like AccuQuote (accuquote.com), LifeInsure.com (lifeinsure.com), or FindMyInsurance.com (findmyinsurance.com). All you do is enter your basic information such as your age, health status, and the amount of insurance you want, and you'll be given policy prices from numerous companies. After you review the quotes, you can request an application and get more information about the plan if you want.

When you've identified a company that offers a good price, check the insurance company's rating on a site like Standard & Poor's insurance ratings (standardandpoors.com). If an agent is helping you shop for life insurance, you should look for quotes from at least five different companies.

Obtaining a life insurance policy probably will require a physical exam or at least a visit from a nurse for a blood pressure check and various other tests. When you've secured a life insurance policy, maintain the best health possible you can in case you need to shop for new coverage.

As with any insurance, the hope is that you won't need it. In the meantime, you'll have the peace of mind of knowing your family will be taken care of in the event of your death.

Health Insurance

If you have employer-sponsored health insurance, consider yourself lucky even if the shares of premiums and copays you're responsible for have increased. Just over half of Americans are covered by insurance provided by employers, although most companies require employees to share some of the costs.

For those who don't have employer-sponsored health insurance, about 19 percent rely on Medicaid, about 18 percent have Medicare, and the remaining roughly 13 percent buy their own coverage or get it through another source.

If your employer doesn't provide coverage, or if you are self-employed, you'll need to buy your own health insurance, either from a private company or through the federal Health Insurance Marketplace (healthcare.gov), operated by the federal government under the provisions of the Affordable Care Act.

If you don't have insurance, or you want to change to another company, you'll need to do some comparison shopping to see what's available. There is, however, help available. You can call the Marketplace Call Center at 800-318-2596 to compare plans, enroll, get more information, or start or finish an application.

An easy way to go is to find an insurance agent or broker near you who is qualified to assist you in locating a policy that meets your needs. There's a Find Local Help option on the Marketplace website at localhelp.healthcare.gov that can provide names of people in your area who can help you find either a Marketplace plan or a private one. You don't pay for the service because brokers are paid by the insurance company or companies whose plans they sell.

You also can use an online health insurance seller, which is a service that offers health plans from a number of different insurance companies. You can compare prices and plans and enroll with the company you prefer. One of these companies is HealthMarkets (healthmarkets.com). At its website, you can enter some information and get health insurance policy quotes to compare.

Just be aware that these companies might try to upsell you and sometimes offer additional products like long-term-care insurance or annuities. Don't be distracted by or persuaded to purchase something you don't need.

If you meet certain income requirements, you can qualify for savings on Marketplace. If you don't qualify for lower costs because your income is too high, you can still buy insurance on Marketplace, but be sure you understand the plan and know what your copays and deductibles are.

If you're leaving a job where you have an insurance plan, look into the possibility of extending your coverage when you leave. COBRA (Consolidated Omnibus Budget Reconciliation Act) requires your employer to continue your health coverage after a job loss, death of an employee, divorce, or attaining a certain age (as when a child reaches an age and is no longer covered under the plan). Your employer is required to offer COBRA coverage for 18 months after you quit your job or 36 months for other situations, such as divorce. You have to pay for the insurance, but at least you'll be covered and your insurance won't lapse.

If you are buying from a private company, it pays to look around. Big insurers like Blue Cross Blue Shield, Aetna, or Humana often can get better rates from health-care providers and are more stable than some smaller companies. Look for a plan that has the highest lifetime maximum benefits you can find and is guaranteed to be renewable.

A medical savings account is another option for certain people. As the name implies, this is a savings account created for the purpose of paying for medical expenses, attempting to make medical insurance more affordable. It works in conjunction with qualified major medical insurance and can be used to help pay deductibles and expenses insurance doesn't cover.

Generally, these plans are options for people who are self-employed, who work for a company with 50 or fewer employees, or who themselves employ 50 or fewer workers. The Internal Revenue Service (IRS) offers a form on medical savings accounts, Publication 969, Health Savings Accounts and Other Tax-Favored Health Plans. Access it at irs.gov/publications/p969.

Disability Insurance

What would happen if you had a serious accident while skiing or cleaning out your gutters that resulted in a head injury? Pretty gruesome to think about, right? Nobody is immune to accidents or injury. You have a greater chance of being disabled by age 65 than dying, and if you were hurt and unable to work for a long period of time, you'd be out of luck.

You'd be a little less out of luck, though, if you had disability insurance, which would provide you with an income to live on until you could work again. If you can't afford to be without a paycheck for an extended period of time, you'd better have disability insurance.

There are two types of disability insurance coverage: short term (usually for up to three or six months) and long term (beginning after six months).

Most large companies provide disability insurance to employees who are unable to work because of a physical or mental disability. If you work for a small company or are self-employed, you might have to buy this insurance on your own. If you don't work, you can't get disability insurance.

How much disability insurance you need depends on how much money you have. If you've been living paycheck to paycheck and have no money saved, you'd better have insurance to cover as much of your income as you can purchase. Generally, short-term liability coverage gives you 100 percent of your pay and long-term gives you 60 percent, so look for those plans when you're shopping around. If you have enough money in the bank to support yourself for 6 months or a year, you can skimp a little on coverage.

Disability insurance becomes increasingly important as you have dependents. If you're married and your spouse doesn't work or doesn't earn enough to support both of you, you can't be without it. If your spouse is making enough to support both of you, it's not as important. If you have kids, however, you've got to have disability insurance, unless your spouse makes enough money to support the entire family for an extended period of time.

Be sure you know what's included in your disability coverage if you get it through work. Many people don't take the time to find out, and you can't depend on the benefits department to seek you out and tell you you're eligible for coverage. Most companies have short-term and long-term provisions, so if you find out you need an operation and will be out of work for a couple weeks, you'll want to know whether you're eligible for benefits.

Also be sure the short-term and long-term disability provisions "match," so that once you are on disability, you continue to receive benefits without having to incur another elimination period, or the number of days you must be disabled before the insurance kicks in.

If you need to buy your own disability insurance, go for the longest elimination period you think you could handle. This will result in a significantly lower rate. A 90-day elimination period is often recommended, but you'd need to be able to support yourself (and your family, if applicable) for that period of time.

Also, be sure you understand how the policy defines "disabled." Some policies require that you be hospitalized to receive benefits. You should look for a policy that will keep paying you as long as you're unable to perform your job duties.

Don't depend on government programs such as Social Security or workers' compensation to provide you with benefits in the event of a disability. With Social Security, you must be off work for at least 6 months before you can file for Social Security benefits. And even if you are eligible for coverage, your benefits won't be as much as you need. Also, your chances of being injured off the job are probably as good, or better, as those of being injured at work. You need coverage in the event of any disability.

Property Insurance

You're required to buy property insurance before you can get a mortgage, so if you own a home, you have homeowner's insurance.

Review your policy at least yearly. Most agents will be happy to sit down and go over the policy with you. Be sure to update the policy as needed, such as if you extensively renovate or add onto your home. You'll want to be sure that your policy provides enough coverage so you'd be able to rebuild it at current prices if it was extensively damaged or destroyed. Some banks require that the limit of your insurance policy is based on your mortgage, which may not be enough to replace the home, if needed.

You'll also want to assess whether your policy provides enough protection for your possessions. If they're insured for actual cash value, your policy will pay less money for older items than you paid for them new. If you get them insured for replacement cost, your policy will pay to replace the items, regardless of when you purchased them originally. You'll usually need to pay about 10 percent more for replacement cost, but if you've got a lot of expensive items you'd need to replace, it may be worth the extra money.

Also consider purchasing coverage for additional living expenses, which would pay the costs of temporarily living somewhere else while your home is being repaired or rebuilt.

Homeowner's insurance includes liability protection, which covers bodily injury or property damage that you, family members, or pets cause to other people. If someone falls down the steps while coming out of your house, you won't be responsible for the cost of their injuries. Most homeowner's policies provide a minimum of $100,000 in liability insurance, but it's advisable to consider upgrading the policy to give you at least $300,000 to $500,000 in coverage.

Also, you could consider an umbrella policy or excess liability policy, which are policies that provide coverage that's greater than your standard limits. These policies kick in after you've exhausted the liability coverage in your policy, giving you added protection. They also may provide broader coverage than standard policies.

If you're renting an apartment, you need renter's insurance if you have a lot of stuff you want to protect. Damage to the building is not your responsibility, but if your TV or laptop is stolen or damaged, you need insurance if you want to replace it without paying out of pocket. If you have a bunch of good computer equipment or musical instruments or a rare-coin collection, you definitely should look into renter's insurance.

As with homeowner's insurance, the best bet for renters is to get a policy that provides replacement value. It will cost a little more, but it will pay you what it would cost to replace your TV or computer at the current purchase price, not the price you paid five years ago.

Auto Insurance

You must have car insurance because the liability risk if you're in an accident is too great to ignore. Auto insurance is expensive, but it's required by law in nearly every state, with the exception of New Hampshire and Virginia. Even if you live in one of those states, however, you can't afford to be without it.

Different types of coverage are associated with car insurance, but the one required by almost all states is liability. Liability coverage is twofold: bodily injury and property damage.

Bodily injury liability coverage protects you against lawsuits in the event someone is injured in an accident that you've caused. Although it varies from state to state, most states impose a minimum amount of bodily injury coverage, between $25,000 and $50,000 per person and up to $100,000 per accident. If you lend your car to someone else to drive, remember that the insurance follows the car. That means your coverage is the primary insurance in the event of an accident, counting as an accident on your record and increasing your future policy premiums.

Although it sounds like $100,000 is a lot for bodily injury coverage, experts say that to protect your assets in case you're sued, you should have up to $300,000 in coverage. If you buy only the minimum amount, it might not cover all your liability in the event of a lawsuit.

Property damage liability covers damage to other cars and property that's caused by your car. It would not only cover the cost of fixing a car you hit, but also pay to repair or replace the fence you ran over. Most states require a minimum of $10,000 in property coverage, although many require significantly more.

If you have a loan on your car, you should have collision coverage and comprehensive coverage, even if it's not required in your state. Collision coverage pays for damage to your car if you're in an accident, or pays to replace a car that's totaled. Comprehensive coverage protects you from car theft or weird things that could happen to your car, such as a tree falling on it or it being damaged during a riot, fire, or flood.

If you get hit by someone who doesn't have any insurance or has inadequate insurance (not as unusual as you might think), you'll need uninsured or underinsured motorist coverage. This insurance covers your medical expenses and lost wages if you're injured by an uninsured or underinsured motorist.

An optional auto insurance coverage is gap insurance, which protects you from depreciation. As soon as you buy your car, its value begins to decrease. So if you're leasing or financing the car, the depreciation leaves a gap between the value of the car and what you owe on it.

Let's say you finance $30,000 for a new car. Two years after you get it, the car is totaled. You still owe $25,000 on the vehicle, which, due to depreciation, is now worth only $20,000. Your insurer will pay you $20,000—the value of the vehicle, but $5,000 less than what you still owe on the car. If you have gap insurance, it will cover (minus the deductible) the difference between the payment you get and the money you still owe on the car.

The cost of vehicles has increased dramatically in the past couple years, meaning that many people are having to borrow more money to pay for them and then are making minimum monthly payments. That increases the chances of you finding yourself underwater if your car is totaled or stolen.

Because the average car depreciates 20 percent in value during the first year you have it, gap insurance can be a good idea. Luxury vehicles, which tend to be packed with a lot of features that may not be as highly valued by the next buyer, tend to depreciate faster than more basic models. Vehicles with the fastest depreciation, according to U.S. News & World Report, include the Ford Expedition, the BMW 7 Series, the Volvo S90, the Audi A6, and the Lincoln Navigator.

The Insurance Information Institute recommends gap insurance if any of the following apply:

- The car is financed for 60 months or longer.
- Your down payment on the car was 20 percent or less.
- The vehicle you bought depreciates quickly.
- You leased the vehicle. (Some lease agreements may require that you purchase gap insurance.)

If you meet any of these criteria or feel you'd have a hard time paying off your vehicle if it was totaled or stolen, you might want to consider gap insurance. When purchased through a major insurer, gap insurance should cost less than about $60 a year. Shop around to see what's available.

When you rent a car, your policy provides coverage unless it states otherwise. Read your policy, and check with your insurance company before you go on a trip if you aren't sure you'll be covered. Also, your US policy probably only covers you in the United States and Canada, so if you'll be renting a car in a different country, you'll need a separate policy from the rental company. Also, if your car insurance deductibles are high, you should purchase coverage from the rental company.

There's a big difference in auto insurance rates, and a poor driving record will dramatically increase your insurance rates, so shop around.

Look for cars with good safety records (the Insurance Institute for Highway Safety's Highway Loss Data Institute provides a list of these at iihs.org/ratings /top-safety-picks), and stay away from hot sports cars if you're interested in keeping your rates down. If you're shopping for a new or used car, learn how rates vary from model to model before making your purchase.

If you're over 25, you'll generally get a better rate than someone who is younger. Also, being married, living in what is considered a safe neighborhood, and having a relatively short work commute (driving less than 7,500 miles per year or not using your car for work) also will lower your insurance rates.

Chapter Summary

Insurance is all about protecting what's important to you, so don't be tempted to skimp or skip buying the policies you need. Protecting yourself and your family is not only a sound financial decision, but also one that provides peace of mind and security in the event of misfortune.

Looking Ahead

If some days seem like a blur to you and those days stretch into weeks or months, you're by no means alone. Science has definitively determined that perception of time significantly changes as we age, causing it to seem to pass by more and more quickly. Because life happens fast, it's smart to begin planning for your future early.

In Part 3, you learn about retirement accounts and how maximizing them when you're young gives you a great head start on a secure and comfortable retirement. We look at investing outside of retirement accounts, covering stocks, bonds, and funds and taking a look at cryptocurrency and real estate investments. We also touch on some investment strategies, taxes, and estate planning, and, because it's never too early to start, discuss how you can start thinking now about what your retirement will look like in 30 or 40 years. Retirement might seem very far off, but the years pass quickly.

Chapter 11

Saving for Retirement

We touched on the subject of 401(k) plans in Chapter 4, but there's a lot more to know about retirement accounts and how important they are to your future.

Depending on the age at which you fall within the millennial generation, retirement might seem like a concept for consideration in the distant future or it might feel like a life event that's coming up a little faster than you expected. Regardless of whether you're 20, 30, or 40 years out, retirement is a topic that should be at the forefront of your financial planning.

You'll read a lot more about retirement, including how to figure out how much money you'll need to retire, in the last chapter of the book. For now, we want to familiarize you with some systems that enable you to start saving—or continue to save—for your retirement early. As you read in Chapter 4, the earlier you start saving, the more time your money has to work for you through the beauty of compound interest.

In this chapter, we look at two popular retirement savings vehicles, 401(k)s and individual retirement accounts (IRAs), both of which offer tax advantages when left in place until you reach the age when you're eligible to withdraw funds.

401(k) Plans

Although they've only been around since the 1980s, 401(k) plans have become one of the most widely used and popular vehicles for retirement savings. These company-sponsored investment plans offer tax advantages because your savings aren't taxed until you withdraw them.

As of 2023, you can contribute up to $22,500 a year into a 401(k) account, and your employer can match some or all of your savings. If you're 50 or older, you can add an additional $7,500, bringing your contribution up to $29,000.

If you work for a school, hospital, or nonprofit organization, you're likely to have a 403(b) plan, which is similar to a 401(k), with some variations.

Both 401(k) and 403(b) plans are named after sections of the tax code. For practical purposes, they're very much alike in the way they work as retirement vehicles. They have the same basic contribution limits, both offer Roth options, and participants in each type of account need to be at least 59½ before they're able to take distributions without penalty. The accounts are taxed in the same manner (more about that a little later), and in both cases, the employer can make matching contributions, although they're not required to.

The major difference between 401(k)s and 403(b)s is the status of the employer offering the plan. If you happen to be employed by both a for-profit and a nonprofit organization, you're allowed to contribute to both types of retirement plan, but you're still limited to the $22,500 contribution limit between the two accounts.

Participation in 401(k)s

It's difficult to imagine why someone who has a retirement plan available to them would not participate in it, but it happens. According to the US Department of Labor, 68 percent of private workers had access to an employee-sponsored 401(k) plan in 2021, but only 51 percent of the workforce contributed to them, even if the plans had a company match. Of state and local government workers, 92 percent of workers had access to retirement benefits, but only 82 percent participated.

Maybe these employees don't realize the plans are available or understand how to enroll in them. Or maybe they feel they don't earn enough to be able to have the money taken out of their paychecks. We don't know.

What we do know is that the US Census Bureau reported in 2022 that 49 percent of Americans between the ages of 55 and 66 had no personal retirement savings. For those in that age group who did have savings, the median balance was just $89,716—far below what's considered necessary for a comfortable retirement.

To combat this problem, Congress passed the SECURE Act in 2019. SECURE stands for Setting Every Community Up for Retirement Enhancement, and it's intended to reform the retirement system. It has made it easier for small businesses to set up 401(k) plans for employees and provided tax credits to employers who offered 401(k) auto enrollment.

The SECURE Act was stepped up in late 2022, when Congress passed SECURE Act 2.0, which *requires* many employers to automatically enroll employees in 401(k) plans. Effective in 2025, all employees who are eligible to participate in their employer's 401(k) plan will be automatically enrolled instead of having to sign up for the plan. Automatic contribution amounts will be set by the employer and must range from between 3 and 10 percent of an employee's salary. Contribution amounts must increase by 1 percent each year until they are at least between 10 and 15 percent. This law, however, applies only to employers offering new 401(k) or 403(b) plans. Businesses with existing plans are grandfathered, meaning that not all employees will fall under the auto enrollment provision.

Automatic enrollment is a good thing because businesses that offer only voluntary enrollment plans have a much lower rate of participation than those with auto-enrollment plans. Companies that auto enroll new hires get about a 90 percent participation rate, compared to only about 28 percent participation at companies that have only voluntary enrollment. And companies that auto enroll found their employees contribute more.

People who don't want to participate in a 401(k) plan can opt out of auto enrollment, but most do not. Small businesses with 10 or fewer employees will not need to participate in auto enrollment, along with businesses that are newer than three years old. Churches and government plans are exempt.

Taking Advantage of an Employer Match

If you remember from Chapter 4, 401(k)s sometimes offer an additional savings incentive by way of an employer match. The amount of the match varies greatly from company to company, with some employers offering only plans that employees can contribute to with no matching contributions.

If you're really lucky, your employer will match your contribution dollar for dollar up to a certain percentage of your paycheck. The most typical match is for every dollar an employee contributes up to 6 percent, the employer throws in 50 percent. By taking advantage of the match, you get an automatic 50 percent return on your money. Not taking advantage of an employer match is like leaving money sitting on the table—not a good idea!

Some companies trying to attract new hires in competitive marketplaces may offer matches or partial matches to contributions up to 10 percent or even higher. Not taking advantage of those opportunities while they're available can have a real negative effect on your retirement.

Some firms, but fewer than ever, match an employee's contributions with company stock. Company stock can be a good thing, but it isn't *always* a good thing.

If you're with a company that's matching your 401(k) contributions with company stock, be sure to keep a close eye on the value of your account and how the stock is performing.

Investing in Your 401(k)

The money you contribute to your 401(k) is invested. You get to decide where by choosing from a list of investment options provided through your employer plan. If your employer has the 401(k) account in various mutual funds or a family of funds (which provide a variety of fund choices within the same company), you could divide your money between stocks and bonds with perhaps some fixed-interest-rate investments or money market funds thrown in for good measure.

Understandably, selecting investments can be a daunting proposition for someone who knows next to nothing about investments. But experts say the process of choosing these options has served as a crash course for a lot of young people who otherwise would know nothing about investing money. They say selecting investments is not that complicated if you keep it simple.

Employers are prohibited by the Department of Labor from offering investment advice regarding their employees' 401(k)s and can be held liable if they do. Financial advisers, however, have come up with some guidelines to direct employees in investing their 401(k) plans. Your employers' 401(k) should have a financial adviser you can talk with about your allocation.

Most advisers suggest investors in their 20s and 30s put at least 60 percent of their money in a large US company stock fund such as the T. Rowe Price Capital Appreciation Fund. The rest, they say, could be divided among international stocks, small company stocks, and bonds. Your company should provide meetings about the various investment choices and how they pertain to you. If it doesn't, ask to have the service provided because it's required by law. You must understand your choices; your future depends on it.

Keep in mind that your 401(k) money is a long-term investment, and you shouldn't plan to use it until your retirement. This makes it conducive to equities—what most people consider the stock market—where you have to accept that your money is in for the long haul and be willing to ride out the market's ups and downs.

When to Adjust Your Contributions

It's likely that when you first start contributing to a 401(k), it will be at a minimal level. And that's okay because some contribution is better than none. Just remember that you always should contribute enough to get a company match, as discussed earlier.

It is imperative, however, to increase your contribution level as you get raises. Remember, you can contribute up to $22,500 a year, so as your salary goes up, be sure your 401(k) contribution goes up, too. It's easy to save what you never see, and the salary increases are new money to you, so put some or all of it away for your retirement instead of making bigger contributions to Uncle Sam. If you keep increasing your contribution level by 1 or 2 percent a year, over time, you'll have a lot more money put aside for your retirement than you ever imagined possible, without much pain at all.

Another easy way to build up your 401(k) is to contribute all or part of a bonus into it. Your account gets a nice contribution, even when your paycheck doesn't change. This is a great way to supplement your annual contribution level.

The idea of contributing 5, 10, or 15 percent of your salary is daunting, and depending on your circumstances, you may not be able to make increases every year. But gradually increasing your contribution levels makes your account balance grow one step at a time.

401(k) Tax Advantages

Historically, a great advantage of traditional 401(k) plans is that the money you put into them is both pretax money and tax-deferred money. That means you win twice.

Your 401(k) contributions are taken out of your salary before your salary is taxed for federal income taxes. The contributions are still subject to Social Security taxes, and some states subject the contributions to state and local income taxes. Still, not having to pay federal income tax on the money you contribute is a great benefit.

The money you contribute is tax-deferred, which means you don't pay any tax on it, or the money it earns for you, until you withdraw it, either prematurely or during retirement. An individual in the 25 percent tax bracket pays 25¢ less tax on every $1 invested in a 401(k). Here's another way of looking at it: if you're in the 25 percent tax bracket and invest $100 per month in your 401(k), your federal tax liability is $300 less per year than if you didn't invest in the 401(k).

Employers now are able to offer Roth 401(k)s. The money you invest in a Roth 401(k) is posttax, with only the employer contributions and the earnings tax-deferred. This can be a good investment for people in their 20s and 30s who generally fall into lower tax brackets. By investing in a Roth 401(k), your contributions go in posttax, but when it's held for at least 5 years and not touched until you reach age 59½, the earnings can be withdrawn tax free.

If you believe you could end up being in a higher tax bracket after retirement, paying taxes on the contribution now and withdrawing in a higher bracket later leads to a net savings on the amount in the Roth 401(k).

Managing Your 401(k) When Changing Jobs

It's likely you'll have numerous employers during your years of working, and every time you change employers, you'll need to address your 401(k) plan. Basically, you have four options for what to do with your 401(k) when changing jobs:

- Roll over the account to your new company's plan

- Leave the account where it is

- Cash out the account

- Roll over the account to an IRA

If you transfer your 401(k) account to the plan your new company offers, your savings are held in the same place, there are no tax implications or early withdrawal penalties, and your money continues to grow for your future. Just be sure your new employer's plan allows for a rollover; some do not.

You also can leave your 401(k) plan in place with your old employer, if that's permitted, and if it's cash neutral, which means there would not be a transaction that would require net cash. Some plans allow you to maintain the account without changes indefinitely, while others require that you transfer your assets within a particular time period. There probably will be a cost to you when you transfer. If your 401(k) savings are less than a certain amount—often $5,000— you might be forced out.

Cashing out your 401(k) account generally is not a good idea because the whole point of it is to preserve funds for your retirement. If you're under the age of 59½, you'll probably get slammed with a 10 percent early withdrawal penalty, plus you'll have to pay taxes on the distribution. Unless there's a compelling reason to liquidate the account, it's always better to keep the money in a retirement account.

Another option is to roll over your money into a traditional individual retirement account (IRA). (You'll read about IRAs later in this chapter.) When your money is safely within an IRA, you can choose different investment options with the account or convert the account to a Roth IRA after paying any income tax that's due.

Be sure to consider all these options carefully and think about which makes the most sense for you. The whole point is to enable your money to grow so it's available when you need it.

Understanding Vesting

Vesting is the length of time you're required to work for a company before you're entitled to the funds your employer has put into your retirement account on your behalf. There are two types of vesting: cliff and graduated.

Cliff vesting, which is usually five years, means you must work for your employer for five years before you're entitled to the matching funds placed in your 401(k). If you change jobs after only two years and your company has five-year cliff vesting, you'll only have your own contributions available to move elsewhere. If you leave this employer after five years, you receive the employer's match as well as your own contributions.

This is something to think about if you're planning on changing jobs. If there's just a short time period left before you are vested in the plan and you stand to lose a significant amount of employer contributions if you leave, you might want to reconsider and stay until you meet the cliff vesting timeframe.

With graduated vesting, you're partially vested after a certain period of time with the company but must remain longer to become fully vested. Graduated vesting is often used as a tactic by employers to retain employees. If your employer has a six-year vesting schedule, for example, you'll be partially vested after two years, but you need to stay with your employer for six years before you're 100 percent vested, as illustrated in the following table.

Years Employed	Percent Vested
After 2 years	20
After 3 years	40
After 4 years	60
After 5 years	80
After 6 years	100

When you change jobs, whether you're vested or not, you still have your own contributions to your 401(k). You can withdraw these funds (but don't forget income tax liability and penalty), roll them over into an IRA, or even possibly roll them over into your new employer's 401(k) plan.

If your new employer has a 401(k) plan, see if you can transfer directly from your former employer's 401(k) plan to your current employer's. If you can't, roll the funds into a separate IRA and then roll them into your new 401(k) later, if permitted. Rolling the funds into an IRA enables you to avoid having to pay taxes at the time you do so, and your retirement savings will continue to grow at a tax-deferred rate. Also, you'll avoid the penalties associated with cashing out your 401(k).

Getting Money from Your 401(k) Early

Unfortunately, sometimes it's absolutely necessary to get money from your 401(k) account before you are of the eligible age of 59½. In certain situations, you may withdraw from your 401(k) for hardship, but you must demonstrate real need to your employer to be able to do so. In some cases, your employer will let you borrow against your 401(k) plan and deduct the repayment from your paycheck. The money you repay goes right back into your account, and you pay yourself, not a bank, with the principal and interest. This is considered a loan—not an early withdrawal—so you're not subject to the taxes and penalties you'd normally have to pay.

You can borrow up to $50,000 or half of the assets in your 401(k) account, whichever amount is less. If your vested savings are less than $10,000, you still can borrow up to $10,000. Generally, a 401(k) loan must be repaid within five years, but if you borrowed the money to buy a house, that time will be extended. You can pay back the loan sooner than five years without penalty.

The big downside to taking out a 401(k) loan is that you cannot contribute additional funds to the account while you're paying off the loan. All your payments are considered payments toward to the loan. Because you're not increasing your retirement savings, your potential for growth is negatively affected.

If you make a withdrawal from your 401(k) before the eligible age, which is different from taking a 401(k) loan, expect some stiff financial consequences. You'll pay a 10 percent penalty, and the money is taxable, which can be a significant blow at tax time. The IRS directs that people who withdraw funds from their 401(k) plans have 20 percent withheld from the money to be used for tax payment. The problem is, that amount usually isn't enough money to pay for both the penalty and the taxes owed on the withdrawal.

For example, if you withdrew $5,000 from your 401(k) plan and had the standard 20 percent withheld ($1,000), you would receive $4,000. But if you were a taxpayer in the 24 percent bracket, you'd owe $1,200 in taxes, plus $500 for the penalty, for a total of $1,700. The 20 percent taken out wouldn't cover those costs, and you'd be $700 short on April 15. Not a nice surprise!

Still, the 401(k) is your money, and you can get it if you have a real need—and if you're willing to pay the penalties.

Individual Retirement Accounts

An IRA is a type of retirement savings plan that anyone who earns money working can contribute to. An IRA is tax-deferred, meaning you don't pay taxes until you withdraw money from the fund. IRAs are popular because they allow you to invest in a wide range of assets with varying degrees of risk.

Investing in an IRA

Investing in an IRA is a bit different from investing in a 401(k) account. Contributions to an IRA are made by the individual account owner, or by an employer in the case of a SEP-IRA, which you'll read more about a bit later. An IRA can be self-directed or non-self-directed, with non-self-directed by far the more common choice.

A non-self-directed IRA, often just called a traditional IRA, includes only stocks, bonds, mutual funds, exchange-traded funds, and other common types of investments. A self-directed IRA gives investors many more choices, including options like precious metals and real estate. Because of the types of investments they hold, self-directed IRAs carry more risk than non-self-directed accounts. Most traditional banks and brokerages don't offer self-directed IRAs to customers. If you want one, you need to research what investments are available within different funds and choose the fund and investments you want.

If you prefer a non-self-directed IRA, you can use an online broker or robo-adviser for investment management, either choosing the investments yourself, as you would with a 401(k) account or relying on a robo-adviser to consider your preferences and choose investments for you. In either case, a brokerage firm manages the account.

Fees vary depending on whether you choose an online broker like Schwab, Fidelity, or Merrill Edge, or a robo-adviser, which tends to have lower fees. Unless you're very investment-savvy or interested in studying investment strategies and keeping up with market conditions and changes, a non-self-directed IRA is probably a better choice than a self-directed one.

Both traditional and Roth IRAs can be either self-directed or non-self-directed.

Traditional IRAs

As you read, anyone who earns money can open and contribute to an IRA, even if, within certain income restrictions, you also contribute to an employer-sponsored retirement account like a 401(k). In 2023, the maximum contribution limit was $6,500.

Someone who makes less than the maximum allowable contribution amount can contribute up to the amount they've earned, but not more. If you have no income from a job but receive taxable alimony money, those funds can count as qualifying income for an IRA. And if you're not being paid to work, such as if you've elected to stay home and care for children, your working spouse can contribute up to the maximum allowable amount to an IRA in your name.

Let's look at how it breaks down. If you're single and do not have an employer-sponsored retirement plan, you can put up to $6,500 a year in an IRA. The full contribution is a dollar-for-dollar deduction from your taxable income on your income tax return.

If you're single and do have an employer-sponsored plan, but your annual adjusted gross income is $68,000 or less (as of 2023), you can contribute up to $6,500 to your IRA and deduct the full amount. If your income is between $68,001 and $78,000, your deduction will be prorated, depending on how much you earn. If you make more than $78,000 a year, you can contribute to the IRA, but you get no deduction.

If you're married and file a joint federal income tax return, have an employer-sponsored plan, and your annual adjusted gross income is $109,000 or less, you can deduct the full amount. If you earn between $109,001 and $129,000, the deduction will be prorated. If you earn more than $129,000, you can contribute but won't get a deduction.

For workers over age 50, there's a "catch-up" provision for those contributing to an IRA. As of 2023, workers who are over age 50 can contribute an extra $1,000 to an IRA for a total of $7,500 a year.

If your spouse doesn't have a retirement plan at work and you file a joint tax return, your spouse can deduct their full $6,500 contribution until your joint income reaches $184,000. After that, the deduction is prorated until your joint income is $218,000, at which time you can't deduct the IRA contribution.

Even if you can't deduct the contributions, they still help out with taxes because the income earned within the IRA is tax-deferred, which means you'll pay no tax on it until you withdraw the money. It's not as great as tax-deductible, which reduces the amount of your current taxable income, but it's the next best thing.

You'll need to take required minimum withdrawals from a traditional IRA when you reach age 72 or 73, with the withdrawals taxed as ordinary income. If you make withdrawals before you turn 59, you'll have to pay income tax and, in most cases, penalties.

Congress passed legislation in 2022 that raised the age you have to start taking required minimum withdrawals from 72 to 73, starting in 2023. If you turned 72 in 2022, you had to take your first withdrawal that year. If you didn't turn 72 until 2023, however, you didn't have to take your first withdrawal until you turned 73 in 2023.

IRAs are good savings vehicles, but if your IRA contributions aren't deductible, be sure you take advantage of the programs on which you can get a tax deduction, such as 401(k)s, first.

Roth IRAs

The Roth IRA, a variation on the basic IRA, has been popular since it was introduced in 1998. The maximum contribution limits are the same for Roth IRAs as for traditional IRAs—$6,500 or $7,500 for those age 50 or older—but the Roth IRA is different from the traditional IRA in several ways. Many financial experts agree it is better than the traditional IRA for people with the right circumstances, especially for those in their 20s and 30s.

With a Roth IRA, you contribute after-tax dollars. That doesn't reduce the amount of your taxable income, but your contributions and earnings on the contributions can grow tax free. And as long as the account has been open for at least five years, at age 59½, you can withdraw the funds tax free and penalty free.

Because you've already paid tax on your Roth IRA contributions, as opposed to the pretax money you invest in a traditional IRA, you don't have to pay tax on the income and appreciation on a Roth. If you have at least 20 years in which to let the funds grow, a Roth IRA probably is preferable to a traditional IRA.

As long as you hold the funds within the Roth for five years, you never have to pay tax on the account again. You'll get all those earning completely tax free, which is a very appealing feature of the Roth. Contributions to a Roth IRA, however, are not tax-deductible.

You can withdraw your Roth money without penalty any time after you reach 59½, but you're not required to take it out when you reach 72 or 73, as you are with traditional IRAs. You can let your money sit there if you want to, continuing to grow, tax free. You even can leave the money and all the earnings there to pass on, tax free, to your heirs.

There are income limits to Roths, though. If your income is more than $153,000 (as of 2023) and you file your taxes as single, you can't get a Roth IRA. If you and your spouse have a combined income of more than $219,000, you're not eligible for a Roth IRA. If you've already contributed to a Roth IRA and your earnings increase so you're not eligible to make additional contributions, the money you have in the account will remain invested and continue to earn interest. If your earnings vary, you might be eligible to contribute to a Roth in certain years but not in others.

SEP-IRAs

If you are self-employed, you can consider a SEP-IRA, or a Simplified Employee Pension IRA. SEP-IRAs are not very complicated and are a great deal for a person who is self-employed or owns a business with only a few employees. Basically, a SEP-IRA is a retirement plan for self-employed persons or small company employers in which, as of 2023, contributions of up to $66,000 a year or 25 percent of income, whichever is higher, are permitted.

SEP-IRAs allow people who are self-employed or who are owners of small companies to add more funds to a retirement account than they can with a traditional IRA. The interest you make in a SEP-IRA is not taxed until you take out the money.

The money you contribute to a SEP-IRA is deducted from your taxable income, so your contribution can save you a lot on federal and maybe also state taxes, depending on where you live. You can open and contribute to a SEP-IRA up until the day of your tax-filing deadline.

SEP-IRAs are advantageous for people who need to save on their own. They might sound intimidating, but you can have a SEP-IRA anywhere you could have a traditional IRA. It just requires a little additional paperwork. Ask your tax preparer or financial consultant about changing your IRA to a SEP-IRA.

The disadvantage of a SEP-IRA for a small business owner is that you are required to contribute the same percentage of income you contribute for yourself for each of your employees, which can be a daunting proposition.

Timing Your IRA Contributions

You can make an annual contribution to your IRA anytime between January 1 and the filing deadline (normally April 15) of the following year. So you can make a 2024 IRA contribution between January 1, 2024, and April 15, 2025. You should know, however, that the earlier you stash some money in your IRA, the better.

If you fund an IRA in January or February, the funds begin to work, tax-deferred, with gains starting immediately and accumulating for the entire year. You get 15 months of deferral by funding your IRA in January rather than waiting until it's time to file your tax return in April of the following year.

If it's not financially feasible to fund your IRA all at once, you might consider contributing some money each month, beginning in January.

Final Thoughts on Saving and Investing When You're Young

You might be tired of reading this, but we can't overstate the value of starting to save—whether it's in a savings account, a retirement account, or another type of investment account, which you'll read more about in the next chapter—as soon as you're able to do so.

If two people save $100 a month toward retirement, or any other purpose for that matter, but one starts at age 25 and the other at age 35, the person who started early will have nearly twice as much saved by the time they're 65.

Chapter Summary

Time is the greatest tool you have for building wealth, ensuring you have choices, and setting yourself up to be comfortable when you are no longer earning a salary. The sooner you begin saving, the better. Be sure you're contributing as much to a 401(k) or IRA as you're able, and pay attention to your 401(k) account if you change jobs, preferably leaving it where it is or rolling it into an IRA to continue realizing tax advantages and keeping your money invested. And unless it's absolutely unavoidable, resist the temptation to take money from a retirement account before the eligible age because you're likely to face tax consequences and fees.

Chapter 12

Investing

If you're paying your bills every month on time, have three to six months' worth of wages in an emergency fund, are contributing part of your income to a retirement account, and have enough left over to enjoy life, count yourself fortunate.

Most people, regardless of how much money they have, are feeling squeezed these days due to inflation, rising interest rates, and the threat of a recession. And more than half of all Americans—58 percent, in fact—were living paycheck to paycheck at the beginning of 2023, according to a CNBC Your Money Financial Confidence Survey.

It can seem counterintuitive, but if you can parlay your current feelings of anxiety about your money into taking action to benefit your future self, you'll be ahead of the game. Again, it's because your money will have more time to work for you and grow, even if you can just put aside small amounts now.

In this chapter, we look at some common investment vehicles outside of retirement accounts, such as stocks, bonds, mutual funds, index funds, and exchange-traded funds. We also consider cryptocurrency, a type of investment that's been hotly debated as the asset has swung wildly from one direction to another. Real estate is another type of investment, and you don't have to buy land or buildings to get in on the game, so we spend a bit of time on that.

First, though, let's spend a little time to understand risk—both the risks of investing and the risks of not investing.

Investing Risks

Often, when Sarah talks to someone about investing in stocks, mutual funds, or another investment vehicle, they tell her they think it's too risky and they don't want to take the chance of losing their money. That's a common attitude, and it's okay. It's good, in fact, to consider the possibility of risk in terms of investing your money.

The Risks of Investing

Let's start by confirming that, yes, there are risks associated with investing. If you invest in something like Treasury bonds, which are considered a safe investment, the risks are minimal. If you invest in something like stocks or options or commodities—or worse yet, in cryptocurrency—your risk can be substantial.

Here's the catch, though: the more risk you're willing to take, the more potential you have for higher returns, as well as for greater losses. One of the keys to investing is knowing how to manage risk. Proper risk management, which is simply the process of identifying risks, analyzing those risks, and making your investment decisions based on either accepting or rejecting them, is key to successful investment.

The amount of risk you're willing to accept is known as risk tolerance, and there are three levels: aggressive, moderate, and conservative. Someone who is an aggressive investor has a high risk tolerance and is willing to risk losing money in exchange for potentially better results. A conservative investor has a low risk tolerance and looks for investments that aren't likely to jeopardize the capital.

A moderate investor, of course, falls somewhere between those two camps with a medium risk tolerance.

Risk tolerance is different from risk capacity, which is how much risk you're able to manage without it keeping you up at night. Someone earning a high salary who has no dependents and little debt has the capacity to take greater financial risks than someone who has a mortgage and three teenagers looking forward to going to college.

Risk tolerance is more of an attitude and is less likely to change than risk capacity. If you've got a high risk tolerance for investing, you're likely to have a high risk tolerance for other endeavors as well.

The Risks of Not Investing

Everyone wants to see great returns on their investments, but you always should evaluate risks before deciding where to invest your money. You learn more about strategies to help you minimize risk and make smart investment choices, and also about finding a financial adviser to help you, in the next chapter. For now, let's flip the conversation around and look at the risks of not investing.

If you keep all your money in a traditional savings account that pays less than 1 percent interest, your money will be safe, but it won't be working very hard for you. You will have forfeited the opportunity to grow your money in a meaningful way with capital gains, dividends, and other earnings that occur when you invest your money in stocks or other vehicles.

We recently saw an interesting chart from the investment firm Charles Schwab. It pointed out that research shows that even investors who bought into the stock market at the "wrong time," meaning when the price of stocks was at the highest rates of the year, generally fared twice as well with returns as those who left their money in cash investments. Investors who bought stocks when prices were at their lowest point of the year showed the best returns, of course, and those who invested regularly at the beginning of each year, regardless of stock costs, came in second.

Let's look at the hypothetical outcomes for four investors, each of whom invested $2,000 a year over 20 years, with a total investment of $40,000:

- Invested when stock prices were at their lowest: earned $175,126
- Invested at the beginning of each year: earned $162,410
- Invested when stock prices were at their highest: earned $141,371
- Invested money only in cash investments: earned $64,386

Another risk to your money when it's sitting in that savings account is inflation. You couldn't have been alive in the early 2020s and not have heard about inflation, which skyrocketed to 8.9 percent in 2022, the highest level since 1981. It doesn't take an economist to understand that money earning less than 1 percent interest decreases in value when inflation keeps eating away at it.

The average annual rate of inflation since 1913 has been a little over 3 percent. Even that moderate amount of inflation can cause your money to decline in value and purchasing power.

Let's move on to some different types of investments, starting with stocks.

Stocks

You hear a lot of talk about stocks and the stock market. Basically, stocks are a security that represent ownership in the company that issues them. When you buy stock in Amazon or Tesla, you're buying a tiny piece of those companies. If the company prospers, you as a stockholder share in its profits and benefit from any rise in the market value of the stock. If the company runs into problems, the value of your investment could decline.

A company that has given ownership to the public through shares of stock is called a public company, and it makes information available to investors. A privately held company is one owned by either those who founded it, managers, or a private group of investors.

Because their prices tend to fluctuate suddenly and sometimes sharply, stocks are considered more risky than bonds or cash investments. Over time, however, stocks have offered the highest returns of the three asset classes—as well as the best hedge against inflation.

If you're going to start investing in the stock market, we recommend that you do some research beyond the scope of this book. There's a lot to know about choosing stocks, knowing the best times to buy and sell stock, investment strategies, investment psychology, and other topics. We get into some of that information in the next chapter, but there's a lot we can't cover in this book.

For now, let's look at what the stock market is, some different types of stocks, stock market indexes, and the concept of bull and bear markets.

Stock Market Basics

The *stock market* is a generic phrase that encompasses the trading of securities. The security can be a bond or a stock, and it's traded on an exchange. There are two major exchanges in the United States:

- New York Stock Exchange (NYSE)
- National Association of Securities Dealers Automatic Quotation System (Nasdaq)

There also are smaller exchanges based on the cities where they're located, such as the NYSE Chicago, formerly the Chicago Stock Exchange, and the Miami Stock Exchange (MS4X). The American Stock Exchange (AMEX) was the third-largest exchange after the NYSE and the Nasdaq, but it was acquired by the NYSE in 2008 and became NYSE American.

The NYSE was founded in 1790 and is considered the granddaddy of all American exchanges. To be able to be listed on the NYSE, a company must have at least 400 shareholders and 1.1 million shares, or the stock that is held by company shareholders, outstanding. Before the terrorist attacks in New York City on September 11, 2001, people could visit the NYSE's building on

Wall Street. Most of the trading once done on the floor there is now done electronically.

The Nasdaq is the largest electronic screen-based market. It was created in 1971 and is considered more modern than the NYSE. It has lower listing fees, which is what a company has to pay to be listed on a stock exchange, than the NYSE, and it boasts some of the largest companies, including the tech giants Meta, Apple, Amazon, and Google.

The NYSE and Nasdaq are open Monday through Friday from 9:30 a.m. to 4 p.m. Eastern Time. There's premarket trading from 6:30 a.m. to 9:30 a.m. and after-hours trading from 4 p.m. to 8 p.m., when most online brokers allow retail investors to place trades. The major markets close for nine trading holidays a year and several half days. Trading hours of smaller exchanges vary.

Different Types of Stocks

In case you're thinking that a stock is a stock is a stock, that's not quite the case. There are different types of stock, some of which you'll read about here. Generally, though, when someone refers to "stock" they're talking about common stock.

Common Stock

Common stock is the type of stock mentioned previously that represents ownership in a company. Investors get a share of the company's profits, usually paid to them in dividends, which are the funds a company pays regularly to shareholders. Common stock is sometimes called ordinary shares. Shareholders of common stock have a say in company policy such as voting on corporate policies and electing officers, based on how many shares of stock they own.

Many companies only issue common stock, as opposed to both common and preferred stock. As the name suggests, it's the most common type of stock.

Examples of companies that offer common stock include Alphabet Inc., American Express, Apple, Colgate-Palmolive, Discover Corporation, JPMorgan Chase, and Microsoft Corporation.

Preferred Stock

Preferred stock is a class of stock that gives shareholders different rights than those with common stock. You generally get higher dividends with preferred stock than with common stock, and the dividends are fixed at a certain rate. With common stock, the value of dividends can change or even be reduced to nothing. Holders of preferred stock get their dividends before holders of common stock. Also, if the company goes bankrupt, preferred shares have a greater claim on being repaid than shares of common stock.

The downside to preferred stock is that, because the dividends are set at a fixed rate, there is limited potential for capital gains; the value of preferred stock is primarily that it provides income through dividends. With common stock, the value can increase greatly as the company grows and becomes more profitable.

Consider this: Apple went public, meaning it first started selling its stock, on December 12, 1980. Investors at the time paid $22 per share for Apple stock. An investment of $1,000 in Apple stock in 1980 would have been worth $127,000 at the end of the first quarter of 2022. And with the value of the dividends added in, the value was $162,500. That's the beauty of getting in early with a company that's poised for great growth.

On the other hand, preferred stock carries less risk than common stock. In fact, preferred stock is often compared to bonds because it has a set redemption price that a company will at some point pay to redeem it. Someone who owns preferred stock will hold it for a specified amount of time and then turn it back to the company. Also, preferred stock does not carry voting rights, so shareholders have no say in how the company is run.

Examples of companies that offer preferred stock include Bank of America, Georgia Power, Goldman Sachs, JPMorgan Chase, MetLife, and Wells Fargo.

Growth Stock

Another type of stock is growth stock, which, as the name implies, is stock that's expected to grow at a rate that's faster than average. Growth stock tends to experience growth when the economy is growing and when interest rates are low. Tech stock is often considered growth stock.

Note that a company's stock can be classified as more than one type of stock. A growth stock, for instance, also could be considered a cyclical stock, as its value may be effected by the performance of the economy.

Examples of company stock that is considered growth stock include Alphabet Inc., Amazon, Apple, Block, Etsy, Meta Platforms, Netflix, Salesforce, Shopify, and Tesla.

Value Stock

On the other side of the equation are value stocks, which are stocks that trade at relatively low prices compared to the company's earnings and long-term potential for growth. They're typically issued by businesses that have been around for a while and trend toward health-care, financial, and energy companies. Value stocks tend to do well when the economy is weak or in recovery because consumers continue to need the products and services offered by the companies. Most value stock, but not all, pay dividends.

Examples of company stock that is considered value stock include AT&T, Berkshire Hathaway, Johnson & Johnson, Nike, Procter & Gamble, Target, and Walmart.

Income Stock

Income stock provides regular income through higher-than-average dividends. The companies that offer them are generally stable. Income stock typically does not appreciate in value as much as growth stock, but they're desirable for people looking for a regular source of income.

Examples of company stock that is considered income stock include Consolidated Edison, Federal Realty Investment Trust, McDonald's, NextEra Energy, Realty Income, Verizon, and Waste Management.

Blue-Chip Stock

Blue-chip stock comes from well-established companies that have high market value. They have successful track records of generating profits and are typically industry leaders. Conservative investors tend to like blue-chip stocks because they aren't usually overly volatile.

Examples of company stock that is considered blue-chip stock include 3M, American Express, Boeing, Chevron Corporation, Coca-Cola, Costco, IBM, and Johnson & Johnson.

Cyclical Stock

Cyclical stock is tied to the performance of the economy and tends to follow economic cycles of expansion, peak, recession, and recovery. When the economy is on an upswing, cyclical stocks tend to follow suit. When the economy tanks, cyclical stocks tend to go down as well. Companies that issue what is considered cyclical stock typically manufacture goods that sell well when the economy is good but not so well when consumers cut their spending during lean economic times.

Examples of company stock that is considered cyclical stock include American Airlines, Apple, Expedia, Halliburton Company, Lowe's, Nike, Nucor Corporation, and Walt Disney Company.

Noncyclical Stock

On the flip side of cyclical stocks are noncyclical stocks, which tend to remain fairly constant in value regardless of what's happening with the economy. Companies that issue noncyclical stock are those whose products and services consumers always will need. Noncyclical stock is considered recession proof.

Examples of company stock that is considered noncyclical stock include Altria Group, Colgate-Palmolive, General Mills, Kellogg Company, Kraft Heinz Company, PepsiCo, and Procter & Gamble.

Defensive Stock

Defensive stock tends to provide steady returns in most conditions. Like noncyclical stocks, defensive stocks are sold by companies that offer essential products and services, like health care and utilities.

Examples of company stock that is considered defensive stock include CVS Health, ExxonMobil, General Motors, Johnson & Johnson, Lockheed Martin, NextEra Energy, Procter & Gamble, and Walmart.

Penny Stock

Penny stock is valued at less than $5 per share and is considered speculative, in that trading them is based largely on guesswork instead of any solid information. Some penny stock is traded on major stock exchanges, but many are traded through smaller markets. Companies whose stock is considered penny stock are likely those you've never heard of, although there are some companies like True Religion Jeans and Monster Beverage Corporation whose stock started out as penny stock before the company took off.

Examples of penny stock include Ardelyx, Blue Sphere Corporation, JCPenney, Nordic American Tankers Limited, Snowline Gold Corp., and SpectraScience.

ESG Stock

A type of stock that's gaining recognition and popularity is ESG stock, which stands for environmental, social, and governance. These stocks are issued by companies that emphasize protecting the environment, working toward social justice, upholding ethical practices, and promoting other social causes. Millennials have embraced ESG stocks in recent years because the companies that issue them reflect their values.

Examples of ESG stock include Best Buy, Cadence, IDEXX Laboratories, Intuit, Lam Research, Microsoft Corporation, NVIDIA, Salesforce, Texas Instruments, The Home Depot, and West Pharmaceutical Services.

There are other kinds of stock in addition to these, but understanding how the stock of different types of companies tends to perform can help you balance your portfolio as you get into stock investing.

Key Stock Market Indexes

A market index is an indicator of performance for a designated group of investments. If you want to see how the stock market is doing, taking a look at the major indexes is how you can do that.

Here are the top three US stock market indexes:

- Standard & Poor's (S&P) 500 Index
- Dow Jones Industrial Average
- Nasdaq Composite index

Some indexes track the movements of companies in many market sectors. The S&P 500, for example, tracks the performance of 500 of the largest companies in the United States. Other indexes track the performance of companies within a certain sector. The Nasdaq Composite index, for example, tracks the performance of more than 3,000 technology-related companies. The Dow Jones Industrial Average follows 30 large US companies that issue blue-chip stocks.

Other market indexes you hear about often include the following:

- Bloomberg US Aggregate Bond Index, aka the USAgg, which tracks the US bond market
- Russell 2000 Index, which tracks 2,000 smaller companies (With market capitalization between $300 million and $2 billion, these companies are known as small-cap companies.)
- Wilshire 5000 Total Market Index, which is a broad-based index made up of about 3,450 publicly traded companies

There are many other stock indexes in the United States and throughout the world. Financial markets around the world have become increasingly connected due to globalization, and often what happens to the market in one country affects what happens to markets elsewhere.

Bull and Bear Markets

The stock market is always on the move—sometimes at a pace that's barely noticeable, and at other times in a much more dramatic fashion.

When the market is going up, it's usually a slow, gradual process. When it goes down, however, it's often sudden and startling. You might recall that during the early days of the COVID-19 pandemic in March 2020, the Dow Jones Industrial Average Index dropped at least 2,000 points—huge losses—on three separate days. Those kinds of drops get the attention of investors everywhere and can wreak havoc on future market performance.

Bear Markets

When the market is down, it's known as a bear market, referring to a bear's practice of hibernating. During a bear market, investors tend to start selling off their stock, putting their money into hibernation instead of leaving it in the market where it could be exposed to further losses.

A market generally must fall by 20 percent before it's considered a bear market.

A sudden drop in the market sometimes is attributed to a market correction, which is a drop that occurs as the result of inflated stock prices. A market correction does not necessarily mean that the market has entered a bear market period.

Bull Markets

A bull market, on the other hand, is an up market in which prices are rising and expected to continue to rise. The imagery here is supposed to invoke that of a bull charging forward with its horns upward, describing investors who run full tilt at the market to purchase stock and put their money to work for them.

Fortunately, bull markets historically last much longer than bear markets. Since 1928, the average length of a bear market has been 286 days, while the average length of a bull market has been 1,011 days. That's why it's almost always a mistake to panic and sell off your investments during a bear market. If you wait it out, the market will recover, and your investment will regain its value.

Bonds

Stocks represent a share of ownership in a company, but bonds are more like an IOU you get from a company or government entity you loan your money to. When you buy a bond—either a corporate bond issued by a company or a government bond issued by the US government or a government agency—you agree to loan your money with the understanding that you'll get back the amount you loaned when the bond reaches its maturity date, along with periodic interest payments, usually twice a year. You can think of owning a bond as securing a stream of future cash payments.

If a company issues a $10,000 bond that pays 6.5 percent interest and is due on June 15, 2026, and you invest in that bond, what you're actually doing is lending the company $10,000 until June 15, 2026. Meanwhile, the company promises to pay you 6.5 percent interest, or $650 a year, on your $10,000.

Interest rates on most bonds are set for certain periods of time and will not change within those periods. The interest rates on some bonds, such as US Savings Bonds, are periodically adjusted for inflation.

Bond Risks and Returns

Bonds typically carry less risk than stocks, but they're not 100 percent safe. Something to keep in mind about bonds: if the federal funds rate, or fed rate, which is the interest rate set by the Federal Reserve, drops while you're holding the bond, the value of the bond increases. That's because most bonds carry a fixed interest rate that doesn't change when the fed rate changes. If the interest rate paid on the bond is higher than the prevailing interest rate—the one set by the Federal Reserve—investors will buy bonds to take advantage of that interest rate, and the demand will drive up the price of the bonds. If the prevailing interest rate raises, however, the value of your bond drops because investors no longer prefer the lower fixed interest rate paid by a bond.

If you buy corporate bonds, there's a chance the company could default on them. However, Treasury bonds you buy from the US government are widely considered a safe investment. (More on Treasury bonds, bills, and notes in Chapter 4.)

Because bonds are considered a safer investment than stocks, you're not likely to realize returns as high. Investors who have low risk tolerance are often drawn to bonds, and there are good reasons to include them in your portfolio. At a young age, however, stocks and some other forms of investment should be a bigger part of your portfolio than bonds.

You'll normally get higher interest rates on a bond you're going to hold for a long time, rather than for just three or six months. Every now and then, however, as we are seeing as we write this in July 2023, the interest rates on shorter-term bonds are higher than those on bonds you'd hold for a longer term. This is known as an inverted yield curve, and it's often—but not always—viewed as an indicator that the economy may be headed toward recession.

Investor Confidence and Interest Rates

Think about it this way: the bond market competes with the stock market for investors' money. As you've read, the downside of buying bonds is that your potential for return is limited. The upside is the security you get with bonds.

Interest rates on US Treasuries can be indicators of overall confidence in the economy. If market conditions seem uncertain, investors shy away from the stock market and buy bonds instead. If the economy is looking good, investors anticipate that stock values will increase, and they buy stocks instead of bonds. With the stock market looking attractive to investors, demand for Treasury bills goes down and the government is forced to raise the interest rates on them to compete with the stock market.

Despite a lot of economic uncertainty in 2022 and 2023 caused by increasing interest rates, ongoing inflation, political uncertainty, war, and other factors, the stock market performed well in the first half of 2023, recouping the majority of losses felt in the first three quarters of 2022. Although interest rates on shorter- and longer-term bonds increased dramatically during that time, it's interesting that in the middle of July 2023, interest on a 3-month Treasury security was higher than the rate on a 10-year bond.

The following table shows interest rates as of July 25, 2023, which indicate an inverted yield curve, with short-term interest rates higher than longer-term rates.

Term Length	Interest Rate
3 months	5.405%
6 months	5.471%
9 months	5.377%
1 year	5.364%
2 year	4.990%
3 year	4.565%
5 year	4.209%
10 year	3.909%

This inverted yield curve is a signal that investors are uncertain about what lies ahead and may be anticipating putting their money into bonds instead of stocks. It's an indication that, although the economy might look okay over the short term—say the next three months—there's a lot of uncertainty about its performance over the longer term—say the next year.

Since World War II, every inverted yield curve has been followed by an economic slowdown or a recession within a year to 18 months. Everyone interested in the economy is keeping an eye on this current situation. You should, too.

Mutual, Index, and Exchange-Traded Funds

Mutual funds, index funds, and exchange-traded funds (ETFs) are similar types of investment vehicles, but they have some significant differences in the way they're managed and what they're intended to achieve.

Mutual Funds

A mutual fund is a professionally managed portfolio of stocks, bonds, and other types of investments. The fund pools the money of many investors to purchase the securities it contains. Most 401(k) accounts are invested in mutual funds; you also can invest in a mutual fund on your own.

A mutual fund can be compared to a pie. If the value of the mutual fund goes down, the pie, including your slice of it, gets smaller. If the value increases, the pie gets bigger.

Mutual funds can be advantageous because they offer diversification, which can reduce risk. Some mutual funds contain just a handful of securities, but others can have thousands of separate issues. That means if one type of security loses value, another type may gain in value and offset the loss. When you buy a mutual fund, you're buying a package of different types of securities, which can help you build a diversified portfolio quickly.

The goal of an actively managed mutual fund is to outperform market averages by having professionals choose investments they think will cause the value of fund to go up. Mutual fund managers are trained to ensure the fund's investment remains consistent with its investment objective.

You can sell mutual funds at the end of any day. There's no penalty for early withdrawal, although depending on the fund, you might have to pay fee to redeem your investment.

There are different kinds of mutual funds. Some invest only in stocks, while others focus on bonds. Balanced mutual funds invest in a variety of asset classes such as stocks, bonds, money market funds, and alternative investments such as hedge funds or venture capital. A money market mutual fund contains short-term, safe debt instruments, mostly government Treasury bills. If you buy a money market fund, you shouldn't expect big returns, but you'll be guaranteed to get your principal back. The interest rates on these funds are linked to the interest rates on bonds because they're heavily invested in them. In mid-2023, money market funds were yielding 5 percent interest.

Index Funds

An index fund is a type of mutual fund that invests in a specific list of securities, such as stock issued only by companies that are listed on the Nasdaq Composite index. That's an easier and less-expensive investment strategy than having professionals research and hand-pick from thousands of securities, so index funds have fewer fees associated with them than mutual funds do. Because there's no one actively managing an index fund portfolio, investing in an index fund is considered passive investing.

The performance of an index fund is based simply on price movement of the individual stocks within the index, not a professional managing the fund and trading stocks as they see fit.

The objective of an index fund is to mirror the performance of the market index the fund is based upon. If an index fund contains stocks of companies listed on the S&P 500 index, for instance, its goal is to perform as well as those stocks perform. It's betting that the value of the stock will go up over time, taking the value of the fund up with it.

The most popular US index funds track the S&P 500, but some other indexes are also widely used, including the Bloomberg US Aggregate Bond Index, the Wilshire 5000 Total Market Index, the Nasdaq Composite index, and the Dow Jones Industrial Average (mentioned earlier in the chapter) and also the MSCI EAFE Index, which includes foreign stocks from developed countries other than the United States and Canada.

Index funds can be bought and sold at the end of every trading day, but many investors choose to hold them for long periods of time. They are considered a form of passive investing—they're monitored but not frequently traded.

Exchange-Traded Funds

An ETF operates much like a mutual fund, but unlike mutual funds, ETFs can be purchased or sold on a stock exchange, just the way regular stock can be. That can make them easier to sell than mutual funds.

An ETF can contain many, diverse types of securities like mutual funds, or it can be based on the contents of an index, like an index fund. Like mutual funds, ETFs are pooled funds. Many ETFs have lower fees than other types of funds.

ETFs are valued for the diversity they provide, and they're thought to have more transparency than mutual funds because anyone can find the price activity for a particular ETF. The amount of holdings an ETF has is disclosed every day to the public, unlike mutual funds that only disclose holdings monthly or quarterly.

Like stocks, you can buy and sell ETFs throughout the day, not just at the end of the day. You'll need to pay a commission when buying and selling most ETFs.

ETFs also have some tax advantages over mutual funds, something you'll want to consider if you intend to buy them.

Cryptocurrency

Cryptocurrency, or crypto, is a type of currency that can be used to buy goods and services online. Because it fluctuates in value, it also can be traded, much like stock. Many investors—although there's debate about whether trading cryptocurrency is investing or speculating—have purchased crypto and held onto it in hopes that its value would increase and they could sell it for a big profit.

The first cryptocurrency was Bitcoin, which was introduced in 2009. Some people use *bitcoin* to refer to all crypto, just as one might say *Kleenex* when referring to all brands of tissue. Although it's still the biggest player, Bitcoin is now just one of about 10,000 cryptocurrencies that have been introduced and are publicly traded.

The total value of all cryptocurrency rises and falls almost constantly. According to CoinGecko, which claims to be the world's largest independent cryptocurrency data aggregator, crypto's global value as of July 23, 2023, was $1.25 trillion. Of that total value, Bitcoin represented $583 billion. That global total was 17 percent higher than at the same time the previous year, but far lower than in November 2021, when the total value of all cryptocurrency assets climbed past $3 trillion.

Those kinds of swings, and the uncertainty about cryptocurrency in general, make it a risky investment to be sure. Also, fraud surrounding cryptocurrency is common, adding another layer of risk.

Crypto is decentralized, meaning it's not affiliated with any bank. It's purchased and sold through crypto exchanges, the best-known of which in the United States is Coinbase. Coinbase is licensed and fully regulated, but not all cryptocurrencies are.

Because cryptocurrency is fully digital, there's no physical money involved. Crypto is stored in a digital wallet that's held either in an online exchange or offline on a device similar to a USB drive.

Warren Buffet, along with some other prominent investors, has expressed opposition to cryptocurrency as an investment. Buffet has declared he has never owned crypto and never will. We might not be as opposed to the investment vehicle as Buffet, but because cryptocurrency is unregulated, we share his hesitation. If you feel you must add some crypto to your portfolio, look into crypto ETFs. They're regulated and less risky than some other forms because their holdings are diversified.

Real Estate Investments

Investing in real estate seems different from putting money into the stock market or buying some mutual funds or ETFs, but real estate can be a viable investment. There are a few ways to invest in real estate, some of which are much more hands-off than others.

You could buy a property and rent it for income. This can be a great idea if you, for instance, buy a house with two separate living spaces and live in one while renting out the other. Or as you've probably watched on HGTV, you could buy properties, fix them up, and sell them for a profit, a practice known as house flipping.

A type of real estate investment you may not be familiar with is a real estate investment trust, or REIT. REITs are similar to mutual funds in that they pool funds from investors and use the money to invest in real estate. The purchased properties are leased, and the income generated is distributed as dividends to the shareholders.

Some REITS contain targeted real estate sectors, like strip malls, hotels, or office complexes. Others contain real estate in specific geographic areas, like the Middle East or the San Francisco Bay Area.

If you're a hands-on type of person, buying and managing a rental property can generate a good income stream, but there are downsides, such as dealing with bothersome tenants and keeping up with maintenance and repairs to the property.

Investing in real estate can be beneficial because it provides diversification, an investment strategy designed to minimize risk. (You'll read more about the importance of diversification in the next chapter.) The real estate market typically is affected by factors that don't affect the value of stocks and bonds. So if the stock market loses value, it's not likely that the real estate market will lose value at the same time. There also are some tax benefits to owning, renting, or managing real estate.

How to Buy and Sell Securities

Buying and selling stocks and other types of investments might sound intimidating, but after you've done it a few times, you'll see that it's quite easy.

To buy and sell stocks, mutual funds, and other securities, you need to open an account with a stockbroker or a brokerage firm. Stockbrokers and brokerage firms are authorized to make transactions on stock exchanges on behalf of their clients. These types of accounts are known as brokerage accounts.

A full-service broker is a person who can advise you on buying and selling stocks and other securities while also helping you with issues such as retirement planning and estate planning. As you can imagine, working with a full-service brokerage can be beneficial, but it also can be pricey because brokers usually charge a fee on each trade you make, and clients of management services often must pay a percentage of their total assets in fees each year.

A discount broker is a company that enables you to buy sell stocks and other investments online. It's a sort of self-service operation. Most millennials favor online brokers, which offer low commissions and trading fees and user-friendly online trading platforms. Many discount brokers also offer educational tools and resources to help you choose and manage investments.

Many brokerage firms offer both full-service and discount brokers. NerdWallet, an American personal finance company, offered this list of the 11 best discount brokers as of July 2023, citing no commissions and low or no account fees:

- Fidelity Investments (fidelity.com)
- Interactive Brokers (interactivebrokers.com)
- Merrill (ml.com)
- E*TRADE (etrade.com)
- J.P. Morgan (jpmorgan.com)
- Webull (webull.com)
- TD Ameritrade (tdameritrade.com)
- Robinhood (robinhood.com)
- Ally Invest (ally.com/invest)
- Firstrade (firstrade.com)
- Charles Schwab (schwab.com)

You also could invest using the services of a robo-adviser, which makes trades on your behalf based on your responses to a survey it provides and algorithms. Most robo-advisers create portfolios that are heavy on ETFs, although some can trade stocks, bonds, and other investments. Robo-advisers have lower fees than a full-service or discount broker, and you normally don't need much money to get a brokerage account set up. If you set up an account with a robo-adviser, it's advisable to establish and stick to a planned deposit schedule to grow your portfolio.

Chapter Summary

As you've no doubt gathered from reading this chapter, there's a lot to learn about investing your money and many options for doing so. Once you've got your emergency fund set up and your retirement accounts going, and you're managing your monthly bills with no problems, you should consider starting to put some money in stocks or some of the other investment vehicles mentioned in this chapter. Setting up an account or two and making regular contributions can give you a great start on your investment portfolio.

Chapter 13

Enhancing Your Investments

Nearly all forms of investing come with some risk, but there are strategies you can use to manage risk and improve your chances for success in the market. One of those strategies, as you've read over and over by now, is to start investing as early as you're able. And once you've started, make regular investments, even if they're small. There are some other strategies, too, such as asset allocation, diversification, having a handle on the fees you're paying, being mindful of your investing timetable, and rebalancing your portfolio when necessary.

We look at those investment strategies in this chapter, as well as the topic of financial advisers—when you might benefit from having one and what to look for when choosing one.

The Importance of a Diversified Portfolio

You read in Chapter 12 that mutual funds, some of which contain a variety of securities, can be a good investment choice, and that investing in some real estate can provide diversification because it's not subject to the same factors that affect the stock market. If you had stocks and real estate in your portfolio (which is a collection of any and all of your financial investments), it's likely that the real estate would hold its value, even if the value of stocks went down. Conversely, if the real estate market was in trouble, chances are your stock investments would be doing okay.

When you have a mix of assets, your portfolio is diversified. Diversification is the strategy of building a portfolio that contains different expected risks and returns—of not putting all your eggs in one basket.

It can be tempting to throw all your investment money at stocks when the market is hot, but when it goes down—as it inevitably does—all your investments will have lost value. Investments that add diversification to your portfolio are valuable because they give you a mix of assets to help reduce the risk of market volatility. When the stock market takes a dive, the returns on bonds may be rising and CDs remain stable. Assets perform differently in different economic times.

When you have different types of assets, you're increasing the chances that not all of your investments will lose value at the same time.

The Four Main Classes of Assets

There are different ways of grouping asset classes, but most financial analysts agree on four major investment categories:

- Equities
- Fixed income
- Cash
- Alternative investments

Equities are stock, or shares of ownership in a company. Some stocks result in dividend payments in addition to their potential to increase in value over time.

Fixed income securities are bonds that pay interest at regular intervals until the security matures, at which time the principal on the bond is returned to the investor.

Cash and cash equivalents include investments that can be converted into cash easily, such as money market funds, Treasury bills, and CDs with three-month maturation times. Some economists argue that cash isn't really a form of investing and shouldn't be included as an investment category, but it's necessary for its liquidity. If you need to get your hands on assets quickly, cash reserves are where you'll look.

Alternative investments cover a wide swath, including real estate, cryptocurrency, precious metals, hedge funds, collectibles, peer-to-peer loans, and others.

Determining the Allocation Mix That Makes Sense for You

You can find dozens of calculators and models to help you figure out the best asset mix for your circumstances, but generally, it comes down to three factors. Ask yourself these questions:

- How long will my money be invested?
- What are my short-term and long-term investment goals?
- What is my risk tolerance?

How your assets are allocated should change over time. A longtime rule of investing is to subtract your age from 100 and base your stock ownership on that number. If you're investing at age 30, your portfolio would contain 70 percent stock and 30 percent bonds, with other formulas factoring in to provide for alternative and cash investments. If you were 50, your allocation of stocks and bonds would be about evenly divided, and by the time you were 75, only one quarter of your assets would be in the form of stocks.

That rule of thumb has shifted more recently, however, with some advisers recommending that you subtract your age from 110 or 120 to account for increases in life expectancy. A lot of people live 20 or 30 years after retiring, meaning that your money has to continue to work for you longer.

Your asset allocation also should account for short-term and long-term investment goals. If you're saving for a short-term goal—generally considered one you'll need to fund within five years—you may be best served by putting money in cash or a cash equivalent fund, like a money market account. That avoids the chance that the value of your assets will drop and not have time to recover before your target date, whether that is when you'll need a down payment on a house, money to pay for a wedding, or another financial goal.

A goal that's five to ten years in the future is considered an intermediate goal and could be something like paying for a college education. To fund these goals, you should consider some investment in stocks and bonds. You could accomplish that with balanced mutual funds, which contain stocks, bonds, and sometimes money market accounts. They're designed for investors who are looking for gains that don't involve overly high levels of risk and can be helpful for meeting your mid-range goals. Of course, a 529 college savings plan also is a good investment option for education expenses.

Long-term goals, such as funding a retirement, are those that are more than 10 years down the road. Because stocks normally offer the best returns over time, even considering the risks they carry, your portfolio should be concentrated on them. Balancing different types of stock, such as growth stock with value stock or defensive stock with cyclical stock can reduce your risk because those stocks tend to counterbalance each other—when cyclical stocks go down in value, defensive stocks generally hold their value. You also can balance funds within other assets to reduce risk.

Your risk tolerance also will play a role in how your assets are allocated. We've already determined that some people are naturally able to tolerate more risk than others. Sarah has had clients in their 70s who were more risk tolerant than some in their 40s. If you have a long investment timeline, you should consider a buying strategy that has higher potential for reward, despite the fact that those investments carry more risk. But if the thought of losing money causes you real distress or disrupts your sleep or other aspects of life, you'll need to adjust your strategy to account for that risk aversion.

If you have a financial adviser (more about that in a bit), they can help you with asset allocation. If not, consider investing in a target-date fund, a mutual fund that holds several asset classes that can be reallocated as your circumstances change. If you set up a 2055 fund, for instance, your money will be spread out across asset classes and then moved around to accommodate aging or other change in a way that will provide the best returns while lessening your risk.

Choosing Securities

You can spend years studying how to become a better-than-proficient investor in the securities market. You can spend hours and hours researching and comparing dozens of companies to decide which stocks to choose. If you want to do that, great; you'll learn a lot.

For our purposes here, however, we'll share some understandable, easily doable steps for choosing stock.

Study the Market

To start, take a look at the market. The majority of stocks perform as the overall market is performing. If the broader market is going up, the value of about three quarters of stock within the market will be rising, too, meaning that buying stock when the market is trending higher might boost your chances of a beneficial trade.

You'll also want to look at the moving averages of a couple of major indexes to get an idea of the general trend in prices during a given period. That can help you gauge the market's general direction during that period.

In addition, pay attention to events that could affect your trade by shaking up the market, such as a Federal Reserve announcement of an interest rate increase.

After you've gotten an overall view of the market, identify an industry or market sector that seems appealing. This can be based on some piece of financial news you've heard or read or some personal knowledge of a business sector. There are guides that can help you track the performance of various sectors, enabling you to see which have done well and which may have faltered. Bloomberg, for instance, offers a sector performance chart that's updated frequently. Looking at it on early August 2023, the chart offered this information about 11 market sectors and the overall performance of all sectors.

	% Price Change
All sectors	+0.06
Communication services	+0.36
Health care	+0.01
Consumer discretionary	−0.01
Materials	−0.06
Financials	−0.09
Consumer staples	−0.13
Utilities	−0.17
Information technology	−0.23
Real estate	−0.39
Industrials	−0.40
Energy	−0.47

If the economy seems uncertain, it's normally good to focus on a defensive sector, such as health care, utilities, or consumer staples.

When you've identified a sector, you can use a stock screener tool to check various factors relating to different companies. Brokerages and some other companies offer stock screeners, some for no charge. If you have an account with a brokerage company, a screener should be available for you to use.

When you've narrowed down your list to several companies, take a little time to look at some details. Look for red flags like a lawsuit filed against the company or a product recall. Check each company's earnings, financial statements, and ratings, comparing one against the other.

After you've whittled down your list even further, look at the stock's trend line, which will give you a good idea of the direction in which an investment's value might move.

Exchange-Traded Funds

When considering exchange-traded funds (ETFs), you'll want to look at the underlying index. Remember that an ETF is a basket of securities that trade on an exchange, similar to stocks. Some indexes are similar, but others look and perform very differently. To assure sufficient diversification, consider an ETF that is based on a broad, widely followed index rather than one that is limited to a geographic focus or just a few industries.

Choose an ETF that has sufficient assets—the common threshold is that it contains at least $10 million in assets. One with assets below that threshold probably will have limited investor interest, which decreases its viability.

Another thing to consider is the level of trading activity. The most popular ETFs have trading volumes of millions of shares every day, while others barely trade at all. ETFs with high trading volumes are more liquid than those with low volumes, which is important when it's time to exit the ETF.

Mutual Funds

If you're considering investing in mutual funds, you'll want to find out what a particular fund contains. Just like stocks, some mutual funds are designed for growth while others focus on value. So, as with stocks, your timeline, purpose for investing, and risk tolerance should be considerations.

Remember that funds that are actively managed by a fund manager who buys and sells securities have higher fees than those that are managed passively, meaning they use a buy-and-hold strategy by tracking a specific market index. Compare the fees and ask yourself if active management is worth the extra cost.

Studies have shown there is little difference in the performances of actively managed and passively managed funds.

Also be sure to check what other fees you'll be charged because they can impact your investment returns.

You won't get it right every time when you're starting out, but soon these steps will become second nature and you'll establish a rhythm for choosing stocks. Remember to keep records of how your picks perform, and learn from your mistakes.

Staying in for the Long Term

Holding on to investments for a long time has been found to be one of the best methods of building wealth over time. The stock market gains value in most years—36 out of the 47 years between 1975 and 2022.

A long-term investment strategy is described as keeping investments, including stocks, bonds, ETFs, and mutual funds, for longer than a year. Research has shown that long-term investments almost always perform better than investments that are frequently traded as their owners try to time their holdings.

It can be difficult to let investments sit as their value decreases. The natural instinct is to get rid of them in an attempt to minimize your losses, but that can hurt you in the long run.

We know the stock market increases and decreases in value—it's simply the nature of how it performs. What's important to remember is that when the value of stocks goes down, it's normally a temporary situation. If you resist the urge to sell them on their way down, you'll still have them when the market recovers and their value returns. Selling them eliminates your ability to benefit when they regain their value.

It's also good to keep in mind that a down market is a great time to add stocks to your portfolio. You can buy when the price is down and wait for it to come back up.

Long-term investing also can save you money in capital gains taxes and fees. If you sell a security at a profit within a year of buying it, your proceeds are taxed as ordinary income. Depending on your adjusted gross income, that rate could be as high as 37 percent. But if you sell the security at a profit after having held it for more than a year, your earnings are taxed as long-term capital gains with a maximum tax rate of 20 percent.

Holding on to securities for a longer period also results in fewer fees than when you buy and sell regularly. Remember that it's important to know what fees you're charged for transactions. You can do that by checking your account after a transaction or by asking a representative of the brokerage you use to buy and sell securities.

Working with a Professional Financial Adviser

If you haven't given much thought to your personal finances or done the work of exploring your options and figuring out where you stand financially, probably the worst thing you can do is go out and hire a financial adviser, assuming the adviser will take care of everything and you'll never have to think about your finances again. On the surface, it sounds like a good idea: let somebody else worry about it, right?

The problem with hiring a financial adviser when you have no knowledge of your own finances is that you're placing a lot of trust, and some of your most valuable assets, in the hands of a person you may know nothing about—or even someone you *do* think you know something about. Many people have trusted their finances to someone who turned out to be untrustworthy.

It also could be that the financial "expert" you hire is not an expert at all. Basically, just about anybody can claim to be a financial adviser. Finances, investments, taxation, and the like are all very complicated topics that take years of education to acquire the knowledge to do the job well. Not everyone can be an expert, and it's imperative that you find someone who has the knowledge you're looking for.

Millennials, some of whom endured the Great Recession and are fighting their way out of student debt, are not lining up at traditional financial advising firms the way members of previous generations did. Your generation likes to do things differently, and many are skeptical of capital markets and financial advisers. So while not denying that they need financial advice, many young adults are looking for it in some nonconventional ways … and some financial services providers are getting onboard.

Know Thy Finances, Know Thy Adviser

The preceding section isn't meant to scare you off from hiring someone to help you with your finances if you've gotten to the point where you need it. Nearly everybody can use some help sometimes. The point is, the more you know about your personal finances, the easier it will be for you to find a qualified, trustworthy financial adviser, which is a broad term for a professional you hire to help you make decisions about your finances.

When you understand your finances, you'll be able to ask intelligent questions of potential advisers and understand their answers. You'll know what they're talking about when they throw out phrases like "full-service broker" or "fee-only adviser." You won't feel stupid asking questions about your own money because generally, you'll know exactly what you're talking about. Armed with prior knowledge, you'll work together with the adviser to put your money to the best possible use.

A financial adviser is called an *adviser* because it's their job to *advise* you on the best uses of your money. Ultimately, however, it's your money, and you're in charge of what happens to it.

Do You Need a Financial Adviser?

You might need a financial adviser for many reasons. Maybe you're faced with a complicated financial situation regarding the sale or purchase of a property, or perhaps you want some advice about which stocks and bonds to buy. Maybe you're setting up a college fund or getting really serious about your retirement fund. Or it could be that you earned a big bonus you'd like to maximize in some sort of investment.

The reason for, and the point at which, you seek help with your finances is entirely up to you. Whether you're leaving a job and deciding what to do with the $15,800 you have in your 401(k), or you've inherited $200,000 from your grandmother, you might feel that you need some financial advice from time to time.

Understanding Fiduciary Responsibility

Financial advisers are divided into two groups: those who have a fiduciary obligation to put you first (this includes most Registered Investment Advisers) and those who work for a brokerage firm and cannot be a fiduciary (this includes stockbrokers and sometimes insurance agents).

The fiduciary relationship is a legal relationship between two or more persons in which the adviser is legally bound to …

- Provide the highest ethical advice.
- Act at all times with a higher standard of care and legal manner for your sole benefit and interests. A fiduciary adviser must always put the interests of the client first.
- Advise you exactly what the charges will be and how they will be paid. This is known as full disclosure, which is different from just handing you a contract. With full disclosure, you know exactly what you are paying for the advice.

Fiduciary advisers have a duty to avoid any situation in which their personal interests and fiduciary duty to their clients conflict and also a duty not to profit from their fiduciary position without disclosure of the fees charged.

The Who's Who of Financial Advisers

When discussing some of the different kinds of financial advisers, the issue can become a little complicated. A financial adviser by any other name may, or may not, be a financial adviser.

We explain some of the common classes of financial advisers in the following sections. There's a wide range of training, certification, and experience among financial advisers. Remember that the type of adviser you need depends on your circumstances, and you should never hire someone just because she has a title you think sounds impressive.

Financial Planners

The term *financial planner* often is used to describe anyone who offers financial advice or services. It frequently is used interchangeably with *financial adviser*.

A financial planner, as the name implies, is someone who designs financial plans of action. They may design and carry out the plan, or their clients may choose to execute the plans they design.

Financial planner is a very broad categorization, so if you're looking to hire one, be sure you know what credentials or other titles may come along with it. For starters, financial planners can be certified—or not.

Certified Financial Planners

A very large group of people in this country are called certified financial planners. They've all earned the Certified Financial Planner (CFP) credential, a national certification that requires certificants to have a fiduciary relationship with their advisees.

Earning the CFP credential involves working through a home-study program and passing a cumulative, six-hour test. Designees must have three years of financial work experience and promise to adhere to a code of ethics. Work experience should include financial planning, investments, or banking. CFPs are also required to take 30 hours of continuing education courses every two years to stay current on industry happenings.

Financial Consultants

Another type of financial planner is the financial consultant. A financial consultant provides an overview of financial information and options so you can choose the products that make the most sense for you.

Financial consultants generally won't produce a plan for your finances; they'll only offer information and advice. The assumption is that the consultant is fee-only, and they won't receive a commission on any products sold. Be sure to ask your consultant how they will be paid.

Certified Public Accountants and Personal Financial Specialists

More and more certified public accountants (CPAs) are becoming financial consultants. The American Institute of Certified Public Accountants now has a special designation, called a personal financial specialist (PFS), for CPAs who have three years of financial planning experience and pass a six-hour test. Unless you purchase a product, CPAs usually are paid on an hourly basis.

Many people depend on their CPA for financial help, regardless of whether or not the CPA is designated a PFS.

Insurance Agents

You might not normally think of an insurance agent as a financial planner, but some agents specialize in financial planning. They usually have either a Chartered Life Underwriter (CLU) or Chartered Financial Consultant (ChFC) designation, or both, as mentioned in Chapter 10. These are designations by The American College of Financial Services in Bryn Mawr, Pennsylvania, given to persons who complete and pass an eight-course program. Often, the program of study can be designed in the agent's area of expertise.

CLUs and ChFCs need continuing education. The designations, although not mandatory to do financial planning, show a level of expertise and experience as well as indicate the agent's commitment to ethical practices.

Money Managers

A money manager is a financial adviser who, after reviewing your parameters, risk tolerance, and total financial picture, agrees to handle your funds, make trades on your behalf, and buy and sell stocks and bonds for you. A money manager normally is employed by investors who have a substantial amount of money.

Money managers typically receive a percentage of the market value of their client's account as compensation—approximately 1 percent of the value of the assets on an annual basis. As an example, a money manager who has $200,000 under management and charges an annual fee of 1 percent would earn $2,000 per year from the account. They probably would charge the fee quarterly, which is $500 per quarter or $166.67 per month.

Some financial advisers, especially those who cater to millennials, bill monthly. The adviser charges a fee each month to make and manage a financial plan, with the thought that young people are used to making monthly payments for services such as gym fees or streaming services.

Many money managers have a Chartered Financial Analyst (CFA) designation. Look for this designation if you're thinking about hiring a money manager.

Meeting with Potential Advisers

It's important to find somebody who understands and shares your views and philosophies on investments and financial planning, so don't hire someone without first having a meeting to get to know that person. Remember, you should have some good financial information and understanding under your belt before the meeting because you've been doing your homework and reading about investments and other financial matters that may affect you.

But let's get one thing very clear before we start: don't forget, even for a minute, that *you* are the person who will be hiring the financial adviser, and *you* will be paying *their* fees. It's not the other way around. Many people are intimidated by professionals because they feel stupid or uninformed around them. That's why you meet with advisers in the first place. It's understood that they have more expertise in the finance area than you do, and hopefully, you can benefit from their knowledge. That's the point, right? You don't need to impress the financial adviser; they need to impress you.

When you're with your prospective adviser, you need to ask some questions. Here are some questions to ask the financial advisers you consider:

- How long have you been in this business? As with most professions, experience is important. You want to find someone who fully understands the financial industry and all its nuances and who has lived through the ups and downs of the market.

- How have you prepared for this job? You'll want to know about your potential adviser's education and previous job experience.

- What was your job before you became a financial adviser? Look for a logical progression, such as moving into a financial adviser position from a banking job. If the progression doesn't seem logical, ask for an explanation.

- How will you tailor my investments to fit my age and retirement goals? You want someone who understands you, your generation, and your financial goals.

- Can you put me in touch with some other clients whose financial situations are similar to mine? References are very important. If you talk to other clients and don't get all the information you're looking for, don't be afraid to ask the candidate for more names.

In addition to these questions, ask to see their Uniform Application for Investment Adviser Registration, or as it's more commonly known, their Form ADV, Parts 2A and 2B. This provides a financial planner's background and tells whether they or their firm have been in any trouble in the past with the law or with investment regulatory offices. If an adviser refuses to make this form available, it should set off warning bells.

Finding an Adviser Online

Most brokers offer online services, including the biggest firms like Charles Schwab, Fidelity, J.P. Morgan, and TD Ameritrade. Robo-advisers also are popular. These online investment platforms provide automated investment and portfolio management advice based on algorithms to determine asset allocations and automated rebalancing for investors. No human financial adviser is involved.

With robo-advisers, each client's portfolio is structured to achieve optimal returns at every level of risk. A key investing approach robo platforms use is to invest in low-cost ETFs that minimize embedded investment costs. Because they utilize technology rather than active management by a human financial adviser, robo-advisers charge significantly lower fees than what most financial advisers typically charge. If you're concerned about costs and fees, robo-advisers or online brokerage options might be your best bet.

Many people like robo-advisers, partly due to the lower costs and also because of their affinity for and trust in technology. Plus, robo-advisers are available to investors who are just starting out with limited funds and tend to not be particularly attractive clients to financial firms.

If you're going to employ an online adviser, either the human variety or a robo-adviser, do your homework and compare both the services offered and the fees charged. Here are some things to look for:

- Quality trade executions
- Online newsletters and reports to keep you informed about what's happening in the financial world
- 24-hour phone service
- Personal access to representatives in case you need face-to-face service
- Customized stock alerts to let you know when something is happening that might affect your account

Also, be sure to find out the various ways in which you can access your accounts. Is an interactive voice-response phone system or online chat feature available? In addition, look for apps that enable you to access your accounts from your phone or tablet.

Go with Your Gut

There's one more important factor to consider when you're choosing a financial adviser: your gut. Some people click, and others don't. Although you should never hire somebody just because you like them, you probably shouldn't hire somebody you don't like either.

Every financial adviser should be able to show you a code of ethics he or she adheres to. Don't be afraid to ask about it. If the adviser can't or won't show it to you, you probably should look elsewhere.

The investing goals of many younger adults vary from those of previous generations, and it's important to find an adviser who understands your goals and knows what's important to you. If you love to travel and are adamant that you don't want to wait until you're retired to see the world, find an adviser who will help you achieve your travel goals while still ensuring your retirement account is healthy.

If you find an adviser you like and feel they're a good and competent professional, you might have a match. You need someone who will take the time to talk with you, teach you, answer any and all of your questions, and be there for you. If you don't like someone, it probably will be very hard to work together effectively, even if they're considered the best financial adviser in the business.

Don't be afraid to ask about fees and to compare them to what other advisers charge. Find out whether the adviser is fee-only or sells products on commission.

If a financial adviser stands to make big money on commissions from selling certain types of financial products, watch out. You might be pressured to buy products that are more beneficial to your adviser than they are to you. An adviser who does this is more salesperson than financial adviser, and that's not what you need. Some of the best financial consultants are commissioned salespeople; you just need to understand how they're paid and ask if there's a product available with a smaller commission.

When you first meet with someone you think you might hire, ask whether or not they get a commission from products they sell. If they say they don't but you're getting a bad feeling, you can check them out.

All advisers are required to register with the Securities and Exchange Commission (SEC) in Washington, DC, or their state SEC, and they all must fill out the Uniform Application for Investment Adviser Registration, mentioned earlier in this chapter. Ask the adviser for a copy of that form, and if they can't produce it, check with the SEC to be sure of their registration.

You also can check out the status of any Certified Financial Planner by using the verification function on CFP Board's website at cfp.net/verify-a-cfp-professional.

If you feel that your financial adviser has cheated you or has done something unethical, you can look for help by contacting a securities lawyer. Or you can seek arbitration, which is the hearing and determination of a dispute between parties by a third party. You can do this either by hiring an attorney to represent you in arbitration, or by representing yourself in arbitration. Before you hire an attorney, contact the Financial Industry Regulatory Authority (FINRA) at 301-590-6500 or finra.org. FINRA's website lets you file a complaint online. You'll need to file one before a SEC auditor will investigate the complaint.

Ultimately, the decision of which financial adviser to hire is up to you. Consider all the factors, throw in your gut feeling, and go for it. Watch out for red flags like too-high fees, conflicts of interest, or past bad behavior. If your finances are relatively uncomplicated and you're willing to put in the time and effort to stay on top of them, a professional financial adviser probably isn't necessary. You can easily use a robo-adviser or online brokerage to help you along. As you gain wealth and your financial situation becomes more complex, however, a trusted adviser can be a great asset.

Chapter Summary

Investing your money becomes easier the longer you do it. When you're starting out, it's important to understand the significance of diversification and to keep an eye on how your assets are distributed among the four main classes:

equities, fixed income investments, cash, and alternative investments. You should have a basic understanding of how to assess the overall stock market and various market segments and how to choose a stock, ETF, or other security. Whether or not you work with a financial adviser is your choice, but if you go that route, you should understand the differences in designations and choose a highly regarded adviser who is a good fit for your situation.

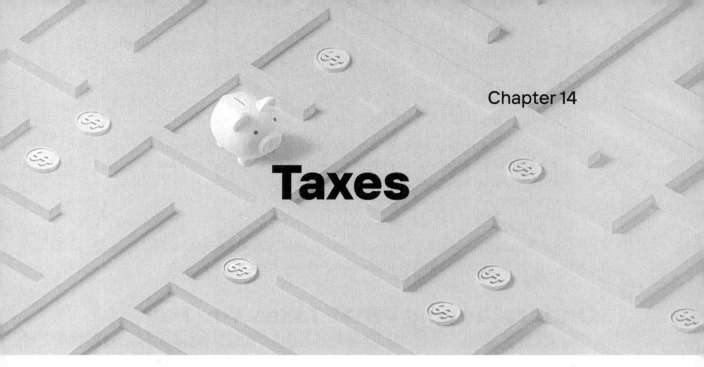

Chapter 14

Taxes

Regardless of how you earn your money, you're going to have to hand over some of it in federal and, in most places, state and local income tax. Depending on your circumstances, you'll also pay other types of taxes, such as property tax, Social Security tax, sales tax, and excise tax (which is a tax imposed on certain goods or activities such as alcohol, tobacco, gasoline, and airline tickets).

Nobody likes paying taxes, but as the late US Supreme Court Justice Oliver Wendell Holms once said, "Taxes are the price we pay for a civilized society." According to Credit.com, your taxes go toward paying the following government expenditures, in order of money spent:

- Government debt

- Social Security

- Medicare

- Other health-care programs, such as Medicaid, the Children's Health Insurance Program, and health-care market subsidies funded under the Affordable Care Act

- National defense

- Veterans benefits
- Safety net programs such as nutrition and food assistance, housing assistance, unemployment compensation, foster care, and certain tax credits (Safety net spending increased enormously during the COVID-19 pandemic.)

In this chapter, we take a closer look at what taxes you pay and how much, and what you can do minimize the amount of tax you have to pay.

Understanding What Taxes You Pay

Americans spend almost 30 percent of their incomes on taxes each year, so it's beneficial to understand how and why you're parting with all that hard-earned money. Basically, most taxes fall into one of three categories: taxes on income, taxes on property, and taxes on goods and services.

Taxes on Income

The federal government and nearly every state impose income tax on individuals and businesses, along with tax on interest income, which is income you get from bank accounts, bonds, and money market accounts. You're also likely to have to pay city wage tax. If you live in Alaska, Florida, Nevada, New Hampshire, South Dakota, Tennessee, Texas, Washington, or Wyoming, you don't have to pay state taxes on your income.

Federal tax rates are based on income. The more money you make, the higher your tax rate is. In 2023, federal income tax rates ranged from 10 percent to 37 percent. State and local taxes generally have much lower rates. These tax rates don't change very often because changing them requires Congress to pass major tax legislation, but the upper and lower income amounts for each bracket are adjusted every year to account for inflation. That means you could end up in a higher or lower tax bracket each year depending on your income and may have to pay a different tax rate on your income in any given year than you did the previous or subsequent year.

The following tables show federal tax brackets for four categories of tax filers: single, head of household (those who are single and maintain a home for a qualifying person such as a child or relative), married but filing separately, and married and filing jointly.

2024 Single Filer Tax Brackets

Taxable Income	Tax Rate
$0 to $11,000	10 percent
$11,001 to $44,725	12 percent
$44,726 to $95,375	22 percent
$95,376 to $182,100	24 percent
$182,101 to $231,250	32 percent
$231,251 to $578,125	35 percent
$578,126 or more	37 percent

2024 Head of Household Filer Tax Brackets

Taxable Income	Tax Rate
$0 to $15,700	10 percent
$15,701 to $59,850	12 percent
$59,851 to $95,350	22 percent
$95,351 to $182,100	24 percent
$182,101 to $231,250	32 percent
$231,251 to $578,100	35 percent
$578,101 or more	37 percent

2024 Married Filing Separately Filer Tax Brackets

Taxable Income	Tax Rate
$0 to $11,000	10 percent
$11,001 to $44,725	12 percent
$44,726 to $95,375	22 percent
$95,376 to $182,100	24 percent
$182,101 to $231,250	32 percent
$231,251 to $346,875	35 percent
$346,876 or more	37 percent

2024 Married Filing Jointly Filer Tax Brackets

Taxable Income	Tax Rate
$0 to $22,000	10 percent
$22,001 to $89,450	12 percent
$89,451 to $190,750	22 percent
$190,751 to $364,200	24 percent
$364,201 to $462,500	32 percent
$462,501 to $693,750	35 percent
$693,751 or more	37 percent

Something important to understand about federal tax brackets and tax rates is that the rates are marginal tax rates. A marginal tax rate is the amount of tax paid for every additional dollar earned as income. You don't pay the same amount of tax on every dollar you earn. If you're a single filer who earns $100,000 a year, for example, your taxable income falls in the 24 percent federal bracket. But that doesn't mean all your income is taxed at 24 percent, due to marginal tax rates. Instead, your taxable income is broken into chunks based on the tax brackets. Your income up to the top level of the first bracket is taxed at the applicable tax rate and then the next highest tax rate kicks in for income up to the top level of the second bracket.

Here's how it breaks down: Of that $100,000 of taxable income, the first $11,000 is taxed at 10 percent, the next $33,724 is taxed at 12 percent, and the next $50,649 is taxed at 22 percent. Any income left over, which in this case would be $4,627, is taxed at 24 percent. This method of taxation is known as progressive taxation and is meant to tax people according to how much they earn. You can see how it results in lower tax bills, especially for lower-income earners.

Although they're a big chunk, federal income taxes aren't the only taxes to come out of your paycheck. Employers must subtract payroll taxes from their workers' paychecks and match the amount of taxes deducted. Payroll taxes are also known as FICA taxes because they're authorized by the Federal Insurance Contributions Act. They're used to fund the Social Security system and the federal Medicare program.

The FICA taxes on individual workers are 7.65 percent of income, with 6.2 percent going toward Social Security and 1.45 percent toward Medicare funding. If you're self-employed, you have to pay both the employer and the employee parts of FICA taxes, meaning you're out another 15.3 percent of your income. If you're a self-employed graphic artist who makes $55,000 a year, for instance, 27.3 percent of your income is given to federal taxes. And more will go to pay state and local taxes. But as Oliver Wendell Holms said …

If you realize any capital gains during a given tax year, you'll have to pay taxes on those as well. Capital gains are any profits realized from the sale of an asset such as a home, car, business, stock, cryptocurrency, or bonds.

Fortunately for homeowners, there's an exclusion on gains from the sale of a primary residence: $250,000 if you're filing as single and $500,000 if you're filing as married. That means most homeowners can sell without having to pay capital gains, although skyrocketing home prices have left some sellers facing tax consequences because the value of their homes increased more than the allowable exclusion. The homeowner exclusion is only good for primary residences, not investment property. You are required to have lived in the house for at least two of the previous five years to qualify for the exclusion.

The amount of gains you'll pay tax on from the sale of other assets is the difference between what you paid for the asset and what you sold it for. If you bought an apartment building eight years ago for $225,000 and sold it for $285,000, you'll pay tax on $60,000. You only pay capital gains on an asset when you sell it, not as it appreciates in value while you own it. The good news is that the apartment building you bought eight years ago will be subject to long-term capital gains instead of short-term capital gains.

As you read in the last chapter, long-term capital gains are those levied on assets you've held for more than a year, while short-term capital gains are on assets you've had for less than a year. Long-term capital gains are taxed at 0, 15, or 20 percent, depending on graduated income levels. The tax on short-term capital gains, which are taxed as ordinary income, can be a high of 37 percent, depending on your tax bracket.

Another tax that can affect your income is the estate tax, but unless you're expecting to receive property valued at about $12 million or more, you won't have to worry about this tax.

Taxes on Property

You read about property tax in Chapter 7, so we'll just reiterate here that property taxes vary according to where you live, but they can be prohibitive in some areas. Property taxes are local taxes and normally paid either once a year or monthly as part of a mortgage payment.

The following table shows a state-by-state listing of the average state property tax rate and annual property tax on a median value home as of July 2023.

Property Tax by State

State	Property Tax Rate	Annual Property Tax
Alabama	0.37%	$1,188
Alaska	0.97%	$3,114
Arizona	0.39%	$1,252
Arkansas	0.53%	$1,707

State	Property Tax Rate	Annual Property Tax
California	0.66%	$2,119
Colorado	0.40%	$1,284
Connecticut	1.57%	$5,040
Delaware	0.48%	$1,541
Florida	0.67%	$2,151
Georgia	0.70%	$2,247
Hawaii	0.30%	$963
Idaho	0.46%	$1,177
Illinois	1.78%	$5,714
Indiana	0.74%	$2,375
Iowa	1.25%	$4,012
Kansas	1.15%	$3,691
Kentucky	0.60%	$1,926
Louisiana	0.53%	$1,701
Maine	0.89%	$2,857
Maryland	0.76%	$2,440
Massachusetts	0.94%	$3,017
Michigan	1.06%	$3,403
Minnesota	0.90%	$2,889
Mississippi	0.55%	$1,765
Missouri	0.82%	$2,632
Montana	0.65%	$2,086
Nebraska	1.36%	$4,366
Nevada	0.44%	$1,412
New Hampshire	1.28%	$4,109

Property Tax by State ...

... Property Tax by State

State	Property Tax Rate	Annual Property Tax
New Jersey	1.79%	$5,746
New Mexico	0.60%	$1,926
New York	1.26%	$4,045
North Carolina	0.53%	$1,669
North Dakota	0.52%	$2,889
Ohio	1.27%	$4,077
Oklahoma	0.76%	$2,440
Oregon	0.78%	$2,504
Pennsylvania	1.29%	$4,141
Rhode Island	1.01%	$3,242
South Carolina	0.46%	$1,477
South Dakota	1.03%	$3,306
Tennessee	0.42%	$1,348
Texas	1.25%	$4,012
Utah	0.44%	$1,412
Vermont	1.43%	$4,590
Virginia	0.72%	$2,311
Washington	0.70%	$2,247
West Virginia	0.47%	$1,509
Wisconsin	1.15%	$3,691
Wyoming	0.64%	$2,054

You also can be taxed on personal property, such as cars, boats, planes, RVs, farm equipment, or business equipment like machinery or furniture. When you pay your car registration every year, for example, you're paying a tax on the vehicle.

Taxes on Goods and Services

When you buy a new set of headphones, pay for your dry cleaning, or buy a hamburger and some fries at your local restaurant, you're likely to be charged sales tax on those items. Sales tax is used by states and local governments to generate revenue, and it varies tremendously from location to location.

Sales tax can seem arbitrary, and there are all kinds of strange applications. In Pennsylvania, for instance, you'll pay tax on a bottle of juice if it contains less than 25 percent real fruit juice, but not if the juice contains 25 percent or more real juice. You don't pay tax on toilet paper, but you do pay tax on a box of tissues. A bag of dog food is subject to sales tax, but a bottle of flea and tick shampoo is not. Most food you buy in a grocery store is not taxed, but prepared food in a restaurant is. We're not sure who determines what is taxed and what isn't, but it certainly can seem confusing.

Some cities and counties also impose local sales taxes, which sometimes are higher than the state tax. Colorado, for instance, has a state sales tax of 2.9 percent, but the average local sales tax is 4.89 percent.

Five states—Alaska, Delaware, Montana, New Hampshire, and Oregon—have no state sales tax. The following table shows how the rest of the states compare in sales tax as of July 2023.

Sales Tax by State

State	Sales Tax Rate	State	Sales Tax Rate
Alabama	4%	Florida	1.019%
Arizona	5.6%	Georgia	4%
Arkansas	6.5%	Hawaii	4%
California	7.25%	Idaho	6%
Colorado	2.9%	Illinois	6.25%
Connecticut	6.35%	Indiana	7%
District of Columbia	6%	Iowa	6%

Sales Tax by State ...

... Sales Tax by State

State	Sales Tax Rate	State	Sales Tax Rate
Kansas	6.5%	North Dakota	5%
Kentucky	6%	Ohio	5.75%
Louisiana	4.45%	Oklahoma	4.5%
Maine	5.5%	Pennsylvania	6%
Maryland	6%	Rhode Island	7%
Massachusetts	6.25%	South Carolina	6%
Michigan	6%	South Dakota	4.2%
Minnesota	6.88%	Tennessee	7%
Mississippi	7%	Texas	6.25%
Missouri	4.23%	Utah	6.10%
Nebraska	5.5%	Vermont	6%
Nevada	6.85%	Virginia	5.30%
New Jersey	6.63%	Washington	6.5%
New Mexico	4.88%	West Virginia	6%
New York	4%	Wisconsin	5%
North Carolina	4.75%	Wyoming	4%

There are arguments both for and against sales taxes. Some people claim they're more equitable than property taxes because everyone has to pay them, not just people who own property, and people who consume a lot pay the most tax. The argument against sales tax is that they disproportionately affect poorer people, who end up paying a larger percentage of their incomes in sales tax than people who have more money do.

Another type of tax on goods and services is excise taxes, which, as you read at the beginning of the chapter, are taxes you pay on certain goods or activities. A big excise tax is the federal government's 18.4 percent tax on every gallon of gas purchased. States often add their own excise tax on top of the federal tax. These taxes vary dramatically from state to state. In New York, for example, tax on a pack of cigarettes is $4.35—the highest in the country. Georgia, on the other hand, charges just 37¢ tax on a pack of cigarettes.

You're likely to pay user fees, taxes imposed on a wide variety of services, when you stay in a hotel, drive on a state turnpike, pay your electricity bill, or rent a car. If you buy an expensive piece of jewelry or a luxury car, you may be charged a luxury tax.

Minimizing How Much You Pay in Taxes

You read in Chapter 11 that the contributions you make to a 401(k) plan are pretax and tax-deferred. That means they're deducted from your salary before your salary is taxed for federal income taxes and you don't pay any tax on the money contributed or on the interest earned on that money until you withdraw it from the account fund. That's a win-win for you because it reduces your taxable income.

You also can reduce your taxable income by contributing to a traditional IRA. Contributions made or benefits from some fringe benefits, like educational assistance programs, transportation reimbursements, and group term life insurance, also may be excluded from your taxable income.

Interest on municipal bonds also is exempt from federal taxes and may be tax-exempt at the local and state level as well.

Another method of reducing your taxable income is to set up a health savings account (HSA), which enables you to save money for future health expenses. Not everyone is eligible to open an HSA. To be eligible, you need to have a high-deductible health insurance plan, which is a plan that requires you to pay a certain amount for your care before your insurance company begins payments. If you're young and healthy, a high-deductible plan probably isn't a problem, but if you have a condition like asthma or eczema, those deductible charges can add up quickly.

The money you put in an HSA is excluded from your taxable income, and as with a 401(k), your employer may provide matching funds. Also, your contributions are invested with the potential to increase in value, and any earnings on them are not taxable. The maximum deductible contribution level in 2023 was $3,850 for an individual and $7,750 for a family.

Finding Tax Credits and Deductions

Tax credits and deductions also can reduce your taxable income and the amount of taxes you'll have to pay.

Tax Credits Worth Exploring

Tax credits to look into if you think you might be eligible include the following:

- Earned Income Tax Credit
- American Opportunity Tax Credit
- Lifetime Learning Credits
- Child Tax Credit

The Earned Income Tax Credit allows you to claim credits if you are a low- to moderate-income earner. The amount you can claim is based on your income and the number of children you have, although you can get a modest credit if you do not have children. In 2023, credits ranged from $7,430 for someone who qualifies and has three or more qualifying children to $600 for someone who qualifies and does not have any qualifying children. You won't qualify for the credit if you haven't worked in the year in which you claim it.

The American Opportunity Tax Credit (AOTC) is a tax credit for education expenses that occur within the first four years of postsecondary education. Education expenses include tuition, school fees, and materials needed for courses, but not room and board, transportation, insurance, or medical costs. The maximum annual credit is $2,500 per eligible student. If the student is a dependent, a parent can claim the tax credit. Those eligible must have a gross income of $80,000 or less if filing singly or $160,000 or less if married and filing jointly.

If you don't qualify for the AOTC, you might qualify for the Lifetime Learning Credit, which has less-stringent requirements. If you do qualify, you can claim up to 20 percent of the first $10,000 of eligible expenses at a qualified college or university. The tax credit applies to undergrad and graduate school expenses, and in some cases, you can claim it for continuing education or professional development classes, too.

The Child Tax Credit can reduce your taxable income, and some taxpayers may qualify for a partial refund of the credit. As of July 2023, if your income is $400,000 or less for married and filing jointly filers or below $200,000 for all other filers, you may be able to get a tax credit worth $2,000 per dependent child. The refundable portion, known as the additional child tax credit, is worth up to $1,600. Children must be under the age of 17 and have lived with you for at least half the year in which you claim the credit. You also must have provided at least half of the child's support. This tax credit can significantly affect what you pay in taxes, so if you think you qualify, be sure to do some more research or talk to your tax preparer.

Deductions That Might Apply to You

Deductions can reduce your taxable income and, therefore, the amount of taxes you'll have to pay. You read about deductions you can take as a homeowner in Chapter 7, so we'll just remind you here that they can be substantial and something you'll want to take advantage of if they apply to you.

Some other tax deductions that often apply to millennials include the following:

- You can deduct $2,500 of the interest you pay on your student loans throughout the tax year, although there are income limitations.

- If you contribute money to your alma mater, your synagogue, the Red Cross, your local volunteer fire company, a museum, or another tax-exempt organization, you can deduct your contributions on your tax return.

- If you've switched jobs in the last year, you can deduct job-hunting expenses such as Uber fees or the cost of printing résumés.

- Prior to the Tax Cuts and Jobs Act of 2017, you could deduct certain moving expenses if you moved more than 50 miles in a given year. Currently, only members of the military and their dependents can deduct moving expenses, but the law is expected to revert to its previous status in 2025. So if you're planning a move for that year or beyond, do a little research to find out if any deductions apply to you.

- If you're a business owner, you can deduct up to $5,000 in start-up expenses. If you have a side gig, you can deduct any expense that's necessary to conduct that business.

- The cost of continuing education or professional education training required by your employer can be deducted if you're not reimbursed for it.

- Cell phone deductions might apply if you're self-employed and have a phone you use exclusively for work. Or you can deduct the percentage of your phone bill for which your personal phone is used for business. The IRS looks at these types of deductions, so you might want to get an itemized phone bill to measure your business and personal use and be able to prove your deduction. An employee who uses their personal cell phone for their job can deduct the job-related portion if their employer doesn't reimburse them.

- If you have to pay for work uniforms or other clothing not considered "ordinary," you may be able to deduct those costs on your tax return.

Deductions can be tricky, so be sure you qualify before you claim them on your tax return. Every tax benefit comes with a list of requirements, which can be complex. Ensure you understand the qualifications and limitations before claiming a credit or deduction. Ask your tax preparer or accountant if you have questions concerning deductions.

The Best Ways to Prepare and File Your Tax Returns

Whether you prepare your taxes yourself or hire someone to do it for you is entirely up to you. If your tax situation is relatively simple, like if you have no dependents and just one source of income, completing your tax return will be fairly easy and probably something you can do yourself. Just fill out the basic information and copy the numbers on your W-2 to your tax return.

You can use free tax-preparation software available through the IRS that allows you to file your taxes for free at any of the partner tax sites like OnLine Taxes (olt.com) or 1040NOW (1040now.net). The software is very user-friendly and helps you avoid mistakes. You can access it at irs.gov/filing/free-file-do-your-federal-taxes-for-free.

Other tax software programs recommended by online personal finance magazine *Money* include these, ranked as its top 10:

1. TurboTax (turbotax.intuit.com)

2. H&R Block (hrblock.com)

3. TaxAct (taxact.com)

4. Jackson Hewitt (jacksonhewitt.com)

5. TaxSlayer (taxslayer.com)

6. E-file.com (e-file.com)

7. FreeTaxUSA (freetaxusa.com)

8. Cash App Tax (cash.app/taxes)

9. Drake Tax (drakesoftware.com/products/drake-tax)

10. 1040.com (1040.com)

If your tax situation is complicated, however, there's a case to be made for hiring a professional to prepare your return for you. If you're self-employed; have unemployment income, childcare expenses, or capital gains; or have experienced a life change in the past year that could affect your tax status, it may be a good idea to get some help.

Remember that in addition to knowing the tax laws, a professional will be able to identify credits and deductions that you don't know about.

If you're planning to hire a tax preparer, be sure to ask for their preparer tax identification number because the IRS requires anyone who is paid to prepare or help with preparing tax returns to have one. Check to be sure the preparer's ID number is on your return; that's also required.

You can find a list of qualified tax preparers in your area on the IRS's directory of preparers at irs.treasury.gov/rpo/rpo.jsf. It only includes those who have ID numbers and IRS-recognized credentials.

Chapter Summary

Taxes are a big topic and can seem overwhelming, but when you understand what taxes you're responsible for and how much you'll need to pay, you can start to look for ways to reduce your tax burden and make your taxes more manageable. Learn about any tax credits or deductions you can take advantage of, and think about how to minimize the amount of taxes you'll need to pay by maximizing your contributions to tax-advantaged accounts. Taxes are a part of life to be sure, but there's no reason to pay more than what you have to.

Chapter 15

Estate Planning

If you're thinking that estate planning is a strange topic to cover in a book written for millennials, we understand your confusion. However, estate planning is for anyone who has any assets. And an estate plan includes a will, which should specify who will care for children in the event that their parents die before they are grown—a compelling argument in its own right.

In this chapter, we unpack estate planning and explain why it's so important to people of any age who want to prepare for future eventualities.

Let's start by reviewing what estate planning entails.

What Is Estate Planning, and How Does It Apply to You?

An estate plan is a set of legal documents and instructions outlining what should happen to your assets when you die and specifying who will make decisions for you if you're unable to do so. It also stipulates your end-of-life preferences and may establish a trust, which is a method of transferring assets to beneficiaries by placing them in the hands of a third person called a trustee. (You'll read more about trusts later in this chapter.)

Having an estate plan in place benefits your loved ones by taking a lot of the decision-making off their shoulders. No one wants to have to make difficult decisions about how someone should be cared for, or how to distribute their property after they've died. An estate plan lessens the chance of disagreement among family members resulting from lack of clear instruction. It also can avoid possible complications if you've had more than one spouse, there's a blended family, or there are other extenuating circumstances. It also lays out instructions for end-of-life care and what you want to happen to your body after you've died.

Dividing up your possessions and end-of-life care are not subjects many people like to think about. Chances are, however, that you know of someone about your age who was killed in an accident or died from cancer. Life is uncertain, and being prepared for future events is better than being unprepared.

You can do estate planning on your own; many planning documents and guides are available to help you. If there's anything you don't understand or if your estate is complicated for some reason, we recommend that you work with a lawyer or financial planner with experience in estate planning.

Common Estate Planning Documents

A complete estate plan would include the following:

- Will
- Trusts, if applicable

- Durable power of attorney (for financial decisions)
- Living will
- Medical power of attorney (for health-care decisions)
- Directions for the disposition of your remains
- HIPAA forms (These give permission for certain people to be notified regarding your medical condition.)

Let's start by looking at what a will should contain and how you go about making one.

Last Will and Testament

Everyone should have a last will and testament, which is a legal document that states how your property should be distributed and who the beneficiaries will be; who will care for your children, if they are minors; and sometimes, how beneficiaries should handle the assets they receive.

If we learned anything from the COVID-19 pandemic, it's that life is uncertain and things can happen quickly. And yet, according to Caring.com, a senior living referral service, only about 33 percent of Americans have planned for what should happen in the event of their disability or death. Here's why, according to those who responded to Caring.com's survey, conducted in December 2021:

- 40 percent of those surveyed said they just haven't gotten around to planning.
- 33 percent said they don't have a will because they don't have anything of value to pass on to their loved ones.
- 14 percent who responded said estate planning and having a will written costs too much money.
- 13 percent of respondents said they don't know where to get a will or how to construct one.

Your will is a personal document with room for personalization. You can identify who should get big possessions, like your SUV or the beach house, but also address small items that are meaningful to you, like a guitar, a special photograph, or a locket that belonged to your grandmother. Those wishes can be included in the will or put into a separate document called a letter of instruction, an added piece that can contain whatever you want, such as details about the history of the locket you're leaving for your sister.

A letter of instruction often also addresses issues such as the following:

- Special instructions for a funeral or memorial service
- Detailed lists of possessions to be passed along to specific people
- Locations of all important documents and items
- Lists of all insurance policies, bank accounts, stocks, access numbers, and so forth
- Personal messages to family members and friends

In addition to designating who should receive your assets, your will can name guardians for your minor children, as well as a property manager for any property you've left to your children. If you leave property to minor children, an adult needs to manage it until the children are of age to do so themselves. This is a simplified sort of trust, which was mentioned earlier.

Some people specify what type of care they want for children, especially if a child is disabled or mentally incapacitated. Some people also provide instructions for the care of pets in their wills. If you own your own business, plans for it can be included in your will.

Recently, people have begun creating separate documents called cyberwills, or digital wills, which name a person or persons to access and manage digital assets like online accounts such as banking or investment accounts, social media accounts, and other web content. This type of document usually contains all of a person's passwords or other accesses to online accounts.

A will also should designate an executor, a trusted person who will ensure the wishes of the deceased person are carried out and be responsible for seeing that any owed taxes or outstanding bills are paid. Other duties of an executor may include closing bank accounts, notifying creditors, setting up checking accounts for paying bills, informing beneficiaries and distributing bequests, and filing final income tax returns. Serving as the executor of a will can be time-consuming, so be sure you choose someone who is willing and able to put in the necessary time and effort to ensure it's done properly.

There are different types of wills, but the most common is an attested written will, which is typed and printed; signed by the testator, who is the person making the will; and also signed by two witnesses. Those signatures make the will legally binding, and the act of signing and making the will legally binding is known as executing the will.

After your will has been drafted and executed, you should keep the original copy with your lawyer or financial adviser. It's not advisable to keep the original copy of your will in a safe-deposit box because family members may not be able to access the box without a court order. A safe or fireproof, waterproof box in your home is a better option, as long as someone else knows where it is and has access to it.

Why is it so important to have a will? If you die without one, or without one that's legally recognized by your state, you are said to be intestate, and the court can make decisions on your behalf. That means the court can decide who should inherit your property and, worse yet, if your children are minors, who will become their guardians.

The court of the state where you live would decide who gets any assets you leave behind. A court-appointed administrator would by law gather all the property, pay off any debts, and distribute the remaining assets to beneficiaries who are determined by the court. In most cases, assets would go to a surviving spouse and/or children, but that isn't guaranteed. Any property owned jointly by two spouses would go to the remaining spouse, but anything that is not joint property could be assigned to anyone, as determined by the court.

As for your children, a judge normally would choose a close relative to take parental control or, in the absence of any living relatives, a close friend.

But there's no guarantee to that, and sometimes the state would assume responsibility for children if no family members are willing or able to step in as guardian. If that occurs, children could end up in a group home or foster care with people they don't know—hardly an ideal scenario.

Requirements regarding wills vary from state to state, so be sure to do some research to find out what your particular state requires. Some states allow handwritten wills, for instance, while others don't recognize them as legal documents.

We don't recommend it, but you can make your own will. There are reputable online programs such as Trust & Will (trustandwill.com), LegalZoom (legalzoom.com), or Quicken WillMaker (willmaker.com) with which you can create wills and other estate planning documents. These services ask a series of questions and use your answers to generate a state-specific form that you can download and print. As long as the information you provide is correct and your will is executed according to the laws of your state, an online will should be legally acceptable.

Some services allow you to schedule a call with a lawyer for an additional cost. That person will review the will with you and can assure you that everything has been done correctly. We would encourage you to have an attorney review an online will if you choose to go that route.

Otherwise, an attorney or, in some but not all states, a financial adviser can draft and execute a will for you. Some states allow only an individual to draft their own will or have an attorney do it for them. It will cost more to have an attorney draw up a will than to make your own, but if you can afford to do so, we think the extra cost is well worthwhile.

It might seem like you don't need a will at this point in your life, but if you want the peace of mind of knowing what will happen to your possessions in the event of your death, it's time to think about getting one. This is, again, especially true if you have small children or your own business.

Trusts

Trusts are less common than wills, but they can be valuable tools in estate planning. A trust is an agreement under which a person or organization, called the trustee, temporarily holds property for the benefit of one or more beneficiaries.

The person who creates the trust and transfers property into it is called the grantor. Someone can create a trust and serve as both grantor and trustee, with someone else designated to take over the trust when the grantor dies.

Property can be placed into a trust while the grantor is living or after they die. If property is transferred into the trust while the grantor is living, it's called a living trust. If property is transferred to the trust after the death of the grantor, it's called a testamentary trust. The grantor would have to have prepared instructions for the property to be transferred after their death in a special type of will.

Another distinction in types of trusts is that of a revocable trust or an irrevocable trust. A revocable trust can be changed by a living grantor whenever they see fit to do so. An irrevocable trust, on the other hand, cannot be changed after it's been put into place.

Trusts can be important tools in estate planning because they may have tax advantages and in some cases can save time and money. They can be complicated, however, so if you're considering establishing a trust, please find an expert to help you do so.

Powers of Attorney

A power of attorney is a legal document that authorizes an individual to act on your behalf if you are unable to do so. Power of attorney also refers to the person designated to act on your behalf. The person who appoints someone to act on their behalf is called the principal, and the person designated is called the agent.

You should have powers of attorney for two purposes: to make medical decisions on your behalf if you are unable to do so and to make financial decisions on your behalf if you cannot. The legal document authorizing it and the agent who makes medical decisions for you is called a medical power of attorney. The authorizing document and agent who makes financial decisions is called a durable power of attorney.

Many people designate the same person, often a spouse or an adult child, to fill the roles of both medical and durable powers of attorney. A separate document would probably be prepared for each role. If you don't have a medical power of attorney, a family member is normally called upon to make medical decisions for you—a task that can be very difficult emotionally. If you don't have a durable power of attorney, tasks such as filing taxes and writing checks may go undone, which could work against the financial interests of your family or business.

Like having a will, appointing one or more powers of attorney can assure that your wishes will be carried out. Think carefully about who you'd like to have make decisions on your behalf. Your agents should have the ability to navigate the financial and/or medical fields and have a personality that's assertive enough to assure that they'll advocate for your wishes.

Finally, don't wait to create a power of attorney. If you become incapacitated, it's too late to get one. And no one else can designate a power of attorney on your behalf; you have to do it yourself.

Living Will and Disposition of Remains

A living will, also called a health-care declaration, is a document that states your wishes regarding your health care to your agent, who communicates them to your health-care providers. There are many treatments available for prolonging life, and probably an equal amount of controversy regarding the value of such treatments.

Talking about and making decisions regarding end-of-life care is not easy, but if you want to have control about the type of care and treatments you'll get, it's necessary not only to talk about it, but also to get it in writing in a living will.

Some things to consider when drafting your living will include the following:

- How do you feel about certain medical procedures such as tube feeding, mechanical ventilation, resuscitation, and dialysis?
- What are your thoughts regarding palliative care and hospice care?
- Do you think you'd prefer to be in a medical facility or at home at the end of life?
- Do you wish for your organs to be donated, if applicable?
- What are your wishes for the disposition of your body? Do you wish to be cremated or buried? (Green burials, which are more environmentally friendly than traditional ones, are becoming increasingly popular. Or perhaps you'd wish for your body to be donated for medical research.)

Do some research so you're knowledgeable regarding these matters and then get them in writing. Having your wishes in writing can be a gift to your loved ones, who wouldn't have to guess about what you might want or not want regarding your care.

HIPAA Release Form

A HIPAA release form is an important piece of your estate planning, but one that is often overlooked. This form enables you to choose family members or others with whom your health-care providers can share protected health information.

If you're not sure who you've authorized to receive this information, you should check. You can ask someone in your health-care provider's officer to look up who you've authorized, or you may be able to authorize the HIPAA release form you signed on your health system's online portal.

Also, if you have a child who is older than 18, ask them to be sure you are designated as someone who can get that information. If your adult child is a college student or living away from home for another reason and is injured in an accident, you won't be able to get information about their condition if your name is not on the release form.

Choosing Beneficiaries

If you have accounts like a traditional or a Roth IRA, annuities, transfer-upon-death registrations, or life insurance policies, you've probably appointed one or more beneficiaries to get their contents after you've died. It's important to understand that those beneficiary designations supersede anything written in a will. Even if you've written in your will that your spouse should receive the assets of all your accounts, if someone else's name is listed as the beneficiary on an account, the assets go to the person listed on the account, not the one named in your will.

If you're not sure who the beneficiaries listed on your accounts are, by all means check by calling the bank, brokerage, or insurance company or checking your account details on the organization's website.

It's not too uncommon for a marriage to split up and the beneficiary on an account to remain the former spouse. That can come as a rude awakening if a spouse dies and the second spouse discovers they are not the beneficiary of the assets.

The Importance of Updating Your Estate Planning Documents

Life circumstances change, and your estate plan should change along with it. Documents contained within an estate plan are prone to revision, so you'll want to keep an eye on them and update them periodically.

Perhaps your wishes concerning end-of-life care have changed due to witnessing a friend or relative getting care you would not want. If so, you'd need to update your living will.

If you move to a different state, it's likely that you'll need to update your will. The state where you die is the state that will administer your will, not the state where the will was written. As you read earlier, laws regarding wills vary from state to state. The last thing you'd want is for your family members to find out your will was not legally valid because you failed to update it when you moved.

Marital changes are a very common reason why people change their wills. If you were recently married or divorced, your will should be addressed. It varies by state, but some states require that you must prepare a new will after marrying, even if you already have one.

Also, if someone listed as a beneficiary has passed away, your will should be revised to reflect those changes.

If your assets increase or decrease dramatically after the time you wrote your will, you should amend it to reflect the current value of your assets. Not doing so could make things more complicated for your executor.

If you have another child or grandchild, you'll probably want to ensure they're included in the will. Also, your choice of beneficiaries can change as your children grow.

Legislation regarding state and federal tax laws changes frequently and can affect your assets and overall wealth as well as how you handle that wealth. For example, federal law limits the amount of money a person can give away to family and friends during their lifetime without paying taxes on the money. The limit was raised in 2017 to $11.58 million, but that amount is expected to decrease dramatically when the Tax Cuts and Jobs Act of 2017—the legislation that enabled the amount to be raised—expires in 2025. If that occurs, someone with a large estate may need to find another way to reduce their wealth (and taxes).

Many people leave money to one or more charities in their wills, but allegiances to charities can change over time. A different charity than one you've named in your will could become more important due to a particular event. A change of thinking regarding charities could be another reason to revise your will.

Some of these reasons would apply to trusts, too. Powers of attorney may need to be changed if one of your agents would die, become unable to carry out their duties, or for some reason no longer agree to be your agent. You might want to add someone to your HIPAA release form or remove a name. Just keep in mind that an estate plan is not static and may need to change as you and your circumstances change.

Chapter Summary

Getting an estate plan together can seem like a daunting task, but it's not all that complicated once you understand what it should include. Consult professionals if there are issues you don't understand, or if your financial and/or health situation is complicated. If you decide to draft your own documents, we'll reiterate that it's a good idea to have an attorney have a look at them to assure everything is in order.

Chapter 16

Planning for Retirement

Millennials who start thinking about retirement while they're still millennials are off to a great start. As you read in Chapter 4, letting your money work for you over time is a key element of investing. And as you learned in Chapter 11, getting retirement accounts set up and taking advantage of employer matches gives you a good head start on investing. If you're already saving for your retirement, or if you're even thinking about how to accomplish your financial goals while still putting away some money for retirement, you're definitely on the right track.

Understanding that saving for retirement probably seems like a daunting task at your age, we're telling you that with some discipline and a solid budget plan, you can do it. Keep your main budget categories of spending and saving in mind, remembering that spending includes the taxes you're required to pay. Live within your means, strive to get as much money as you can into some key accounts, and enjoy the feeling of being confident about your financial future.

Determining Your Retirement Timeline

Those of you in the younger cohort of millennials might still be settling into your careers, with *retirement* sounding like a foreign word right now. If you're one of the older millennials who has crossed into their 40s, however, retirement might be something you've started to think about. It's never too early to start planning for your retirement. Trust us—30 or 40 years goes by really quickly.

Retirement planning is simply the process of laying out some goals and figuring out what's needed to achieve them. You can think about what sources of income you might have when you retire, how much money you'll need, your savings goals before you retire, and how you can best manage your assets and risk.

Retirement planning can start at any time; we know people who are in their 60s and just now starting to think about their retirement strategies. The best scenario, however, is to begin planning early so when you reach retirement age, you'll be prepared for it and able to enjoy the type of retirement you envision.

When trying to determine your retirement timeline, consider the following:

- Your current age
- The age at which you'd like to retire
- Your annual household income
- The percentage of your income you're currently saving for retirement
- How much money you currently have in retirement savings
- Any expected income increases
- How much of the income you have now you anticipate you'll need when you retire
- How many years of retirement income you anticipate needing
- The annual rate of return you expect to earn on your retirement savings and investments prior to retiring
- The annual rate of return you expect to earn on your retirement savings and investments after retiring

You've probably noticed that a lot of the information you'll need to compile requires some guesswork. No one knows how long they'll live or how the stock market will perform during the next 20 or 30 years. But making educated guesses will give you a good idea of how much money you'll need and how much you should be striving to save now. You can look at historical returns and calculations to make your best guesses about how well your investments might perform, how long you'll need those investments for income, and how your needs will change when you retire.

Most retirement planners advise that you plan for retirement income of at least 80 percent of your preretirement income because you're going to stop working, not stop living. How much money you'll need when you retire depends on factors like whether you'll need to pay for health insurance, a cost that has grown recently at 6 percent per year; if you plan to downsize to a smaller home or apartment; how much you plan to travel; and so on. Expenses to consider include the following:

- Housing
- Utilities
- Health care
- Transportation
- Food
- Entertainment
- Charitable contributions
- Travel

Basically, you'll need to make a retirement budget. Keep in mind that some expenses, such as health care, tend to increase as you age, while others, like clothing and transportation, tend to decrease.

After you've calculated expenses, consider anticipated sources of income, which you'll read more about later in this chapter. Getting an idea of how much you'll need and how much you'll have can be a guide as you get closer to retirement.

It can be fun to use a retirement calculator that lets you view your goals and gives you an idea of how you're doing with your savings at this point. Forbes, a media company that focuses on business and financial news, recommends the following retirement calculators. All are free to use.

Empower's Retirement Planner (empower.com/personal-investors/retirement-planner) is a new feature of Empower's free financial dashboard and comes highly recommended for its ease of use and ability to provide thousands of investment scenarios automatically.

Fidelity's myPlan Snapshot (fidelity.com/planning/retirement/content/myPlan /index.shtml) lets you enter some basic information like age, income, and savings and then generates a graphical picture of your projected assets.

The Flexible Retirement Planner (flexibleretirementplanner.com) allows you to input a lot of very detailed information to give you a graph of how much your retirement fund is likely to be worth when you need it and how financially secure you're likely to be when you stop working.

The Ultimate Retirement Calculator (nesteggly.com/retirement-calculator) lets you figure in money you'd like to have left in your estate for your heirs when you die and also include one-time benefits you expect to receive, like an inheritance of income from the sale of a business.

Vanguard's Retirement Nest Egg Calculator (vanguard.com/nesteggcalculator) is an easy-to-use tool designed to inform whether the money in your nest egg will be enough to last throughout your retirement. You only input four pieces of information: how many years your savings must last, your current amount of savings, your annual spending, and how your assets are allocated. The calculator will tell you the likely odds of how much your portfolio will generate per year and for how many years with a certain percentage of your assets invested in stocks.

Trying out one or more of these calculators can help give you an idea of where you stand. If you find you're in good shape and on target, carry on! If you find you're behind in savings, think about how you can either earn and save more or reduce your spending to save more. Calculating your progress annually can help keep you on task.

Accelerating Your Retirement Timeline

Most people plan for achieving financial independence between the ages of 60 and 70. "Achieving financial independence" simply means saving enough money to support your lifestyle for the rest of your life without you having to continue to work to contribute to those savings. Three-quarters of Americans work until they're at least 60, with more than half retiring between the ages of 61 and 65.

A growing number of people, however, are eschewing the notion of working for most of their lives and instead are seeking to achieve financial independence at a much earlier age. There's an organized movement of these like-minded people known as Financial Independence, Retire Early (FIRE). They make a conscious effort to spend as little money as possible when they're young in order to be able to save enough to retire when they're in their 30s, 40s, or 50s instead of their 60s or 70s. We're not advocating that you join the FIRE movement, but it's an interesting concept if you want to read more about it.

The degree of participation in the FIRE movement varies. Some people save as much as 85 percent of their incomes, which, as you can imagine, requires them to live extremely frugally. Others strive to live reasonably well while still saving 25 or 30 percent of their incomes—far more than the average investor, who saves less than 10 percent of their income for retirement, according to the US Bureau of Labor Statistics.

Not everyone can participate in the FIRE lifestyle, of course, because there are many people who already work hard and barely have enough money to meet their monthly bills, leaving little to nothing to help increase their savings. Many people, however, can rethink their spending and intentionally increase their savings to speed up their retirement timeline.

The FIRE movement got its start about 30 years ago when a book called *Your Money or Your Life: 9 Steps to Transforming Your Relationship with Money and Achieving Financial Independence*. Written by Vicki Robin and Joe Dominguez, the book was a best-seller, catching the attention of many readers.

Your Money or Your Life challenged readers to consider each of their expenses and figure out a time value for that expense. For instance, someone who earned

$40,000 a year—about $770 a week—and bought a new suit for $200 would need to work for about 10 hours to pay for the suit. Readers were asked to consider whether the suit was worth 10 hours of work when they could have been doing something else with their time, like spending it with family or friends.

In addition, the book asked readers to consider questions like these:

- Do you have enough money?
- Do you have as much time as you'd like to participate in meaningful activities?
- Do you spend enough time with family and friends?
- Do you have enough money saved to pay for normal living expenses for three to six months?
- Are you happy with what you've contributed to the world?
- Does your job reflect your values?
- Do you come home from your job feeling energized?
- Do you find your job to be rewarding and fun?

Those questions spurred interest in the idea of financial independence and early retirement, and the movement continued to grow.

Today, several popular blogs and websites are devoted to FIRE, including Mr. Money Mustache (mrmoneymustache.com), Chief Mom Officer (chiefmomofficer.org), Our Next Life (ournextlife.com), and Financial Samurai (financialsamurai.com).

The FIRE movement isn't for everyone, certainly, but everyone probably could take some lessons from it. Maybe you'll be inspired to check out some of the blogs mentioned and think a little harder before you buy the next thing that catches your eye.

Some people make a game of it by putting the money they would have spent on a new pair of shoes or the large latte into a designated account. When they've saved a certain amount in that account, they move it into a mutual fund or other investment and let the money begin compounding interest.

Social Security, Pensions, and Retirement Savings

Regardless of at what age you retire, you're going to need income. That means you'll need to either continue to earn money by taking a part-time job, having some real estate investment that generates income, or starting a small business to provide income. If you're not earning money, your option is to depend on Social Security, a pension, or your retirement savings.

Social Security

Lots of people depend on Social Security as a major source of income, and many more anticipate that Social Security will be a major source of income when they retire. Of all those depending on it or anticipating depending on it, however, a large percentage report worrying about the future of the program.

Social Security was enacted in 1935 when President Franklin D. Roosevelt signed the Social Security Act into law. It was in the middle of the Great Depression, and many people were desperate for money. The act said that workers would make payroll tax contributions during the course of their working lives and receive benefits when they retired at age 65. Workers started receiving those benefits in 1940 and have been ever since.

A problem for the Social Security system is that the average life expectancy has increased dramatically since 1935, when it was just 61 years. Part of that was due to infant mortality, which was quite high in the 1930s and significantly reduced overall life expectancy. Still, not nearly as many people lived into their 90s as they do today, meaning that the average amount of time that people collected Social Security was significantly shorter.

Social Security benefits amount to more than $1 trillion a year, worrying some economists who think the system is unsustainable as America's population ages and people live longer than they used to. Also, the number of workers contributing to Social Security is decreasing due to a declining birthrate since the post–World War II baby boom. In 2020, there were 2.8 workers for each Social Security beneficiary. In 2035, there will be only 2.3 workers for every beneficiary.

It's projected that without reform, the Social Security trust fund will run out of money by 2034, just short of 100 years since the program was started. That doesn't mean benefits would disappear, but they very likely would have to be reduced.

We hate to be the bearers of bad news, but we think you should understand the problem of relying too heavily on Social Security for retirement.

Pensions

Pensions used to be a common source of retirement income for workers in a wide range of businesses and industries. If you retired from a factory, chances are you'd get a nice pension. If you retired from a banking firm, you'd probably get a pension as well. That pension, along with Social Security benefits, provided a stable financial situation for many retirees.

A pension, formally called a defined benefit pension plan, is a benefit that provides retired workers with income throughout their lifetimes. Companies started moving away from pensions for a variety of reasons, including, of course, cost. The US Department of Labor's Employee Benefits Security Administration reports that the number of pension plans offering guaranteed benefits decreased by 73 percent between 1986 and 2016. Much of that decrease can be attributed to the number of 401(k) plans now available for workers. It costs a lot less for employers to match a percentage of workers' contributions than to set up pension funds that pay retired employees for the rest of their lives.

Public employees are more likely to still get a pension than those who work in the private sector. The Pension Rights Center, an organization that works to ensure American workers will have enough money for retirement, reported that three quarters of all state and local government workers participate in a pension plan, and more are eligible but don't participate.

If you have a pension, consider yourself lucky. An advantage is that you'll know how much you'll get in retirement, which makes it easier to plan. Unlike 401(k)s or IRAs, pensions are usually managed by the company or government agency that offers them and invested in a manner that can keep the plan funded. You should get a notice every year informing you how well funded the plan is. Hopefully, your plan is fully funded, which means it has enough assets to fund its present and future obligations. If you find out your plan is underfunded, that means it doesn't have enough money to fund its obligations. If it's an unfunded plan, it's using company income to make pension payments as it becomes necessary to do so.

If you are eligible for a pension when you retire, you'll need to decide whether to receive a monthly payment or take your pension as a lump sum. Most people take the monthly payment because it provides steady income in retirement. Some pensions include cost-of-living adjustments. If yours does not, you'll need to consider how inflation is cutting into your payments.

If you decide on a lump-sum payment, you'll need to decide what to do with the money. If you have plenty of other resources, you could spend it on a trip or vacation. You could use it to purchase an investment property that you could rent; put the money in an IRA; or create your own pension by buying an annuity, which is a financial product that provides an income stream during a specified period of time.

We would suggest that if you have a pension plan where you work, continue to check on the health of the plan and start to think about whether you'd prefer a monthly payment or a lump sum. As you get closer to retirement, we'd suggest you consult with a financial adviser regarding the best use of your pension money.

Your Retirement Savings

Hopefully, when you're ready to retire you'll have a healthy portfolio of retirement accounts and other investments that will allow you to maintain a comfortable lifestyle for the duration of your retirement. That's the whole point, after all, of planning and saving and thinking ahead.

If you have a 401(k) or a traditional IRA, you'll need to start taking required minimum distributions when you turn 73. That requirement will change to 74 in 2034. Your required amount can be calculated by dividing your account's prior year-end balance by a life expectancy that the IRS designates. Check out the US Securities and Exchange Commission's website at Investor.gov for a required minimum distribution calculator. Remember that your withdrawals are included in taxable income.

If you have a Roth IRA, however, you've already paid the income tax on your contributions. And if you're over age 59½, any increase in value over what you've contributed to the fund won't be taxed when you withdraw it either. Roth IRA contributions can be withdrawn before you turn 59½ if you've had the fund for more than five years because the withdrawals are considered a return of your principal, which was already taxed.

You'll need to sell some investments if you want to withdraw money from a brokerage account, so you'll want to watch the value of any stocks, bonds, mutual funds, exchange-traded funds, or other investments you have, always selling when the values are up. An adviser can help you choose what to sell at the best times and assist you with the sale. It can take a few days for a trade to settle, so you might not see the money in your account right away.

You'll want to look for ways to minimize tax consequences when withdrawing money from retirement and brokerage accounts. If you sell securities at a gain, you'll likely be subject to capital gains taxes.

What About Health Insurance?

Most retirees take advantage of Medicare, the national health insurance program that becomes available when you turn 65. Medicare doesn't cover all health care costs, however, so you'll need to have a supplemental plan to cover things like dental, vision, prescription drugs, and the 20 percent of costs that Medicare does not cover.

We have no idea what Medicare will look like in 20 or 30 years, so we won't spend much time on it here. A bigger concern for you now is considering what you would do if you find yourself having to buy health insurance for yourself or for yourself and your dependents.

You read a little bit about health savings accounts (HSAs) in Chapter 14, but we'll say again that they are a good option and can be particularly valuable in retirement because the money in an HSA can cover expenses that Medicare does not.

If you retire or lose your employer-provided health care before you are eligible for Medicare, you'll need to find your own health-care insurance, which can be quite expensive. If your spouse is working, you might be able to get insurance through their plan, although employers are not required to offer family or spousal insurance. If you lose your job, ask about getting insurance through the Consolidated Omnibus Budget Reconciliation Act, or COBRA.

COBRA requires employers to continue the same health-care coverage an employee had before retiring or leaving a job, either voluntarily or involuntarily, except if job loss was due to gross misconduct. The difference is that you'll have to pay for the insurance. If you're going to be without health insurance, COBRA could provide a short-term solution, so keep it in mind as an option.

You can get a private health-care plan through any company that sells health insurance, but before you do that, as suggested in Chapter 10, look into the Health Insurance Marketplace (healthcare.gov).

It's important to understand that health-care costs normally increase with age and to plan for additional expenses. Although it varies according to location, age, and overall health, a study showed that the average monthly cost of health care for a retired couple is $1,185.

The following table offers some predictions for future annual health-care costs for a retired couple, according to Health View Services, a provider of health-care cost-projection software.

Projected Annual Health-Care Costs for Couples

Age of Couple	Year	Average Annual Cost
70	2024	$16,155
75	2029	$21,164
80	2034	$27,060
85	2039	$34,268

Obviously, those are big chunks of money. Something to consider to help combat those costs is long-term-care insurance, which is insurance designed to pay for long-term-care services in a nursing home or an assisted living facility or for at-home services. This insurance can be expensive, but the cost of long-term care can be prohibitive. Many people have seen their savings wiped out by nursing home costs.

It's recommended that you purchase long-term-care insurance when you're in your mid-50s to mid-60s because costs are lower at that age and you're less likely to be declined for coverage.

The key to being able to afford the health coverage you'll need in retirement is to start planning for it now.

Inflation and Your Retirement Savings

Many people probably weren't thinking much about inflation before it soared to nearly 9 percent in 2022 and became a topic of conversation just about everywhere. The thing about inflation, or the rate at which prices for goods and services increase, is that when you're living on a fixed income, like you will be during your retirement, it causes you to lose buying power.

The average rate of inflation is about 3 percent annually. If you have a fixed income, it becomes worth less each year due to inflation.

Social Security, and some pensions, offer cost-of-living adjustments (COLAs), but they're not always enough to keep up with inflation. Social Security COLA rates vary dramatically and are not guaranteed. They typically are about what the inflation rate is for the year, but not always.

We know it's disheartening to think about, but you really need to consider inflation when deciding where you invest your money and understand that the total amount of money you save won't be worth as much when you retire as it is today.

Working After You Retire

Nearly a third of all people between ages 65 and 69 have jobs, according to the Federal Reserve Bank of Minneapolis. That's more than the number of teenagers who work.

Some people who are of retirement age continue to work because they don't have adequate savings. Others get part-time jobs for something to do or because they enjoy working and being with other people. The number of older workers is expected to rise during the next decade.

Research has shown that working past the traditional retirement age helps keep you mentally sharp, as is the case with Wilmar Jensen, a 95-year-old practicing attorney in Modesto, California. Jensen passed the California bar and started practicing law in 1953, the same year Dwight D. Eisenhower became president. Although he could retire, Jensen said he enjoys working and wants to continue for as long as he's able.

Many older people are perfectly capable of working and have expertise they're eager to share. Increased ability to work from home or on a flexible schedule has attracted many older people back to work.

If you decide to continue working after your retirement age, we hope it will be something you enjoy and that provides some fulfillment. Some popular jobs for people 65 and older include consultant, writer and subject matter expert, teacher, on-demand or delivery driver, customer service representative, retail salesperson, event usher or attendant, tutor, personal care aide, childcare worker, or temporary office worker.

Something important to keep in mind about working after retirement, however, is your Social Security benefits. You can work while receiving benefits, but there's a limit to how much you can earn before those benefits will be reduced if you have not yet reached your full retirement age.

Your full retirement age is when you can qualify to collect 100 percent of your Social Security benefits based on your earnings history. For anyone born in 1960 or later, the full retirement age for benefits is 67.

In 2023, the annual earning limit for those receiving Social Security benefits and not of their full retirement age was $21,240. If you were getting benefits and earned more than that, the Social Security Administration would deduct $1 from your benefits payment for every $2 you earned above the limit. After you hit your full retirement age, there's no limit on how much you can earn and still receive your benefits.

Some retired people start their own businesses, capitalizing on their skills or interests. Glenda, for instance, loves making pottery in her home studio. When she retired from the accounting firm where she worked, she started her own business making and selling pottery at craft shows and artisan events. Nancy makes jewelry in her basement studio and sells it in various gift shops in her area.

Starting and running a small business that has low start-up and operating costs can generate extra income that you may need to live on or that you can use for activities you enjoy. It is not something you should do without considerable thought and planning, however, because it can involve financial risk.

If you're thinking of starting a business, choose one that has low start-up costs to avoid going into debt. A home-based business generally has lower start-up and operating costs than if you need to rent space somewhere. Start small and make your start-up something that takes advantage of your skills, experience, and the contacts you've made during the years.

Be careful if you're tempted to help finance someone else's start-up though. Some people bet their retirement accounts on a successful business venture, but if the enterprise you're helping fund fails, your financial stability could be jeopardized.

What you choose to do after you retire is up to you. You can greatly increase your choices and opportunities, however, by starting to plan for your retirement earlier rather than later. Start planning now to get an idea of how much you'll need when you retire and whether your savings are on track for getting you there. If they're not, now's the time to make some adjustments to get you on the path to a successful, comfortable retirement.

Chapter Summary

Think about what you'd like your retirement to look like. Do you envision moving to a smaller home, or perhaps selling your home and renting an apartment? Would you like to continue working in some capacity, perhaps even starting a small business? What will your health insurance situation look like? It's impossible to see into the future, of course, but envisioning a path to get you there is the first step.

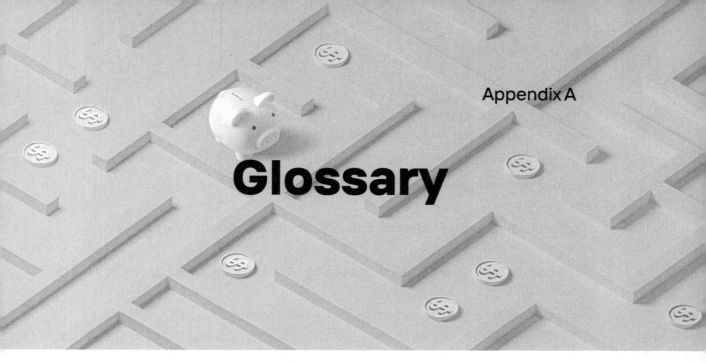

Glossary

401(k) plan   A plan that gives employees a chance to save part of their salaries in a tax-advantaged manner.

403(b) plan   A type of retirement account that's similar to a 401(k); often used by nonprofit organizations.

529 college savings plan   A tax-advantaged savings plan designed to encourage saving for future education costs.

actual cash value   The amount your insurance policy will pay to replace your property, minus depreciation.

adjustable-rate mortgage (ARM)   A mortgage that has an interest rate that can fluctuate.

after-tax contributions   Account contributions from which income taxes have already been deducted.

agent   A person designated to serve as power of attorney for another person.

aggressive investor   An investor who has a high risk tolerance and is willing to risk losing money in exchange for potentially better results.

American Opportunity Tax Credit   A tax credit for education expenses that occur within the first four years of postsecondary education.

annual percentage rate (APR)   The yearly interest rate charged for a loan.

annual percentage yield (APY)   The real rate of return earned on an investment.

annuity   A financial product that provides an income stream during a specified period of time.

arbitration   The hearing and determination of a dispute between parties by a third party.

attested written will   A will that is typed and printed and signed by the person making the will.

average daily balance   The balance of a credit card at the end of each day divided by the number of days in the billing cycle.

balance-transfer credit card   A type of credit card that enables you to transfer debt from one or more cards to the balance-transfer card, which carries a lower interest rate than the previous cards.

bear market   A down stock market. *Bear* refers to a bear's practice of hibernating.

blue-chip stock   Stock of well-established companies that have high market value and successful track records of generating profits.

bodily injury liability coverage   Insurance that protects you against lawsuits in the event that someone is injured in an accident you've caused.

bond   A debt instrument. The issuer promises to pay the investor a specified amount of interest for a period of time and repay the principal at maturity.

bond issuer   The entity that issues a bond.

bull market   An up stock market where prices are rising and expected to continue to rise, like a bull charging forward with its horns upward.

capital gains   Profits realized from the sale of an asset such as a home, car, business, stock, cryptocurrency, or bonds.

cash neutral   An investment strategy involving the sale and purchase of securities within a portfolio that results in zero net cash.

cash value insurance   A policy that combines a life insurance policy with a type of savings or investment account, allowing you to earn interest, or appreciation, on part of the money you pay into the plan.

certificate of deposit (CD)   A type of savings investment in which money is invested for a specified amount of time and the investor is guaranteed a certain amount of interest.

certified financial planner   Someone who has earned the Certified Financial Planning (CFP) credential, a national certification that requires planners to have a fiduciary relationship with their advisees.

collision coverage   Insurance that pays for damage to your car if you're in an accident, or pays to replace a car that's totaled.

common stock   A type of stock, sometimes called ordinary shares, that represents ownership in a company.

comprehensive coverage   Insurance that protects you from car theft or weird things that could happen to your car, such as a tree falling on it or it being damaged during a riot, fire, or flood.

conservative investor   An investor who has a low risk tolerance and looks for investments that aren't likely to jeopardize their capital.

consumer price index   A measure of inflation across the economy.

conventional mortgage   A mortgage loan that's not backed by a government agency and is not federally guaranteed.

credit freeze   A feature offered by the three major credit reporting agencies (Equifax, Experian, and TransUnion) that blocks access to your credit reports. This will protect you if someone attempts to access your credit reports and open fraudulent accounts because the lender or card issuer won't be able to access the information they need to approve opening the account.

credit history   The record of everything pertaining to any credit you've ever had or applied for, all summarized in your credit report.

credit score   A number that informs lenders of a potential borrower's creditworthiness.

credit utilization ratio   A measure of how much of your total available credit you are using at any given time.

cryptocurrency   A type of currency that can be used to buy goods and services online. Because it fluctuates in value, it also can be traded, much like stock.

custodial account   A type of account you control for your child until he or she is of legal age, which is 18, 19, or 21, according to your state's laws.

cyclical stock   Stock that is tied to the performance of the economy.

debt avalanche   A type of accelerated debt repayment plan in which you make the minimum required payments on each source of debt and then allocate any remaining funds to the debt with the highest interest rate.

debt consolidation   A process that combines multiple debts into a single payment.

debt consolidation loan   A loan a borrower takes in order to combine high-interest debts into a single payment.

debt snowball   A debt-reduction strategy in which you pay off debt in order of smallest to largest debt.

debt-to-income ratio   A comparison of how much you owe to how much money you earn.

defensive stock   Stock that tends to provide steady returns in most conditions, often offered by companies that offer essential products and services, like health care and utilities.

defined benefit plan   A retirement plan that guarantees a specific amount of retirement income, such as a pension.

defined contribution plan   A retirement plan that doesn't guarantee income but enables employees to invest money for retirement, often with some employer assistance, such as a 401(k).

diversification   A strategy of building a portfolio that contains different expected risks and returns.

divorce settlement agreement   A formal document that sets forth the terms of a divorce settlement.

down payment   A sum of money you pay up front when purchasing a home, car, or other high-price item.

durable power of attorney   A legal document authorizing an agent to make financial decisions for another person.

earned income tax credit   A tax credit that allows you to claim credits if you are a low- to moderate-income earner.

elimination period   The waiting period before you start to receive insurance benefits.

emergency fund   Money you save to see you through in case you get laid off from your job or face another financial emergency.

escrow account   An account specifically designated to collect and pay property taxes, home insurance, and, if required, mortgage insurance premiums.

ESG (environment, social, and governance) stock   Stock issued by companies that emphasize protecting the environment, working toward social justice, upholding ethical practices, and promoting other social causes.

estate plan   A set of legal documents and instructions outlining what should happen to your assets when you die and specifying who will make decisions for you if you're unable to do so.

exchange-traded fund (ETF)   A fund that operates much like a mutual fund, but unlike mutual funds, ETFs can be purchased or sold on a stock exchange.

excise tax   A tax imposed on certain goods or activities such as alcohol, tobacco, gasoline, and airline tickets.

executor   A person who oversees the will of a deceased person, ensuring their expressed wishes are carried out and taking responsibility to see that any owed taxes or outstanding bills are paid.

financial independence   Having enough money to support your lifestyle for the rest of your life without you working to contribute to those savings.

financial planner   Someone who designs financial plans of action for clients.

fixed-rate mortgage   A mortgage on which the interest rate remains constant during the life of the loan.

foreclosure   The legal process in which ownership of a house transfers from the homeowner to the mortgage lender.

grantor   The person who creates a trust and transfers property into it.

head of household filer   Tax filers who are single and maintain a home for a qualifying person, such as a child or relative.

health savings account (HSA)   A type of investment that enables you to save money for future health-care expenses.

high-deductible health insurance plan   An insurance plan that requires you to pay a certain amount for your care before your insurance company begins making payments.

identity theft   When someone obtains and uses your personal or financial information in some way without your permission.

income stock   Stock that provides regular income through higher-than-average dividends.

index fund   A type of mutual fund that invests in a specific list of securities, such as stock issued only by companies that are listed on the Nasdaq Composite index.

individual retirement account (IRA)   A tax-advantaged personal retirement savings plan.

inflation   The rate at which prices for goods and services increase.

installment loan   A closed-ended, or lump-sum loan, such as a mortgage, car loan, or student loan.

insurance premium   The amount of money you pay for insurance every month, semiannually, or annually.

interest income   Income you get from bank accounts, bonds, and money market accounts.

intestate   The state of dying without a will or without a will that is legally recognized by the state.

irrevocable trust   A trust that cannot be changed after it's been put into place.

judgment of divorce   A document that finalizes a divorce and ends proceedings.

last will and testament   A legal document that states how your property should be distributed and who the beneficiaries will be; who will care for your children, if they are minors; and sometimes, how beneficiaries should handle the assets they receive.

letter of instruction   A document added to your will that can contain whatever type of instruction or wishes you want.

level term life insurance   A type of term life insurance that enables you to pay the same premium for the life of the policy.

line of credit   A preset amount of money from a bank or other lender you can tap into as needed.

listing fees   Fees a company has to pay to be listed on a stock exchange.

living trust   A trust in which property is transferred while the grantor is living.

living will   A document that states your wishes regarding your health care.

long-term capital gains taxes   Taxes on assets that you've held for more than a year.

long-term-care insurance   Insurance designed to pay for long-term-care services in a nursing home or an assisted living facility or for at-home services.

long-term investment strategy   The act of keeping investments, including stocks, bonds, exchange-traded funds, and mutual funds, for longer than a year.

marginal tax rate   The amount of tax paid for every additional dollar of income.

market correction   A drop in the stock market that occurs as the result of inflated stock prices.

market index   An indicator of performance for a designated group of investments, such as the Standard & Poor's (S&P) 500 Index.

medical power of attorney   A legal document authorizing an agent to make medical decisions for another person.

Medicare   America's national health insurance program that becomes available when someone turns 65 years old.

moderate investor   An investor who has more tolerance for risk than a conservative investor but less than an aggressive investor.

money manager   A financial adviser who, after reviewing your parameters, risk tolerance, and total financial picture, agrees to handle your funds, make trades on your behalf, and buy and sell stocks and bonds for you.

money market account (MMA)   A type of savings account that generally pays slightly higher interest than regular savings accounts.

mortgage   A loan you get from a bank or other lender to purchase a home.

mortgage preapproval   A written verification from a lender that you qualify for the amount of money you've applied for.

mutual fund   A professionally managed portfolio of stocks, bonds, and other types of investments that pools the money of many investors.

noncyclical stock   Stock that tends to remain fairly constant in value regardless of what's happening with the economy.

paid time off (PTO) policy   An employer benefit that combines vacation, sick time, and personal time into a bank of time that employees can use as needed.

penny stock   Stock valued at less than $5 per share and considered to be speculative because trading is based largely on guesswork.

pension   An employer benefit that provides retired workers with income throughout their lifetimes.

points   Prepaid interest paid as a fee to a mortgage lender to cover the cost of applying for the loan.

portfolio   A collection of any and all of your financial investments.

preferred stock   A class of stock that gives shareholders different rights than those with common stock.

prenuptial agreement   A legal document that spells out how assets will be divided in the event a marriage fails.

principal   The initial amount of money borrowed for a loan, the amount paid for a bond, or the original sum committed to the purchase of assets before the accumulation of any interest or earnings. Principal also can refer to someone who appoints an agent to act as their power of attorney.

priority obligations   Certain types of debt, such as child or spousal support or federal student loans, that are not eliminated when you file for bankruptcy.

private mortgage insurance (PMI)   Insurance that protects the lender if you default on your mortgage.

privately held company   A company that is owned by those who founded it, by managers, or by a private group of investors.

property taxes   Taxes on property owned that are levied by the municipality and/or school district in which you live.

public company   A company that has given ownership to the public through shares of stock and makes financial information available to investors.

real estate investment trust (REIT)   An investment that pools funds from investors and uses the money to invest in real estate.

refinance a mortgage   To trade in one mortgage for a new one to take advantage of lower interest rates.

replacement cost   The amount your insurance policy will pay to replace the items at their current value, regardless of when you purchased them originally.

revocable trust   A trust that can be changed at any time by a living grantor.

revolving debt   Debt that's open-ended, such as a credit card.

risk capacity   How much risk you're able to manage without having it keep you up at night.

risk management   The process of identifying risks, analyzing those risks, and making your investment decisions based on either accepting or rejecting them.

risk tolerance   The amount of risk you're willing to accept when choosing investments.

robo-adviser   An online wealth management tool offering portfolio management advice that's based on algorithms and doesn't require a human financial planner.

Roth IRA   A variation on a traditional IRA. A Roth IRA offers tax-free growth and tax-free withdrawals in retirement.

secured debt   Debt that's backed by something of value, like a house or a vehicle.

SEP-IRA   A Simplified Employee Pension IRA, or type of IRA designed for people who are self-employed, own a business, or employ others.

shares outstanding   Stock that is held by company shareholders.

short-term capital gains taxes   Taxes on assets you've had for less than a year.

target-date fund   A mutual fund that holds several asset classes that can be reallocated as your circumstances change.

tax-deductible contribution   A contribution that reduces the amount of your current taxable income.

tax-deferred contributions   Money on which you'll pay no tax until you withdraw it from the account.

term   The length of time you hold a bond.

term life insurance   An insurance policy for which you pay an annual premium in exchange for a predetermined amount of money that will be paid to your beneficiaries if you die during the term you're insured.

testamentary trust   Property transferred to a trust after the death of the grantor.

testator   The person making a will.

Treasury bill   A short-term government security that's purchased at a lower price than the redemption value.

Treasury bond   A long-term government debt security with a maturity of 20 or 30 years.

Treasury note   A short- or intermediate-term debt security with a maturity of two, three, five, seven, or ten years. Treasury notes pay a fixed rate of interest every six months.

trustee   A person or organization that temporarily holds property for one or more beneficiaries.

umbrella policy   A policy that provides coverage that's greater than your standard limits.

uninsured or underinsured motorist coverage   Insurance that covers your medical expenses and lost wages if you're injured by an uninsured or underinsured motorist.

unsecured debt   Debt, such as credit cards and medical bills, that does not require collateral.

value stock   A stock that trades at relatively low prices compared to the company's earnings and long-term potential for growth.

vesting   The length of time you're required to work for a company before you're entitled to the funds your employer has put into a retirement account on your behalf.

Resources

In addition to this book, other resources are available to help you keep track of and stay on top of your personal finances. This collection of books, websites, apps, and podcasts can help you find the resources you need.

Books

This list of additional reading includes some books specifically geared toward millennials, while others seek a wider audience. It also includes some books that have stood the test of time and are considered classic guides for those wanting to learn more about personal finances.

Beating the Street
Peter Lynch
(New York: Simon & Schuster, 1994)
Written by investing legend Peter Lynch, this book is written in layman's terms and contains timeless information for investing wisely and making the most of your finances. Lynch is best known as the former manager of Fidelity's Magellan Fund, a mutual fund that between 1977 and 1990 averaged more than a 29 percent return.

Financial Freedom: A Proven Path to All the Money You Will Ever Need
Grant Sabatier
(New York: Avery Publishing, 2019)
This book teaches about saving aggressively when you're young with the goal of retiring early and contains innovative ideas for traveling on the cheap, making money from your living situation, negotiating with your employer, and more. The author is known as the "Millennial Millionaire" and has been featured in more than 400 international media outlets.

How to Adult: Personal Finance for the Real World
Jake Cousineau
(independently published, 2021)
This well-reviewed book explains basic topics such as compound interest, mutual funds, insurance deductibles, and more, using stories, charts, and research. Cousineau is an educator and author.

The Millionaire Next Door: The Surprising Secrets of America's Wealthy
Thomas J. Stanley, PhD, and William D. Danko, PhD
(Boulder, Colorado: Taylor Trade Publishing, 2010)
The book identifies and explores seven traits shared among people who have accumulated significant wealth, including a willingness to live below their

means. Stanley, who died in 2015, was a former professor and author of seven books focusing on America's wealthy population. Danko is a best-selling author.

Money: Master the Game. 7 Simple Steps to Financial Freedom
Tony Robbins
(New York: Simon & Schuster, 2014)
Robbins researched this book for 10 years before writing it, interviewing financial gurus like Warrant Buffet, Ray Dalio, and Jack Bogle. Based on those and other interviews, he compiled their best strategies to help average people get ahead financially. Robbins is an esteemed life and business strategist, as well as an author and philanthropist.

The Psychology of Money: Timeless Lessons on Wealth, Greed, and Happiness
Morgan Housel
(Hampshire, Great Britain: Harriman House LTD, 2020)
Housel shares 19 short stories that explore various ways people think about and make decisions about money. The author is a partner at The Collaborative Fund and a two-time winner of the Best in Business Award from the Society of American Business Editors and Writers.

Rich Dad Poor Dad: What the Rich Teach Their Kids About Money—That the Poor and Middle Class Do Not!
Robert T. Kiyosaki
(Scottsdale, Arizona: Plata Publishing, 2022)
First published in 1997, this book examines how classes conceptualize, work for, invest, and spend their money. Partially based on Kiyosaki's life and the way he watched his father and his best friend's father handle their money, the book has sold more than 32 million copies in more than 100 countries. Kiyosaki parlayed the book into a series of *Rich Dad* books.

The Total Money Makeover: A Proven Plan for Financial Fitness
Dave Ramsey
(Nashville, Tennessee: Thomas Nelson Publishing, 2013)
This book provides tools and encouragement for paying off debt, breaking bad money habits, putting aside emergency funds and retirement savings, and becoming financially healthy. Ramsey is a best-selling author and host of *The Ramsey Show*, a radio program heard by millions of listeners each week.

The Wealthy Barber: Everyone's Commonsense Guide to Becoming Financially Independent
David Chilton
(Sydney, Australia: Currency Press, 1997)
Chilton uses Roy the barber to teach readers good financial habits like paying off credit card balances and using unexpected windfalls to build emergency funds. Written in a humorous manner, the book has been updated several times, with more than 2 million copies sold, and was used as the basis for a television show aired by PBS in 1993. Chilton is the president of a financial consulting firm.

Why Didn't They Teach Me This in School? 99 Personal Money Management Principles to Live By
Cary Siegel
(South Charleston, South Carolina: Simple Strategic Solutions LLC, 2018)
This easily readable book includes eight lessons focusing on 99 principles to enhance financial understanding. Siegel, who wrote the book as a guide for his children, retired as a business executive when he was 45, crediting the early age to having followed the principles of this book.

Websites and Blogs

This list of personal finance websites and blogs was compiled from a variety of online recommendations. The blogs mentioned here showed up repeatedly on lists of recommended sites.

Afford Anything
affordanything.com
Paula Plant was a journalist who loved her work but hated being stuck in a cubicle. She saved money with a vengeance and then used her savings to travel around the world, starting the website and blog when she returned to let others know they could do the same thing. The site's content is varied, with frank talk about inflation, goal-setting, rental property investing, and more.

Broke Millennial

brokemillennial.com

Erin Lowry created the website to provide practical advice for millennials who want to learn more about taking control of their finances. The website is home to a blog that runs the gamut on topics of interest to millennials. Lowry also is the author of the *Broke Millennials* book series.

CentSai

centsai.com

A digital finance community geared toward millennials and Gen-Xers, CentSai uses stories, guides, quizzes, calculators, videos, and more to inform users in an easy-to-understand manner. The site has been featured by CNBC, Huffington Post, *USA Today*, and others.

Clark.com

clark.com

Operated by Clark Howard, a well-known consumer advocate and money expert for more than 30 years, the site contains written, audio, and downloadable content on a variety of financial topics. It provides practical advice on buying a car, ordering groceries for pickup, choosing a mobile phone plan, and so on.

Frugal Rules

frugalrules.com

John Schmoll, who started the website and writes the blog, uses personal stories and experiences to encourage readers to live within their means to achieve financial freedom. As the name suggests, he offers frugal tips and formulas for success, like saving more, taking on less debt, supplementing your income, and keeping expenses low.

Millennial Money Man

millennialmoneyman.com

This site was founded by Bobby Hoyt, a former teacher who graduated from college with $40,000 in student debt that he repaid in 18 months on his teaching salary. Geared toward millennials, his blogs focus on making money, saving money, and paying off debt, and he reviews and recommends tools to help you manage your finances and achieve the lifestyle you're looking for.

Money Crashers

moneycrashers.com

Money Crashers works to "develop a community of people who try to make financially sound decisions." Recent blog posts include "7 Best Cash Management Accounts" and "How to Get a Mortgage Loan If You're Self-Employed with Fluctuating Income." The Money Crashers team includes subject matter experts, financial professionals, financial writers, and business owners who bring their own perspectives to the table.

Physician on Fire

physicianonfire.com

This website is home to the blog written by Leif, a former anesthesiologist who built wealth and retired early. Known to be thorough and well researched, Leif's blog is intended to inform and inspire other physicians and their patients about attaining financial independence.

Well Kept Wallet

wellkeptwallet.com

Well Kept Wallet was founded in 2010 by Deacon Hayes, a personal expert, speaker, author, and podcaster. It contains hundreds of personal finance blog posts in the categories of making money, saving money, and paying off debt. Some titles include "How to Make Money with YouTube" and "How to Improve Your Credit Score After a Divorce."

Wise Bread

wisebread.com

This site contains articles and blogs by a variety of writers, offering different perspectives and opinions on all matters related to personal finance. Its focus is on teaching readers how to spend less and save more, and it offers tips on avoiding common financial pitfalls.

Apps

These apps were compiled from recommended lists by financial sites including NerdWallet, The Balance, Investopedia, and Forbes Advisor.

Albert

albert.com

Designed to serve as a sort of personal financial adviser, Albert analyzes your debt, accounts, and spending and then recommends ways to improve your portfolio. It helps you organize your money into categories, create an Albert Cash bank account, track spending, and receive notifications about overdraft fees and bill increases. The app is free to download, but there's a charge for some features.

Empower

empower.me

Formerly known as Personal Capital, Empower is a wealth management tool that offers an investment component and access to financial advisers. The app's budgeting tool is free, but there is a wealth management fee on investments.

Goodbudget

goodbudget.com

Goodbudget uses a digital envelope system to help you divide funds to be used for different purposes. When the money in one envelope runs out, the app signals you to stop spending in that category. Goodbudget can be synced across multiple devices so partners can readily see how much is available to spend and includes tools for saving on future expenses and paying down debt. There is a free version that includes 20 envelopes, or you can get unlimited envelopes for $8 a month.

Honeydue

honeydue.com

This free app helps couples monitor all of their accounts, including bank, loan, and investment. You can choose the accounts you want to share with each other. It tracks spending, sends bill reminders, and sets spending limits in different categories. There's also a chat feature that lets couples communicate with each other.

Mint

mint.intuit.com

Produced by Intuit, Mint was voted best overall app by several financial sites. It has a variety of features that let you keep track of spending and monitor your credit score. It has simple bill tracking, categorizes your expenses, and is free, with an optional paid upgrade.

Oportun

oportun.com

This app, formerly known as Digit, analyzes your spending habits and transfers money you won't miss from your checking account into a savings fund. It's designed to help you save, borrow, invest, and track your finances and claims that users save thousands of dollars a year, nearly effortlessly. You can use it free for 30 days, after which it's $5 a month.

PocketGuard

pocketguard.com

This app helps you avoid overspending, using an algorithm to track your income, expenses, and savings goals to tell you how much you can spend every day. It's easy to use and free, with an optional paid upgrade.

Simplifi by Quicken

quicken.com/simplifi

This app offers a personalized spending plan that gives you updates on what you have to spend throughout the month. It syncs with your bank accounts to provide a comprehensive picture of your progress and goals. It also tracks your monthly bills and subscriptions, including those you don't use. After a free trial, the app costs $47.99 a year.

Stash

stash.com

The app gives you access to budgeting tools, a taxable brokerage account, a digital checking account, and a debit card with which you can earn stocks when you use it for expenses. You can get a $3 monthly subscription or a $9 per month account that includes $10,000 in life insurance coverage.

YNAB (You Need a Budget)

ynab.com

This app costs $99 a year, but the company makes the claim that new budgeters save $600 in their first two months and more than $6,000 in their first year. It offers a complete budget makeover and comprehensive education and is known for strong customer service. You can try it for free for 34 days.

Zeta

askzeta.com

Zeta is a budgeting app designed for couples, whether or not they share joint accounts. It's geared toward couples who are living together, engaged, married, or new parents, enabling them to sync various accounts to track spending, manage bills, and view their net worth. The app is free, with a paid investment service available.

Podcasts

You can learn a lot while you're out for a run, cleaning your living room, or driving to meet with a client. Podcasts can be entertaining, but they also can be great teachers. They can present perspectives you'd never considered, introduce you to people you never knew, expand your ability to focus and listen without distraction, and leave you with a lot of new ideas and insights.

This list of podcasts is a compilation of some that have come highly recommended from sites like Millennial Money, Investopedia, Business Insider, and Modern Frugality.

BiggerPockets Money

biggerpockets.com/podcasts/money

Released once a week, this podcast features interviews with financial experts who share ideas about how to earn more, save more, spend more wisely, and build wealth. The episodes average more than an hour each, but the content is interesting and provides information you can act on. It's hosted by financial experts Mindy Jensen and Scott Trench.

Brown Ambition

brownambitionpodcast.com

Short episodes feature fun conversation on topics ranging from paying off credit card debt, to asking for a raise at work, increasing savings, setting up custodial accounts for your kids, and navigating shared finances as a couple. *Brown Ambition* was created and is hosted by friends Tiffany Aliche and Mandi Woodruss.

HerMoney

hermoney.com/t/podcasts

Geared toward women at the older end of the millennial cohort, *HerMoney* is hosted by Jean Chatzky but features guests such as Ginni Rometty, former CEO of IBM; nutritionist Ellie Krieger, who offers advice on eating better while saving money on food; Catherine Rampell, an opinion columnist at *The Washington Post* who discusses economic news; Hal Hershfield, a marketing, decision-making, and psychology professor at UCLA who talks about the psychology of saving; and others. Chatzky is a journalist and financial editor for the *TODAY Show*, explaining her ability to attract well-known guests to her show.

Journey to Launch

journeytolaunch.com/podcast

Geared toward those aiming to save enough money to be able to leave a full-time job and go out on their own, *Journey to Launch* explores the pros and cons of quitting your job, common mistakes made by those who are looking for financial independence, paying off student loans, and more. Host Jamila Souffrant teams up with a variety of guests, many of whom are well known in financial fields. Episodes vary in length, with most between 30 and 60 minutes.

Marriage, Kids, and Money

marriagekidsandmoney.com/podcast-archive

Host Andy Hill and his wife, the parents of two children, paid off $50,000 of debt in one year; paid off their mortgage before they were 35; and beginning with savings of $50,000, became millionaires in less than 10 years. His podcasts teach other young families how to do the same with topics such as no-spend challenges, saving and spending, and more.

The Money Guy Show

moneyguy.com/category/episodes

Brian Preston and Bo Hansen, financial planners and wealth managers, explore practical financial matters like how to get the best deal on a car, how presidential elections might affect your finances, and the ins and outs of Roth IRAs. Episodes are released once a week and are about an hour long.

Motley Fool Money

fool.com/podcasts/motley-fool-money

The Motley Fool has been offering financial advice and investing insights to people for 30 years, and its podcasts, including *Motley Fool Money*, get great reviews. Hosted by Dylan Lewis, Deidre Woollard, Ricky Mulvey, and Mary Long, the podcast covers daily business news and financial headlines with a team of investment analysts. Other Motley Fool podcasts include *Market Foolery*, *Industry Focus*, *Motley Fool Answers*, and *Rule Breaker Investing*.

Planet Money

npr.org/podcasts/510289/planet-money

National Public Radio's *Planet Money* podcast breaks down complicated financial topics into understandable, user-friendly advice. Also a daily talk show on NPR, the show claims to be "The Economy Explained." It's got great ratings, is easy to listen to, and is entertaining.

Popcorn Finance

popcornfinance.com/podcast

Produced and hosted by financial analyst Chris Browning, these fun, short podcasts discuss the ins and outs of debt, how your credit score is calculated, how stocks work, and other financial topics. Browning touts the episodes as just about as long as it takes to make a bag of popcorn, making them good for listening to during short commutes.

So Money

podcast.farnoosh.tv

Hosted by Farnoosh Torabi, a financial correspondent, author, and TV personality, *So Money* offers conversations about money strategies and features guests like Arianna Huffington, Margaret Cho, and Seth Godin. On Fridays, Torabi answers questions from listeners. Episodes are released on Mondays, Wednesdays, and Fridays, and each is about half an hour long.

Helpful Forms

Legal documents and estate planning aren't topics people typically think about early in life, but they should be on your radar, especially if you're married or married with kids.

In Chapter 8, we explored the idea of a prenuptial agreement. Whether or not you choose to execute one is up to you, but it's worth thinking about. And in Chapter 15, we explained what wills, powers of attorney, and other legal documents are and why you need to have them.

In this appendix, we include some vital documents for you to read through. These can give you an idea of what information certain forms contain, whether you re-create these for yourself or find versions online.

However you decide to craft your documents, it's always a good idea to have a lawyer review them to ensure they're completed correctly and are legally sound.

Prenuptial Agreement

A prenuptial agreement, sometimes called a premarital agreement, is a contract entered into by two people before the start of a marriage, civil union, or other type of arrangement.

This Agreement is made this _____ day of _____, 20__, between _____, of _____, future husband, and _____, of _____, future wife.

WHEREAS, a marriage is intended to be, soon after the date hereof, solemnized between _____ and _____, and

WHEREAS, each party owns real and personal property which was obtained independently of the other party, and each has made a complete disclosure of his or her property as listed on Exhibit A and Exhibit B attached hereto and made part of this Agreement, and

WHEREAS, each party has been advised and understands his or her rights, and the rights of each party's heirs in the event of the marriage and in the absence of any agreement regarding those marital rights, and

WHEREAS, each party desires to keep all of his or her separate property whether now owned or hereafter acquired, free from any claim of the other party by virtue of the forthcoming marriage, and

WHEREAS, each party declares that he or she has had independent legal advice or the opportunity to secure independent legal advice before entering into this Agreement and that each party acknowledges that he or she fully understands the legal effect of this Agreement, and each party acknowledges the free, knowledgeable, and voluntary execution of the Agreement with no fraud, deceit, or undue influence being exerted and that the same is executed by them with the intent to be bound hereunder, and

WHEREAS, each party desires to set forth his or her mutual agreement and understanding in writing.

NOW, THEREFORE, IT IS AGREED AS FOLLOWS:

1. That all property of any kind or nature, real, personal, or mixed, which belong to a party, shall be and forever remain the individual property of that party (also known hereafter as separate property), including all income therefrom.

2. Each party shall have full right and authority, in all respects the same as if unmarried, to use, enjoy, manage, convey, mortgage, and dispose of all that party's present and

future separate property, of every kind and character, including the right and power to freely, without any spousal claim, dispose of the same by gift or by Last Will and Testament.

3. Each party waives and relinquishes any spousal claim, family allowance, election against the other party's Last Will and Testament, or intestate share in the decedent's separate property.

4. Each party waives and relinquishes, in the event of legal separation or divorce, any claim against the separate property of the other party.

5. Neither party intends by this Agreement to limit or restrict his or her right to receive a transfer, conveyance, devise, or bequest from the other.

6. Each party agrees to execute any documents necessary to accomplish the intent of this Agreement.

7. Each party agrees that this Agreement, may, by mutual agreement, be amended, revoked, or rescinded.

8. This Agreement is legally binding upon each party and each party's heirs, personal representatives, successors, and assigns.

9. This Agreement shall take effect only in the event that the parties become legally married to one another.

IN WITNESS WHEREOF, we have subscribed our names to this Prenuptial Agreement, this _____ day of _____, 20__.

Signed: _____

Signed: _____

Reviewed by: _____

Attorney for: _____

Reviewed by: _____

Attorney for: _____

Last Will and Testament—Basic for Single Person

A basic will for a single person normally designates a personal representative for the deceased, instructions for settling debt, and notes on how property should be distributed.

I, _____, of _____, _____, being of sound and disposing mind and memory, do make, publish, and declare this to be my Last Will and Testament, and I hereby revoke all wills and codicils heretofore made by me.

I. Identification, Definitions, Comments

A. I am a single person.

B. A beneficiary must survive me by thirty (30) days to be entitled to receive a devise.

C. "Issue" is to be construed as lawful lineal descendants and include adopted persons. Issue shall receive any devise by representation, not per capita.

II. Debts, Expenses, Encumbrances, Taxes

A. I direct that my enforceable debts, expenses of my last illness, and funeral and administrative expenses of my estate shall be paid by my personal representative from my residuary estate. At his or her discretion, my personal representative may continue to pay any installment obligations incurred by me during my lifetime on an installment basis or may prepay any or all of such obligations in whole or in part, and my personal representative may, at his or her discretion, distribute any asset encumbered by such an obligation subject to the obligation.

B. I direct that all inheritance, estate, and succession taxes (including interest and penalties thereon) payable by reason of my death shall be paid out of and be charged generally against my residuary estate without reimbursement from any person.

III. Specific Devises

I devise all my personal effects and household goods to _____.
If he or she does not survive me, I devise said property, in equal shares, to _____. If a devisee does not survive me, his or her share devolves to the deceased devisee's issue, or if none survive me, the share devolves, equally, to the surviving devisees.

IV. Residuary Estate

I devise my residuary estate to _____. If he or she does not survive me, I devise my residuary estate, in equal shares, to _____. If a devisee does not survive me, his or her share devolves to the deceased devisee's issue, or if none survive me, the share devolves, equally, to the surviving devisees.

V. Personal Representative

I hereby appoint _____ as personal representative. If he or she cannot serve, I appoint _____ as personal representative. I authorize unsupervised administration of my estate. I request that the personal representative serve without bond, or if a bond is required, that a minimum bond be required. My personal representative shall have all powers enumerated and granted to personal representatives under the Code of the State of _____, and any other power that may be granted by law, to be exercised without the necessity of Court approval, as my personal representative determines to be in the best interest of the estate.

I have signed this Last Will and Testament in the presence of the undersigned witnesses on this _____ day of _____, 20__.

Signed: _____

Testator: _____

The foregoing instrument was at _____, _____, this _____ day of _____, 20__, signed, sealed, published, and declared by the testator to be his or her Last Will and Testament, in our presence, and we, at the testator's request and in his or her presence and in the presence of each other, have hereunto subscribed our names as attesting witnesses.

Witness: _____

Address: _____

Witness: _____

Address: _____

Last Will and Testament—Basic for Married Person with Minor Children

A will for a person who is married and has children is more complicated than one for a single person with no dependents. In addition to designating a personal representative for the deceased and instructions for settling debt and for how property should be distributed, this will addresses guardianship of the children.

I, _____, of _____, _____, being of sound and disposing mind and memory, do make, publish, and declare this to be my Last Will and Testament, and I hereby revoke all wills and codicils heretofore made by me.

I. Identification, Definitions, Comments

A. I am married to _____. I have _____ children: _____, _____, and _____.

B. A beneficiary must survive me by thirty (30) days to be entitled to receive a devise.

C. "Issue" is to be construed as lawful lineal descendants and include adopted persons. Issue shall receive any devise by representation, not per capita.

II. Debts, Expenses, Encumbrances, Taxes

A. I direct that my enforceable debts, expenses of my last illness, and funeral and administrative expenses of my estate shall be paid by my personal representative from my residuary estate. At his or her discretion, my personal representative may continue to pay any installment obligations incurred by me during my lifetime on an installment basis or may prepay any or all of such obligations in whole or in part, and my personal representative may, at his or her discretion, distribute any asset encumbered by such an obligation subject to the obligation.

B. I direct that all inheritance, estate, and succession taxes (including interest and penalties thereon) payable by reason of my death shall be paid out of and be charged generally against my residuary estate without reimbursement from any person.

III. Specific Devises

I devise all my personal effects and household goods to _____. If he or she does not survive me, I devise said property, in equal shares, to _____, _____, and _____. If a child does not survive me, his or her share devolves to the deceased child's issue, or if none survive me, the share devolves, equally, to the surviving children.

IV. Residuary Estate

I devise my residuary estate to _____. If he or she does not survive me, I devise my residuary estate, in equal shares, to _____, _____, and _____. If a child does not survive me, his or her share devolves to the deceased child's issue, or if none survive me, the share devolves, equally, to the surviving children.

V. Personal Representative

I hereby appoint _____ as personal representative. If he or she cannot serve, I appoint _____ as alternate personal representative. I authorize unsupervised administration of my estate. I request that the personal representative serve without bond, or if a bond is required, that a minimum bond be required. My personal representative shall have all powers enumerated and granted to personal representatives under the Code of the State of _____, and any other power that may be granted by law, to be exercised without the necessity of Court approval, as my personal representative determines to be in the best interest of the estate.

VI. Guardian

I appoint _____ as guardian of the person and property of each of my minor children. If he or she cannot serve as guardian, I appoint _____ as alternate guardian. I request that no bond be required for the guardian; however, if such a bond is required, I request that such bond be nominal in amount.

VI. Miscellaneous

If my spouse and I executed wills at approximately the same time, this Last Will and Testament is not made pursuant to any contract or agreement with my spouse.

I have signed this Last Will and Testament in the presence of the undersigned witnesses on this _____ day of _____, 20__.

Signed: _____

Testator: _____

The foregoing instrument was at _____, _____, this _____ day of _____, 20__, signed, sealed, published, and declared by the testator to be his or her Last Will and Testament, in our presence, and we, at the testator's request and in his or her presence and in the presence of each other, have hereunto subscribed our names as attesting witnesses.

Witness: _____

Address: _____

Witness: _____

Address: _____

Last Will and Testament—with Trust for Minor Children

This will designates a trustee to oversee the residual estate of the deceased for the benefit of the deceased's children, addresses guardianship, and appoints a personal representative.

I, _____, of _____, _____, do make, publish, and declare this to be my Last Will and Testament, hereby revoking all former wills and codicils.

I. Identification, Definitions, Comments

A. My spouse is _____. We have _____ children: _____, _____, and _____.

B. "Survive me" means that the person referred to must survive me by thirty (30) days. If the person referred to dies within thirty (30) days of my death, the reference to him shall be construed as if he had failed to survive me, and all devises made herein to or for the benefit of that person shall be void.

C. Whenever used herein, words importing the singular include the plural and words importing the masculine include the feminine and neuter, unless the context otherwise requires.

D. "Issue" of the person referred to means the lawful lineal descendants (except those who are lineal descendants of living lineal descendants) who, at the time they must be ascertained in order to give effect to the reference to them, are either in being or they are in gestation and later born alive. Issue shall take by right of representation, in accordance with the rule of per stirpes distribution. "Issue" includes adopted persons.

II. Debts, Expenses, Encumbrances, Taxes

A. I direct that my enforceable debts, expenses of my last illness, and funeral and administration expenses of my estate shall be paid by my personal representative from my estate as soon as practicable after my death.

B. If any real or personal property that passes by reason of my death is encumbered by a mortgage, pledge, or other lien, I direct that such claim not be a charge to or paid as an administrative expense of my estate, but the person receiving such property shall take it subject to all claims.

C. I direct that the expense of safeguarding, packing, shipping, and delivering any property to a beneficiary be paid as an administrative expense of my estate.

D. I direct that all transfer, estate, inheritance, succession, and other death taxes (together with any interest and penalty thereon) that shall be payable by reason of my death shall be paid out of and be charged generally against my residuary estate without reimbursement from any person.

III. Specific Devises

I devise all my clothing; jewelry; household goods; personal effects; automobiles; boats; athletic and sporting equipment; any collections of stamps, coins, money, or other thing; all books; manuscripts; antiques; works of art; and all other tangible personal property not otherwise specifically devised, including insurance policies thereon, owned by me at the time of my death, to _____. If my spouse does not survive me, I devise said property, in equal shares, to my children _____. If a child does not survive me, his share devolves to his issue if any survive me; if a child's issue does not survive me, the share shall devolve to the other child.

IV. Residuary Estate

A. I devise my residuary estate to _____. If my spouse does not survive me, I devise my residuary estate to _____, of _____, _____, as trustee, in trust, for the benefit of my children, _____, _____, _____, under the following terms and conditions:

1. If there is one child under age twenty-two (22), the trustee shall hold and administer the trust for the benefit of my children. The trustee may pay to the children or expend on their behalf so much of the net income from the trust as the trustee may deem advisable to provide properly for the children's support, maintenance, health, and education. Any income not distributed shall be added to the principal. The trustee may, in his sole discretion at any time, and from time to time, disburse from the principal of the trust (even to the point of completely exhausting such estate) such amounts as the trustee deems advisable to provide for the support, maintenance, health, and education of the children. In determining the amounts of the principal to be so disbursed, the trustee shall take into consideration any other income or property which the children may have from any other source. For all sums so disbursed, the trustee shall have full acquaintance. All such disbursements from the principal shall be charged against the trust and shall not be charged against any child's share of the principal subsequently divided.

2. When the youngest child becomes age twenty-two (22), the trust estate shall be divided equally among my children, those then living and those predeceased but with issue then living. Any child age twenty-five (25) shall receive his proportionate share upon written request to the trustee; any child who is at least age twenty-two (22) but less than age twenty-five (25) shall receive one third (1/3) of his proportionate share upon written request to the trustee and have the remainder of his share administered according to the provisions of Paragraph 1 herein; if any child does not survive but has issue, his share shall be distributed to his issue, or if there is no issue, his share shall devolve to the other children. If none of the foregoing persons survive to receive final

distribution of the trust, the trust estate shall be distributed according to the terms of Paragraph B herein. Notwithstanding the foregoing, the trust shall terminate within twenty-one (21) years of the last to die of the beneficiaries who were living at my death; upon such termination, the trust estate shall vest in and be distributed as provided for herein.

3. No person paying money or delivering any property to the trustee need see to its application.

4. The trustee is entitled to reasonable compensation for services rendered and to reimbursement for expenses.

5. If, at any time, the aggregate principal value of the trust is ten thousand dollars ($10,000.00) or less, the trustee may in his sole judgment terminate the trust and distribute the assets thereof in the trustee's possession to the beneficiary or beneficiaries, at that time, of the current income.

6. Any interest in any trust created by this instrument shall not be transferable or assignable by any beneficiary, or be subject during his life to the claims of his creditors, including spousal support claims from a separation or dissolution of marriage.

7. The trustee shall have all powers enumerated in the Trust Code of the State of _____, as may be amended, and all other powers granted by law.

B. If none of my children nor their issue survives me, I devise my residuary estate to _____.

V. Personal Representative

I appoint _____ as personal representative of this Last Will and Testament; if he is unable or unwilling to serve, I appoint _____ as personal representative. I request that my personal representative serve without posting bond, or if a bond is required, that a minimum bond be set. My personal representative shall have all powers enumerated in the Probate Code of the State of _____, as may be amended, and all other powers granted by law. In addition to powers conferred by law, I authorize my personal representative to exercise absolute discretion, without the necessity of any notice, petition to or order from any court or being required to report to or obtain the approval of any court.

VI. Guardian

I appoint _____, or if he is unable or unwilling to serve, _____, as guardian of the person and property of each minor child who survives me, during his minority. I request that the guardian be permitted to serve without bond or that the bond be a nominal amount.

IN WITNESS WHEREOF, I have subscribed my name to this, my Last Will and Testament, the preceding pages bearing my initials.

Signed: _____

Testator: _____

The foregoing instrument was at _____, _____, this _____ day of _____, 20__, signed, sealed, published, and declared by the testator to be his Last Will and Testament, in our presence, and we, at the testator's request and in his presence and in the presence of one another, have hereunto subscribed our names as attesting witnesses.

Witness: _____

Address: _____

Witness: _____

Address: _____

Will Information Form

A will information form is intended to collect all the information you need to help determine the contents of your will. Lawyers often ask for a will information form so they can offer the best advice concerning a client's will.

Husband: _____

Wife: _____

Address: _____

Child: _____   Age: _____

Child: _____   Age: _____

Child: _____   Age: _____

Bequests

Property	**Beneficiary**
_____	_____
_____	_____
_____	_____

Cash Amount	**Beneficiary**
_____	_____
_____	_____
_____	_____

Residuary

First: Name and relationship (if does not survive): _____

Name and relationship (if does not survive): _____

Name and relationship: _____

Equally or percent share: _____

Second: Name and relationship (if does not survive): _____

Name and relationship (if does not survive): _____

Name and relationship: _____

Equally or percent share: _____

Third: Name and relationship (if does not survive): _____

Name and relationship (if does not survive): _____

Name and relationship: _____

Equally or percent share: _____

Executor

First: Name and relationship: _____

Name and relationship: _____

Second: Name and relationship: _____

Name and relationship: _____

Guardian

First: Name and relationship: _____

Name and relationship: _____

Second: Name and relationship: _____

Name and relationship: _____

Trust

Beneficiary	Age	Share
_____	_____	_____
_____	_____	_____
_____	_____	_____

Distribution Alternatives

All at age: _____   One third (1/3) at age: _____

One half (1/2) at age: _____   Balance at age: _____

Trustee

First: Name and relationship: _____

Second: Name and relationship: _____

Codicil

If you want to make changes to your will after you've created it, you'll need to complete a codicil.

Codicil to the Last Will and Testament of _____
____

I, _____, of _____
_____, do make, publish, and declare this to be the First Codicil to my Last
Will and Testament executed by me on _____, 20__, in the presence of
_____ and _____ as witnesses.

I hereby remove _____ and substitute _____ as
primary guardian, under Article _____ of my Last Will and Testament.

In all other respects, I hereby ratify all the provisions of my Last Will and Testament,
dated _____, 20__.

IN TESTIMONY WHEREOF, I have subscribed my name on this my First Codicil
to my Last Will and Testament all in the presence of the persons witnessing it at my
request, on this _____ day of _____, 20__.

Signed: _____

Testator: _____

The foregoing instrument was signed, published, and declared by
_____ to be his or her First Codicil to his or her Last Will and
Testament, in our presence, in the testator's presence, and in the presence of one
another, and at the testator's request, we signed our names as witnesses to the codicil
this _____ day of _____, 20__.

Witness: _____

Address: _____

Witness: _____

Address: _____

Pet Care Trust Agreement

A pet care trust agreement appoints someone to care for your pet or pets in the event of your death.

This Trust Agreement is made this _____ day of _____, 20__, at _____, _____, between _____, the Settlor, and _____, also serving as the Original Trustee under this Agreement.

The Settlor desires to create a Trust for the purpose of caring for and providing for the benefit and use of my pet _____, by the name of _____, and this trust shall be administered for said pet as enumerated herein:

1. The Settlor has delivered to the Trustee the property indicated in Exhibit A attached hereto, receipt of which is acknowledged by the Trustee of the Trust by signing and dating Exhibit A. That property and any other property that may be received by the Trustee from the Settlor as additions to this Trust shall be held and disposed of by the Trustee in accord with the terms stated in this Agreement.

2. The income generated by this Trust shall be paid to _____, who has agreed to take over the care and custody of my _____ and provide him or her with a loving home.

3. If the income generated by this Trust is not sufficient to provide the necessary care for my pet, the Trustee at his or her sole discretion may use the Trust principal for my pet's benefit.

4. My Trustee shall confer on a regular basis with my pet's caregiver to ensure there are adequate funds to provide for the appropriate care. Funds may be used to provide special dietary food, veterinary examination and treatment costs, medicines, possible operations, and professional grooming.

5. The Trust shall continue until the death of my _____. Upon the death of my pet, his or her remains will be cremated and disposed of according to the instructions provided the pet's caregiver. The Trust shall pay for the cost of this cremation.

6. The Settlor may, by signed instrument delivered to the Trustee, revoke this Agreement in whole or in part or amend it, but no amendment changing the powers, duties, or compensation of the Trustee shall be effective unless approved in writing by the acting Trustee.

7. The Trustee may resign by giving the Settlor written notice thirty (30) days in advance of the effective date of the Trustee's resignation. If there is no Successor Trustee designated, the personal representative of the estate of _____ shall designate a Successor Trustee. The Successor Trustee shall continue to hold title to all assets in the Trust until appropriate distribution can be lawfully made.

8. _____, as the Original Trustee, and all Successor Trustees under this Agreement shall have all powers enumerated under the Trust Code of the State of _____ and any other power that may be granted by law, to be exercised with the necessity of Court approval, as my Trustees, in their sole discretion, determine to be in the best interests of the beneficiaries. Said powers are to be construed in the broadest possible manner and shall include the following and shall pertain to both principal and income, but shall in no way be limited thereto:

    A. To retain any property received from the Settlor without liability for loss due to lack of diversification or nonproductivity.

    B. To invest and reinvest the Trust estate in any kind of real or personal property without regard to any law restricting investment by Trustees and without regard to current income.

    C. To sell any Trust property, for cash or on credit, at public or private sales; to exchange any Trust property for other property; and to determine the prices and terms of sales and exchanges.

    D. To take any action with respect to conserving or realizing upon the value of any Trust property, and with respect to foreclosures, reorganizations, or other changes affecting the Trust property; to collect, pay, contest, compromise, or abandon demands of or against the Trust estate, wherever situated; and to execute contracts, notes, conveyances, and other instruments, including instruments containing covenants and warranties binding upon and creating a charge against the Trust estate.

9. The following provisions govern the administration of this Trust as established by the Settlor.

    A. Any named Trustee of this Trust is relieved from any requirement as to routine Court accountings that may now or may hereafter be required by the statutes in force in any jurisdiction, although he or she is not precluded from obtaining judicial approval of his or her accounts. The Trustee shall be required to account on at least an annual basis to the pet's caregiver.

    This instrument and the dispositions hereunder shall be construed and regulated and their validity and effect shall be determined by the laws of the State of _____.

B. Any Trustee shall be entitled to reasonable compensation for services rendered in administering and distributing the Trust property, which shall be paid in accordance with an hourly rate if the Trustee is an individual. If the Trustee is a corporate fiduciary, it shall be compensated in accordance with its current fee schedule. During the administration of this Trust, the Trustee shall be entitled to reimbursement for expenses.

C. No person paying money or delivering property to a given Trustee need see to its proper application by the Trustee.

D. In the event that _____ dies, resigns, or is unable to serve as Trustee of this Trust, _____ is nominated to serve as Successor Trustee under this Trust Agreement. The Successor Trustee shall automatically assume his or her position as Successor Trustee upon the signing of an oath, without the necessity of any Court order or approval of the same.

10. In the event that there is any balance remaining in this Trust, the balance held in the Trust shall be paid to _____, and said Trust shall terminate.

IN WITNESS WHEREOF, I, _____, have hereunto signed my name as Settlor and as the Original Trustee of this Agreement on the _____ day of _____, 20___.

Settlor: _____

Trustee: _____

Witness: _____

Witness: _____

Appointment of Health-Care Power of Attorney

A health-care power of attorney appoints a representative to make decisions regarding your health care in the event that you are unable to do so.

I, _____, name _____ as representative to act for me in matters affecting my health, in particular to:

(1) Consent to or refuse health care for me.

(2) Employ or contract with servants, companions, or health-care providers for me.

(3) Admit or release me from a hospital or health-care facility.

(4) Have access to records, including medical records, concerning my condition.

(5) Make anatomical gifts on my behalf.

(6) Request an autopsy.

(7) Make plans for the disposition of my body.

I authorize my representative to make decisions in my best interest concerning the withdrawal or withholding of health care. If at any time, based on my previously expressed preferences and diagnosis and prognosis, my representative is satisfied that certain health care is not or would not be beneficial, or that such health care is or would be excessively burdensome, then the representative may express my will that such care be withheld or withdrawn and may consent on my behalf that any or all health care be discontinued or not instituted even if my death results.

My representative must try to discuss this decision with me. However, if I am unable to communicate, my representative may make such a decision for me, after consultation with my physician or physicians and other relevant health-care providers. To the extent appropriate, my representative may also discuss this decision with my family and others, to the extent they are available.

I understand my rights under the Health Insurance Portability and Accountability Act of 1996 (HIPAA) and hereby declare and authorize my representative to have the authority to obtain any health-care information to the same extent I would be able to obtain my own health-care information.

Dated: _____, 20__

Signed: _____

Printed: _____

_____ has been personally known to me, and I believe him or her to be of legal age and capable of making decisions regarding his or her health care.

I am competent and at least 18 years of age.

Witness: _____

Dated: _____, 20__

Witness: _____

Dated: _____, 20__

Health-Care Power of Attorney—Minor Child

This document is used to appoint a representative to make decisions regarding your child or children's health care if you are unable to do so.

I, _____, as parent of _____ and _____, name _____ as representative to act for me in matters affecting each of my children's health, in particular to:

(1) Consent to or refuse health care for my child.

(2) Employ or contract with servants, companions, or health-care providers for my child.

(3) Admit or release my child from a hospital or health-care facility.

(4) Have access to records, including medical records, concerning my child's condition as if I requested those records, being fully aware of federal and State of _____ health-care privacy laws. I understand my child's rights under the Health Insurance Portability and Accountability Act of 1996 (HIPAA) and hereby declare and authorize my child's representative to have the authority to obtain any health-care information to the same extent I would be able to obtain my child's health-care information.

Dated: _____, 20__

Signed: _____

Printed: _____

_____ has been personally known to me, and I believe him or her to be of legal age and capable of making decisions regarding the health care of my child.

I am competent and at least 18 years of age, and I am not a relative of the grantor or his or her children.

Witness: _____

Dated: _____, 20__

Witness: _____

Dated: _____, 20__

Health-Care Information Authorization

This form authorizes that information about your health care can be shared with a designated person or persons.

Name: _____

Address: _____

Spouse: _____

Address: _____

Health-Care Power of Attorney

Primary representative: _____

Address: _____

Secondary representative: _____

Address: _____

Any restrictions on authority? _____   Explain: _____

Burial instructions to be included? _____   List: _____

Living Will

Living will: _____ Yes/_____ No

    Artificially supplied nutrition/hydration: _____ Yes/_____ No

    Health-care representative to decide: _____ Yes/_____ No

Out-of-hospital do not resuscitate declaration: _____ Yes/_____ No

Life-prolonging declaration: _____ Yes/_____ No

Durable Power of Attorney

Health-care decisions by grantee of power: _____ Yes/_____ No

Grantee of durable POA: _____

Grantee of health-care POA: _____

Release of Health-Care Information*

Spouse: _____

Child: _____

Other: _____

*Grantee of any health-care decision must be given this information, usually in that document.

Life-Prolonging Procedures Declaration

A life-prolonging procedures declaration specifies your wishes to have your life prolonged with appropriate measures in the event that you are unable to make that decision known.

Declaration made this _____ day of _____, 20___. I, _____, being at least eighteen (18) years of age and of sound mind, willfully and voluntarily make known my desire that if at any time I have an incurable injury, disease, or illness determined to be a terminal condition, I request the use of life-prolonging procedures that would extend my life. This includes appropriate nutrition and hydration; the administration of medication; and the performance of all other medical procedures necessary to extend my life, to provide comfort care, or to alleviate pain.

In the absence of my ability to give directions regarding the use of life-prolonging procedures, it is my intention that this declaration be honored by my family and physician as the final expression of my legal right to request medical or surgical treatment and accept the consequences of refusal.

I understand the full import of this declaration.

Signed: _____

Printed: _____

City, county, and state of residence: _____

The declarant has been personally known to me, and I believe him or her to be of sound mind. I did not sign the declarant's signature above for or at the direction of the declarant.

I am not a parent, spouse, or child of the declarant. I am not entitled to any part of the declarant's estate or directly financially responsible for the declarant's medical care. I am competent and at least eighteen (18) years of age.

Witness: _____

Dated: _____, 20___

Witness: _____

Dated: _____, 20___

Living Will Declaration

A living will declaration specifies your wishes to not have your life prolonged under certain circumstances if you are unable to make that decision known.

Declaration made this _____ day of _____, 20___. I, _____, being at least eighteen (18) years of age and of sound mind, willfully and voluntarily make known my desires that my dying shall not be artificially prolonged under the circumstances set forth below, and I declare:

If at any time my attending physician certifies in writing that: (1) I have an incurable injury, disease, or illness; (2) my death will occur within a short time; and (3) the use of life-prolonging procedures would serve only to artificially prolong the dying process, I direct that such procedures be withheld or withdrawn and that I be permitted to die naturally with only the performance or provision of any medical procedure or medication necessary to provide me with comfort care or to alleviate pain, and, if I have so indicated below, the provision of artificially supplied nutrition and hydration (indicate your choice by initialing or making your mark before signing this declaration):

_____   I wish to receive artificially supplied nutrition and hydration, even if the effort to sustain life is futile or excessively burdensome to me.

_____   I do not wish to receive artificially supplied nutrition and hydration, if the effort to sustain life is futile or excessively burdensome to me.

_____   I intentionally make no decision concerning artificially supplied nutrition and hydration, leaving the decision to my health-care representative appointed under the laws of the State of _____.

In the absence of my ability to give directions regarding the use of life-prolonging procedures, it is my intention that this declaration be honored by my family and physician as the final expression of my legal right to refuse medical or surgical treatment and accept the consequences of refusal.

I understand the full import of this declaration.

Signed: _____

Printed: _____

City, county, and state of residence: _____

The declarant has been personally known to me, and I believe him or her to be of sound mind. I did not sign the declarant's signature above for or at the direction of the declarant. I am not a parent, spouse, or child of the declarant. I am not entitled to any part of the declarant's estate or directly financially responsible for the declarant's medical care. I am competent and at least eighteen (18) years of age.

Witness: _____

Dated: _____, 20__

Witness: _____

Dated: _____, 20__

Out-of-Hospital Do Not Resuscitate Declaration and Order

This form indicates that you would not want to be resuscitated under certain circumstances if you were stricken when you were outside a hospital setting.

Declaration made this _____ day of _____, 20__. I, _____, being at least eighteen (18) years of age and of sound mind, willfully and voluntarily make known my desires that my dying shall not be artificially prolonged under the circumstances set forth below, and I declare:

If at any time my attending physician certifies in writing that: (1) I have an incurable injury, disease, or illness; (2) my death will occur within a short time; and (3) the use of resuscitation would be unsuccessful or within a short period I would experience repeated cardiac or pulmonary failure and the use of resuscitation would serve only to artificially prolong the dying process, I direct that, if I experience cardiac or pulmonary failure in a location other than an acute care hospital or a health-care facility, cardiopulmonary resuscitation procedures be withheld or withdrawn and that I be permitted to die naturally. My medical care may include any medical procedure necessary to provide me with comfort care or to alleviate pain.

I understand that I may revoke this Out-of-Hospital Do Not Resuscitate Declaration at any time by a signed and dated writing, by destroying or canceling this document, or by communicating to health-care providers at the scene the desire to revoke this declaration.

In the absence of my ability to give directions regarding the use of life-prolonging procedures, it is my intention that this declaration be honored by my family and physician as the final expression of my legal right to refuse medical or surgical treatment and accept the consequences of refusal.

I understand the full import of this declaration.

Signed: _____

Printed: _____

City, county, and state of residence: _____

The declarant has been personally known to me, and I believe him or her to be of sound mind. I did not sign the declarant's signature above for or at the direction of the declarant.

I am not a parent, spouse, or child of the declarant. I am not entitled to any part of the declarant's estate or directly financially responsible for the declarant's medical care. I am competent and at least eighteen (18) years of age.

Witness: _____

Dated: _____, 20__

Durable General Power of Attorney

A durable general power of attorney appoints someone to handle your affairs if you are unable to do so.

KNOW ALL PERSONS PRESENT, that I, _____, a resident of _____, _____, have made, constituted, and appointed and do hereby make, constitute, and appoint _____, a resident of _____, _____, as my true and lawful attorney-in-fact and in my name and stead to do and perform all acts and exercise all powers and general authority with respect to all of the following designated transactions and matters as fully described in the State of _____ Powers of Attorney Act, applying to all powers of attorney created and specified therein, as amended, to wit:

Real property transactions; tangible personal property transactions; bond, share, and commodity transactions; banking transactions; pensions and retirement accounts; business operating transactions; insurance transactions; beneficiary transactions; gifts; family maintenance matters and actions; benefits from military service matters and actions; records, reports, and statement matters and actions; estate transactions; health-care powers matters and actions; and general authority with respect to delegating authority and general authority with respect to all other matters.

IN WITNESS WHEREOF, I have hereunto set my hand and seal this _____ day of _____, 20__.

Signed: _____

Printed: _____

State and county: _____ Social Security number: _____

Before me, the undersigned Notary Public within and for said County and State, personally appeared _____, who signed in my presence the foregoing Durable Power of Attorney and acknowledged the execution thereof to be his or her voluntary act and deed.

Witness my hand and notarial seal this _____ day of _____, 20__.

Signed: _____

Printed: _____

County of residence: _____ Commission expiration: _____

Limited Power of Attorney

A limited power of attorney designates an agent who is authorized to perform certain, but not all, tasks on your behalf. For instance, if you would want someone to handle paying your bills if you are not able to do so but not make financial decisions regarding your investments, that would be a limited power of attorney.

KNOW ALL PERSONS PRESENT, that I, _____, a resident of _____, _____, have made, constituted, and appointed and do hereby make, constitute, and appoint _____, a resident of _____, _____, as my true and lawful attorney-in-fact and in my name and stead to do and perform all acts and exercise all powers and general authority with respect to all of the following designated transactions: _____ _____, as provided for by Section _____ of the Code of the State of _____.

A person may rely in good faith upon any representations and authority of my attorney-in-fact regarding any transaction within the attorney-in-fact's authority as stated herein.

This Limited Power of Attorney and actions taken by my attorney-in-fact properly authorized hereunder shall be binding upon me, my heirs, successors, assigns, legatees, guardians, and personal representatives.

My attorney-in-fact, acting in good faith and under the authority stated herein, is hereby released and forever discharged from any and all liability and from all claims by me, my heirs, successors, assigns, legatees, guardians, and personal representatives.

This Limited Power of Attorney is effective as of _____, and shall terminate upon _____.

IN WITNESS WHEREOF, I have hereunto set my hand and seal this _____ day of _____, 20__.

Signed: _____

Printed: _____

State and county: _____ Social Security number: _____

Before me, the undersigned Notary Public within and for said County and State, personally appeared _____, who signed in my presence the foregoing Limited Power of Attorney and acknowledged the execution thereof to be his or her voluntary act and deed.

Witness my hand and notarial seal this _____ day of _____, 20__.

Signed: _____

Printed: _____

County of residence: _____ Commission expiration: _____

Revocation of Durable Power of Attorney

If you change your mind about the person you appointed to handle your affairs, you'll need to fill out a revocation of durable power of attorney form.

_____ hereby states that he or she hereby revokes the appointment of _____ to serve as attorney-in-fact.

That the date of the Durable Power of Attorney appointing _____ to serve as his or her attorney-in-fact was _____.

That the authority granted to _____ to serve as attorney-in-fact is no longer in effect and he or she shall have no authority to make any further decisions on behalf of the grantor.

That the Durable Power of Attorney was/was not recorded on _____, at the Office of the _____, County of _____, State of _____, as document number _____.

IN WITNESS WHEREOF, I have hereunto set my hand and seal this _____ day of _____, 20__.

Signed: _____

Printed: _____

State and county: _____ Social Security number: _____

Before me, the undersigned Notary Public within and for said County and State, personally appeared _____, who signed in my presence the foregoing Revocation of Durable Power of Attorney and acknowledged the execution thereof to be his or her voluntary act and deed.

Witness my hand and notarial seal this _____ day of _____, 20__.

Signed: _____

Printed: _____

County of residence: _____ Commission expiration: _____

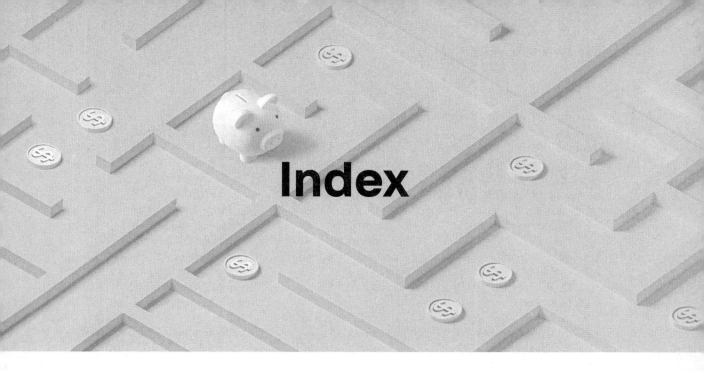

Index